Magnetics 2020

Orlando, Florida, USA
11-12 February 2020

ISBN: 978-1-7138-0805-3

Printed from e-media with permission by:

Curran Associates, Inc.
57 Morehouse Lane
Red Hook, NY 12571

Some format issues inherent in the e-media version may also appear in this print version.

TWST Events
622 3rd Ave, 34th FL
New York, NY 10017
USA

twstevents.com

Additional copies of this publication are available from:

Curran Associates, Inc.
57 Morehouse Lane
Red Hook, NY 12571 USA
Phone: 845-758-0400
Fax: 845-758-2633
Email: curran@proceedings.com
Web: www.proceedings.com

TABLE OF CONTENTS

METROlab
Magnetic precision has a name

NMR Magnetometers: The best gets better

Philip Keller, Magnetics 2020

METROlab
Magnetic precision has a name

Magnetic measurement technologies

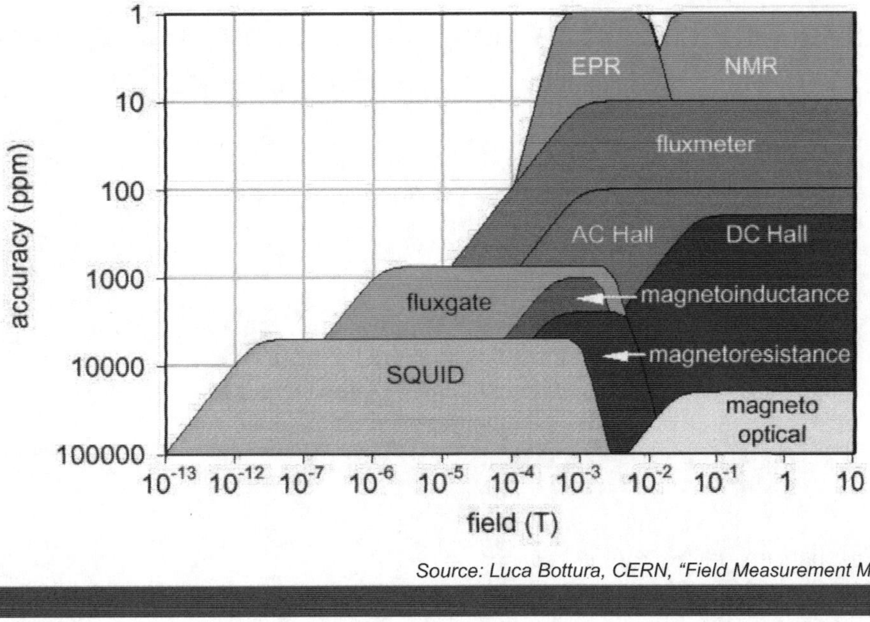

Source: Luca Bottura, CERN, "Field Measurement Methods"

METROlab
Magnetic precision has a name

NMR Precision Teslameters

- Pros:
  - Very precise
  - No drift: time, temperature
  - Total field
- Cons:
  - Uniform fields only
  - Static fields only (?)
  - High fields only (?)
- Application examples:
  - High-precision field mapping (e.g. MRI, accelerator physics)
  - Standards & calibration (secondary standard)
  - Magnet regulation (e.g. accelerators, ion mass spectrometers)

METROlab
Magnetic precision has a name

Nuclear Magnetic Resonance

Quantum-mechanical view:
Zeeman level transition

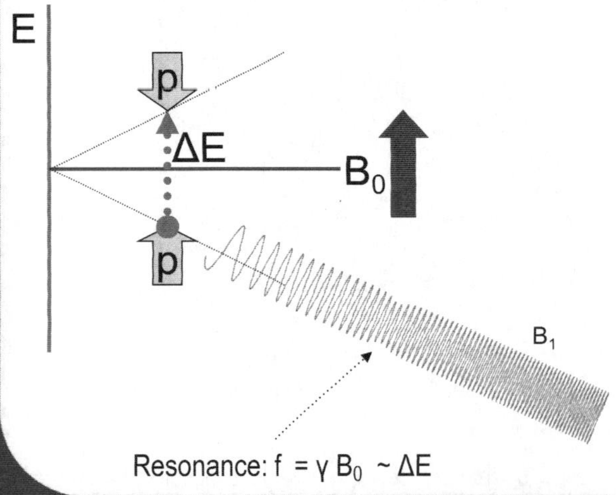

Pseudo-classical view:
Spin precession

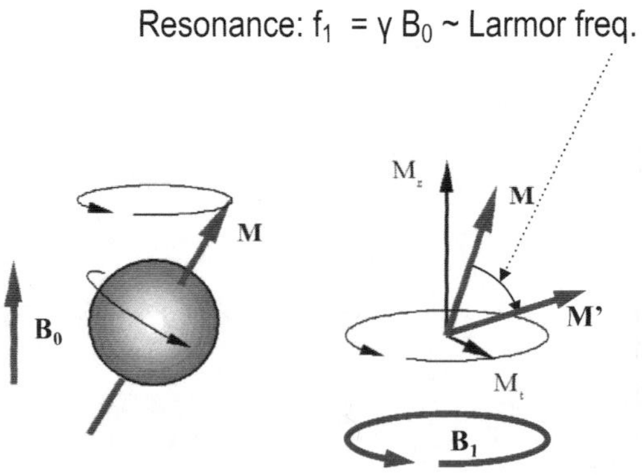

NMR commercial applications

- NMR Spectroscopy (Varian, 1948)

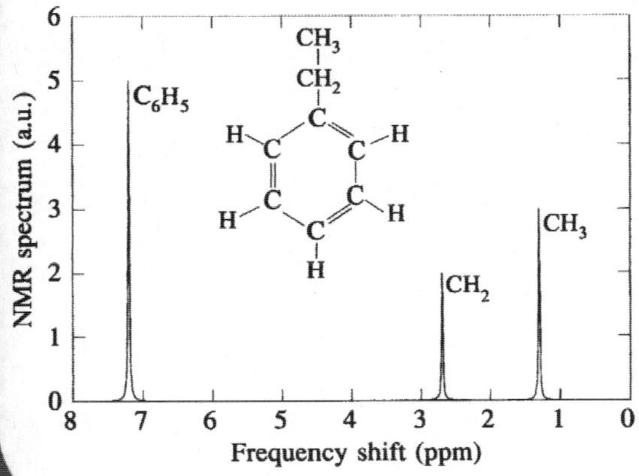

Source: G. Boero, EPFL, PhD Thesis (2000)

- MRI (Fonar, 1978)

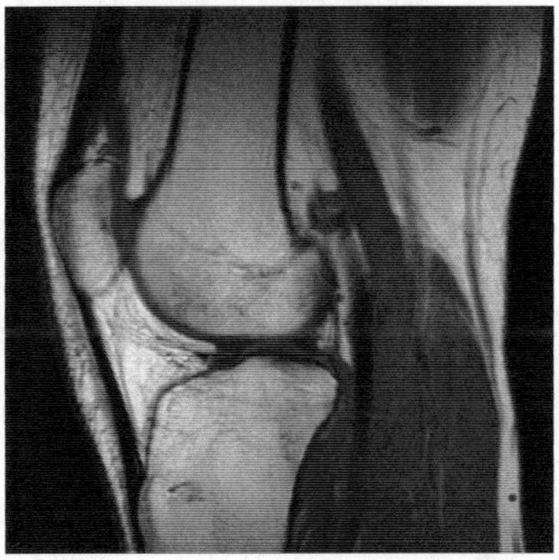

Source: Wikipedia, "MR Knee.jpg" (2006)

NMR magnetometer: recipe

- Sample material: water (^1H), deuterium (^2H), …
  - Single, sharp NMR resonance peak
  - "Reasonable" relaxation time (H_2O ~ 2 sec)
- B_1 excitation coil:
  - ± perpendicular to B_0
  - linear oscillation = superposition of 2 counter-rotating fields
- Radio-Frequency (RF) generator:
  - Wide-band: ~ 1 MHz – 1 GHz
  - Stable: ~ ppb/day
  - Spectrally pure
- Detector:
  - "Continuous-wave" (CW):
    - Inductive bridge, Marginal oscillator, Absorption
  - "Pulsed-wave" (PW):
    - Re-emission
- Modulation for CW: RF frequency or B_0

Magnetic precision has a name

NMR magnetometer: example

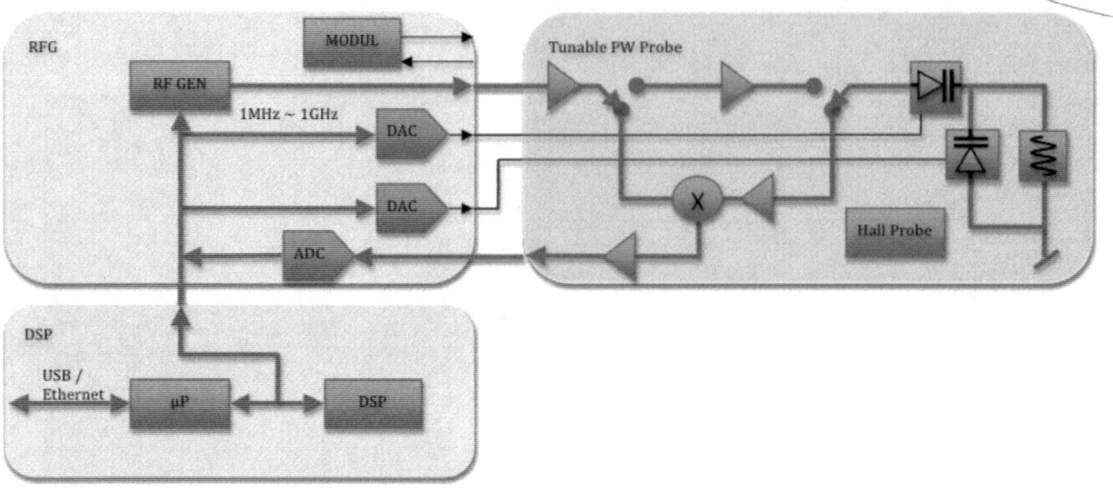

Magnetic precision has a name

NMR magnetometer: example

- Range: 38 mT – 30 T
- Resolution: 0.01 ppm (typical)
- Accuracy: 5 ppm
- Measurement rate: 33 Hz max
- Max gradient: > 1.5 mT/cm

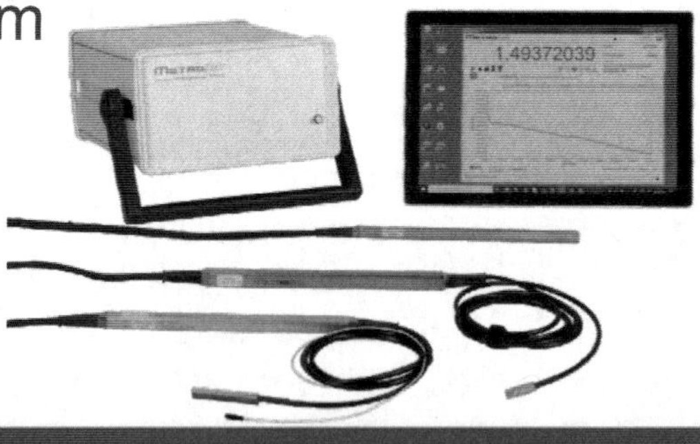

METROlab
Magnetic precision has a name

What "0.01 ppm" really means

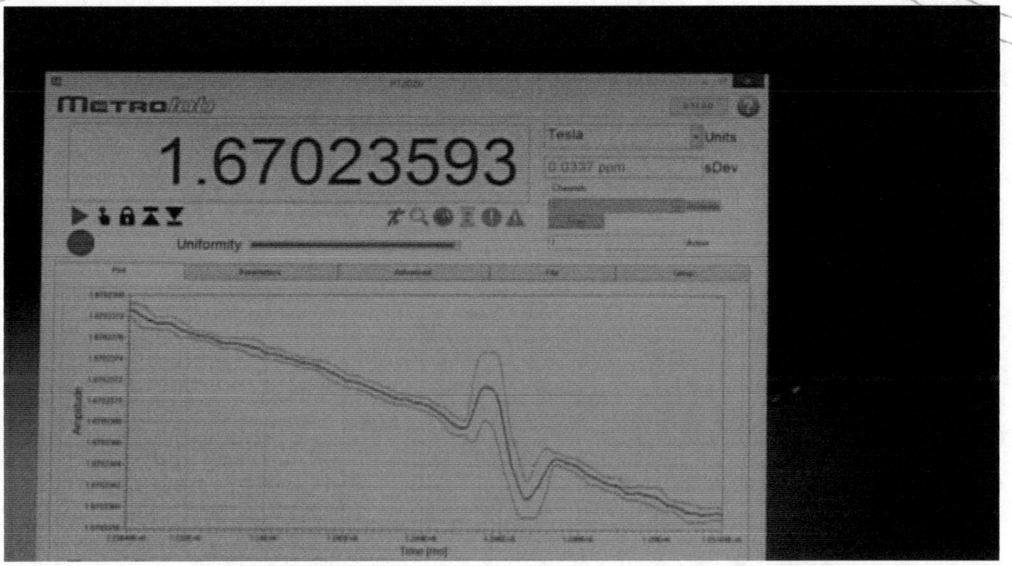

METROlab
Magnetic precision has a name

Challenges: Design optimization

Single-chip integrated transceiver:

- Reduced complexity
- Improved SNR
- Broader bandwidth
- Reduced power
- No ferro-magnetic material

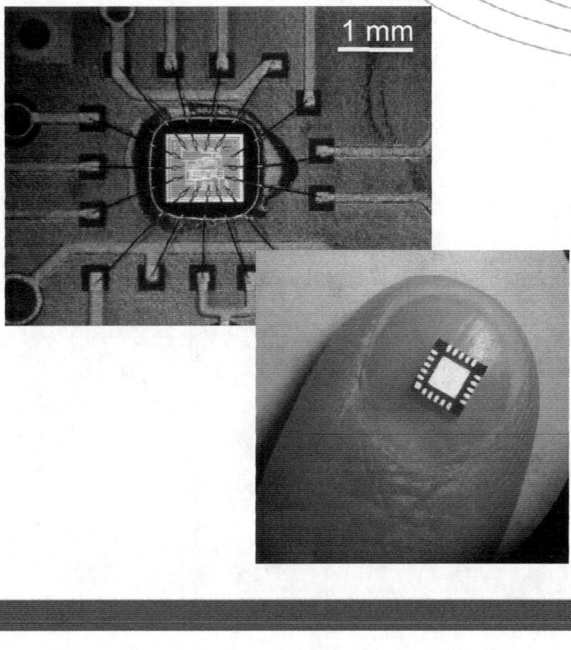

Magnetic precision has a name

Challenge: Rapid field mapping

- Parallelism:
  ≤ 255 probes / array
- Mechanical accuracy:
  < 0.3 mm
- Simplicity:
  - 2D structure
  - Specific geometry
  - Narrow field range

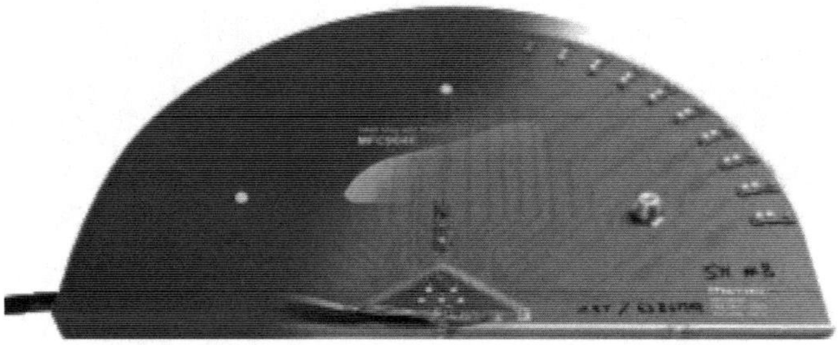

Magnetic precision has a name

Challenge: Rapid field mapping

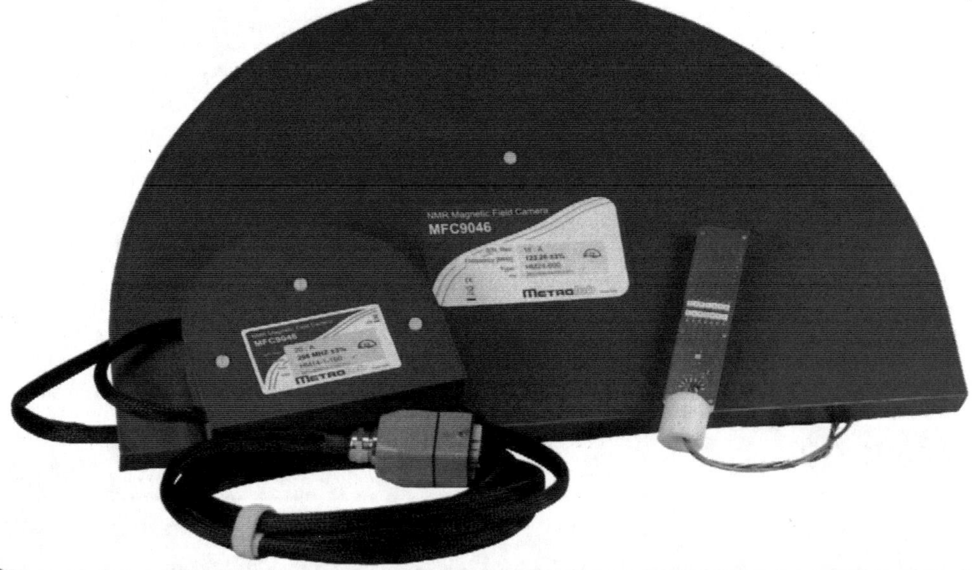

METROlab
Magnetic precision has a name

Challenge: Low fields

- Physical limitation: thermal noise lessens spin polarization, thus NMR signal & SNR
- Possible approaches:
  - Large samples
  - ESR
  - Sensitive detector
  - Pre-polarization

METROLAB Instruments SA — the world leader in NMR measurement

1072 ESR PROBE

MEASUREMENT OF LOW FIELDS : 32 GAUSS AND LESS

- Range : 1072-4: 0.55 to 1.6 mTesla (5.5 to 16 Gauss)
  1072-5: 1.1 to 3.2 mTesla (11 to 32 Gauss)

METROlab
Magnetic precision has a name

Challenge: Low fields

Dynamic prepolarization via Overhauser effect:

- Excite ESR to spin-polarize electrons
- Spin transfer polarizes nuclei
- Measure NMR resonance

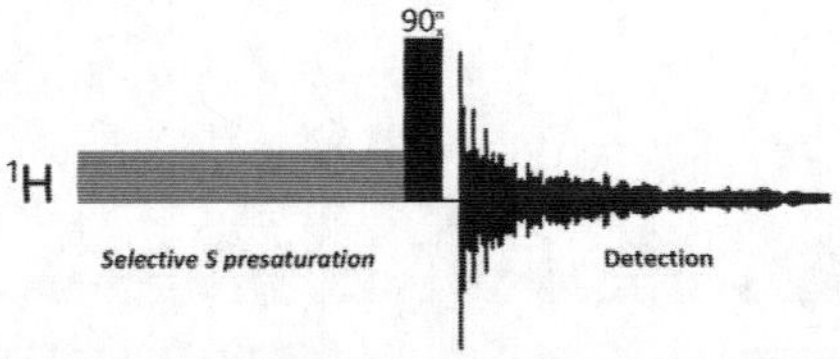

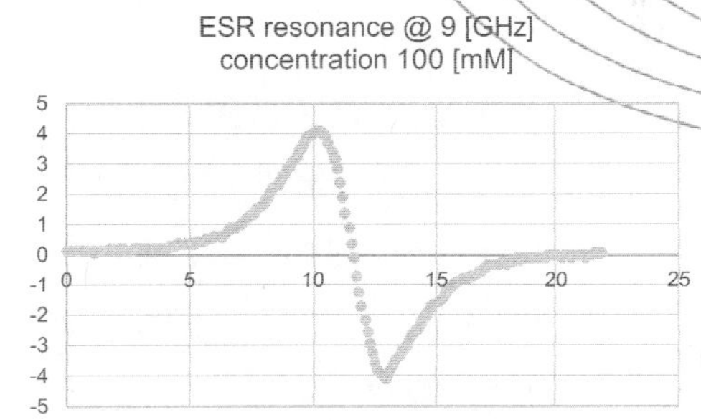

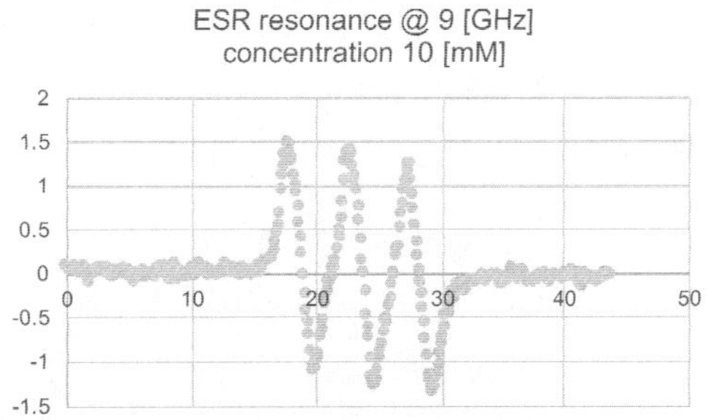

Measurement made @ EPFL / Boero, Tinembart

METROlab
Magnetic precision has a name

Challenge: Rapidly varying fields

- No physical limits: NMR resonant frequency changes instantaneously
- Challenge is data analysis

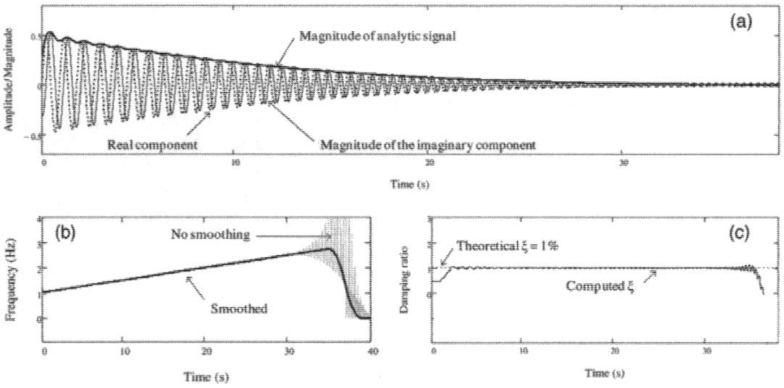

Giovanni Cascante
University of Waterloo

METROlab
Magnetic precision has a name

Conclusions

- NMR provides:
  - Very high precision
  - Total reproducibility
  - **B** vector magnitude
- Pulsed NMR magnetometers are mature
- Pulsed NMR field mappers are commercially available
- Promising solutions exist for low and rapidly varying fields

MAGNETICS 2020

Additive Manufacturing of Magnetic Materials

Dr. Sim Narasimhan
P2PTechnologies
Moorestown ,New Jersey

P2PTech

MAGNETICS 2020

P2P Technologies

- **P2P Technologies is a Division of CS 21 LLC, registered in NJ, USA.**
- **Intellectual Property strategies; Business Strategies**
- **Guidance in material selection and processing of metal powders**
- **Sales of Neo , rare earth, permanent magnets**
- **Global Sales Marketing including India, China, Korea and USA**
- **Seminars on Powder Metallurgy, Permanent magnets for beginners and advanced level**

P2PTech

MAGNETICS 2020

AM of Magnetic Materials

- What is AM
- Application to Hard magnets
- Application to soft magnets
- Conclusions

P2PTech

MAGNETICS 2020

Vocabulary of Additive manufacturing

3D Printing	
Rapid Prototype Rapid Manufacturing	Additive Manufacturing (AM) Additive layer Manufacturing (ALM)
Laser Beam Melting (LBM) Selective Laser Melting (SLM) Selective Laser Sintering (SLS) Direct Metal Laser Sintering (DMLS) Electron Beam melting (EBM) Powder Bed Fusion	Free Form Fabrication (FFF) Solid Free Form Fabrication (SLFF)
Laser Metal Deposition Laser Cladding Direct Energy Deposition (DED) Direct Metal Deposition (DMD) Powder bed Fusion	

In Red most common terminology

P2PTech

EPMA

MAGNETICS 2020

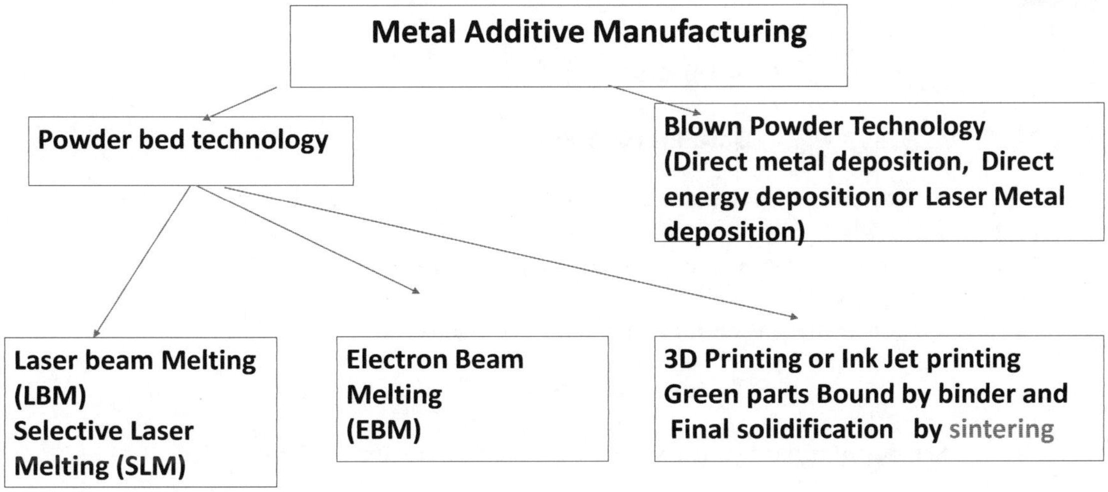

EPMA

P2PTech

TICS 2020

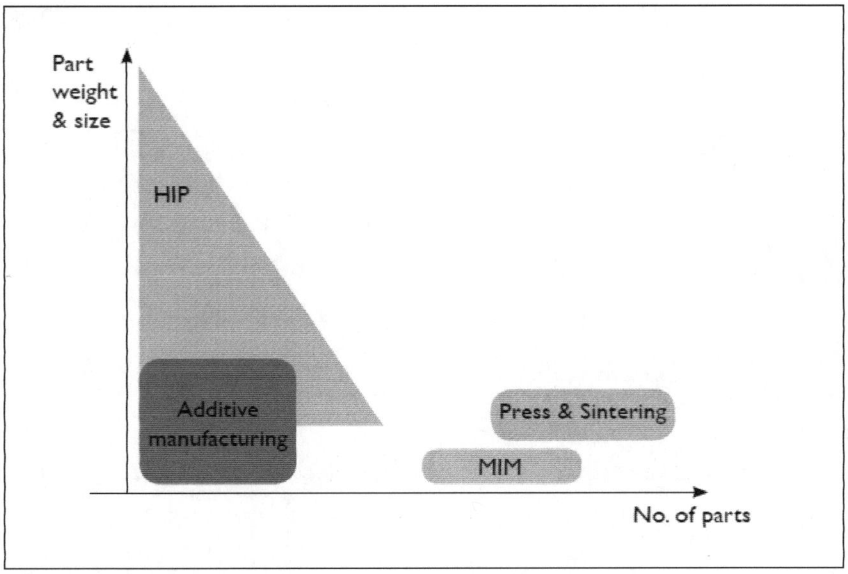

EPMA

P2P

Positioning of various PM technologies according to part weight or size and production series

MAGNETICS 2020

3D Modeling

Data Preparation

Part orientation and support structures , slicing from 3DSlice program

Manufacturing on AM machine

Generation of control data ,production of parts

Post Processing

Removal of support structures and platform, Heat treatment , Finishing

P2PTech

MAGNETICS 2020

Post Processing

Machining
EDM
Peening, Grinding,
Polishing, surface treatment
Heat treatment
Hot isostatic pressing (HIP) to eliminate residual porosities

P2PTech

MAGNETICS 2020

Selective laser melting

Small area is melted and Cooling is rapid and forms nanocrystalline grains

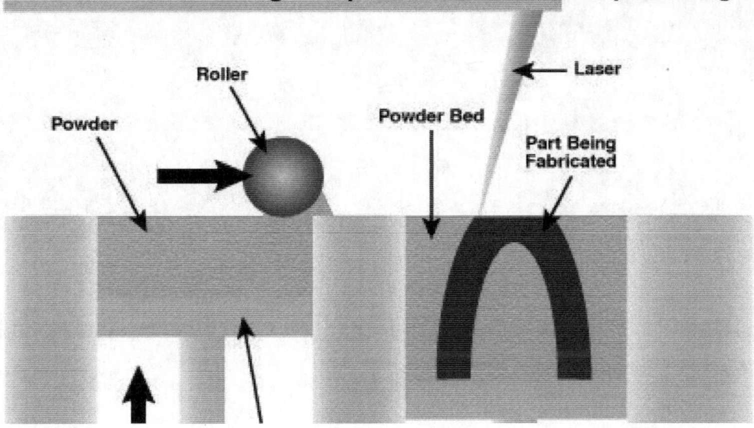

P2PTech

MPIF

MAGNETICS 2020

EOS M290- Hoeganaes Corporation- Cinnaminson, NJ USA

P2PTech

MAGNETICS 2020

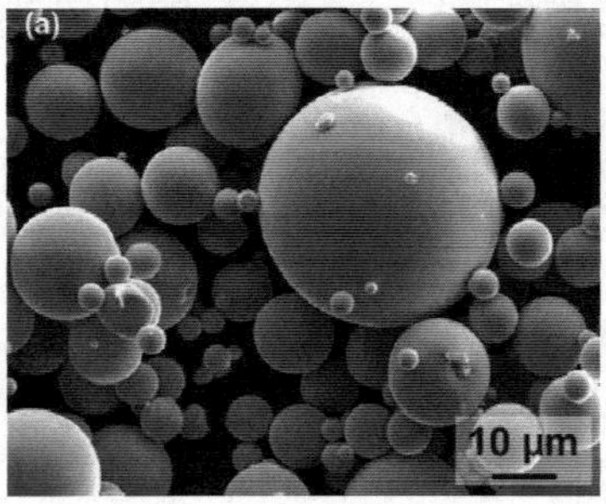

Powder | 3D Simulation | **Actual part With powder attached to it**

Materials Today • Volume

Simon Pauly[1], Lukas Löber[1,2,*], Romy Petters[1,*], Mihai Stoica[1], Sergio Scudino[1], Uta Kühn[1] and Jürgen Eckert[1,2]

P2PTech

MAGNETICS 2020

InkJet Printing

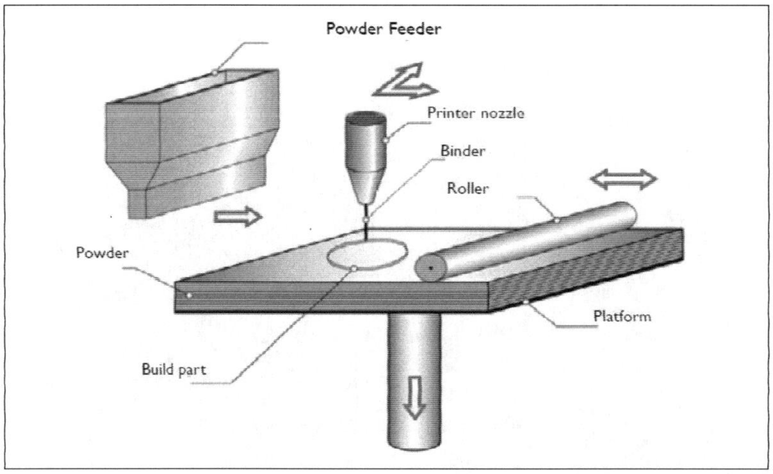

Manufacturers

- Digital Metal
- ExOne

P2PTech

MAGNETICS 2020

ExOne Binder Jet Printer- Hoeganaes Corporation- Cinnaminson, NJ USA

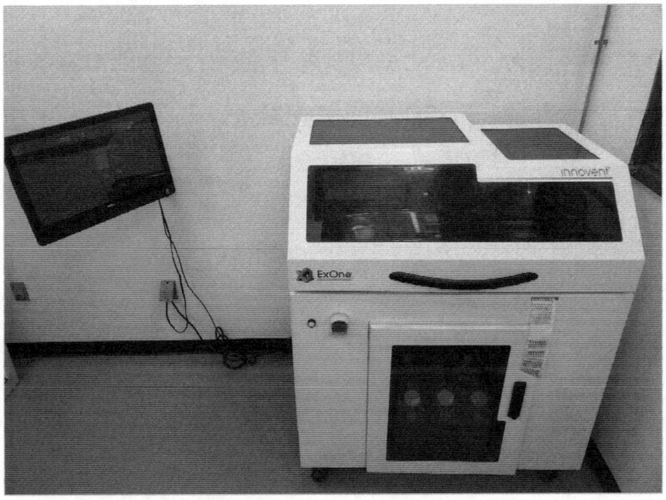

P2PTech

Additive Manufacturing benefits

- Design freedom compared to casting and machining
- 3D shapes and provide material where needed
- Net Shape capability saving raw material costs.
- No Tools Needed. Rapid prototyping
- Constraints on production runs is eliminated

P2PTech

Additive Manufacturing Limitations

MAGNETICS 2020

- Part size is limited to powder bed size of 250mmx250mmx250mm
- Direct deposition can be much larger sizes but build time is slow
- Production runs of 25000/year and hence limited to small production runs
- Non weldable materials cannot be processed
- Anisotropy in the build z direction
- Densities in excess of 99.5% can be achieved ;superior to cast parts

P2PTech

Industry Usage

MAGNETICS 2020

- Aerospace
- Medical
- Tooling
- Automotive and transportation
- Consumer goods
- Etc

P2PTech

Rough estimate of costs

MAGNETICS 2020

	2018	2023
Build speed	**$40cm^3/hr$**	**$80cm^3/hr$**
Machine costs	**$770000**	**$880000**
Machine Utilization	**84%**	**81%**
Steel powder price	**77/kg**	**30/kg**
Post processing costs	**1.05/Kg**	**0.96/kg**
Total cost	**1.6X**	**1.1X**

P2PTech

Cost are decreasing as usage and knowledge grows

MAGNETICS 2020

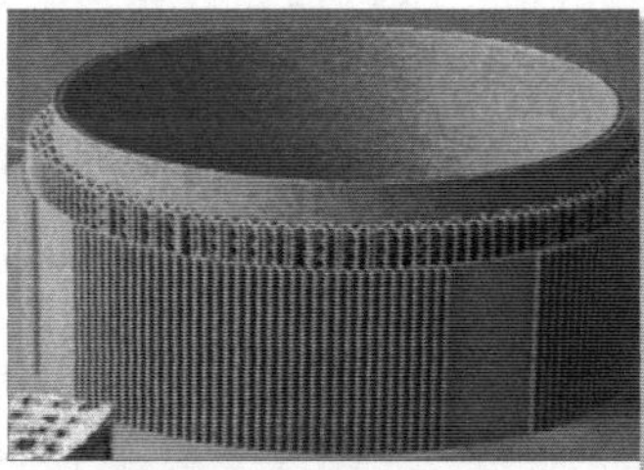

Prototype of heat exchanger for electrical motor with struts of 0.4 mm diameter for COMPOLIGHT project (Courtesy of Fraunhofer IFAM)

EPMA

www.nafems.org

Ni 718 Combustion chamber made by Laser Beam Melting (Courtesy of Concept Laser GmBH) EPMA

Complex shapes are possible with AM

P2PTech

Typical Magnetic Materials and their magnetism origin

MAGNETICS 2020

Origin of Coercive Force	Alloy Systems
Mechanical Hardening	Fe-C, Fe-Cr-C, Fe-Co-C, Fe-W-C, Fe-Co-V, Ag-Ni-Cr, Ag-Mn-Al
Precipitation Hardening and Shape Anisotropy	F-Co-W, Fe-Co-Mo, Fe-Al-Ni, Fe-Al-Ni-Co, Fe-Ni-Cu, Co-Fe-Ti, Fe-Ni-Ti, Fe-Co-W, Fe-Cr-Co
Superstructure Crystal Anisotropy	Pt-Fe, Pt-Ni, Pt-Co
Crystalline Anisotropy	Mn-Bi, Mn-Al, Mn-Al-C, Rare earth -Co, Ba Ferrite, Sr Ferrite, Rare-Earth-Fe-B, Fe 16N2, Sm-Fe-N
Exchange Anisotropy	Co-CoO, Fe-CoO, Rare Earth FeB/Nano Fe
Narrow Domain Walls	DY_3Al_2, Th-Co-Ni
Amorphous and Microcrystalline Alloys	Rare earth-Fe-B, F-Cr-P, Fe-Co-Si-B

P2PTech

MAGNETICS 2020

Permanent Magnetic Materials single domain size

Material	Saturation Induction(T)	Curie temp(K)	Domain wall width(nm)	Single domain radius(nm)	Crystal structure
CoPt	1.0	840	4.5	310	Tetragonal
FePt	1.43	750	3.9		Tetragonal
MnAl	0.75	650	15	90	Tetragonal
MnBi	0.78	630			Tetragonal
$BaFe_{12}O_{19}$	0.48	723	14	290	Hexagonal
$SrFe_{12}O_{19}$	0.47	733			Hexagonal
$SmCo_5$	1.07	1003	3.6	425	Hexagonal
YCo_5	1.06	987			Hexagonal
Sm_2Co_{17}	1.30	1190	6.5	250	Rhombohedral
$Sm_2Fe_{17}N_3$	1.54	749	3.6	190	Rhombohedral
$Nd_2Fe_{14}B$	1.61	585	3.9	107-300	Tetragonal
$Pr_2Fe_{14}B$	1.41	565	4.6	300	Tetragonal

P2PTech **300 nm= 0.3 microns**

Lewis et.al

MAGNETICS 2020

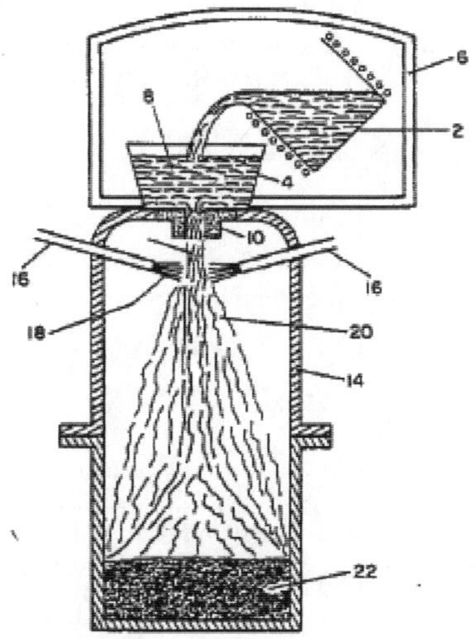

United States Patent [19] — Narasimhan et al.
[11] Patent Number: 4,585,473
[45] Date of Patent: Apr. 29, 1986

P2PTech

MAGNETICS 2020

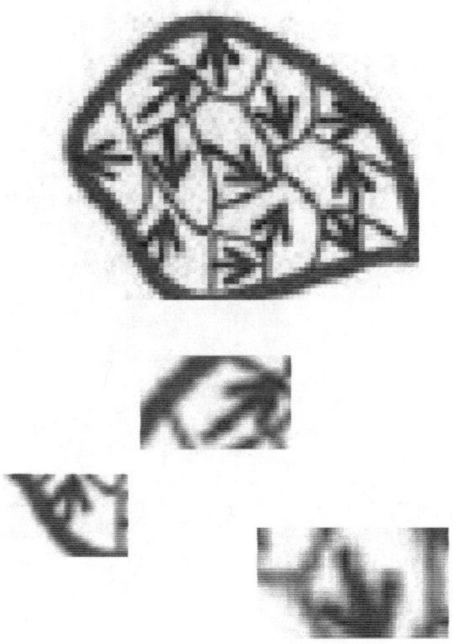

- **Atomizing the melt and quenching does not have sufficient cooling rate(10^3 to 10^5 K/sec).**
- **Each particle has several single domain; so easy to crush and get single domain size grains.**

P2PTech

MAGNETICS 2020

Gas atomized $Nd_2Fe_{14}B$ and $SmCo_5$ powder intrinsic coercive force. Data collected on powders dispersed in liquid paraffin and orienting in a magnetic field of 2000 kA/m(25kOe)

Method of production	Particle size, microns	Ratio of remanence over saturation (indicator of hysteresis loop shape)	Intrinsic coercive force kA/m
$Nd_2Fe_{14}B$ Atomized in Ar, liquid argon quenched	-74	0.38	120((1500Oe)
$Nd_2Fe_{14}B$ Atomized in Ar, liquid argon quenched	-88	0.17	42 (527Oe)
$Nd_2Fe_{14}B$ Atomized in Ar, liquid argon quenched	-100	0.15	36 (452Oe)
$Nd_2Fe_{14}B$ Atomized in Ar, liquid argon quenched	-250	0.12	32 (402Oe)
$SmCo_5$ Atomized in Ar, liquid argon quenched	-300 to +150	NA	1750(22000Oe)
$SmCo_5$ Atomized in Ar, liquid argon quenched	-150+75	NA	1544(19400Oe)

P2PTech

MAGNETICS 2020

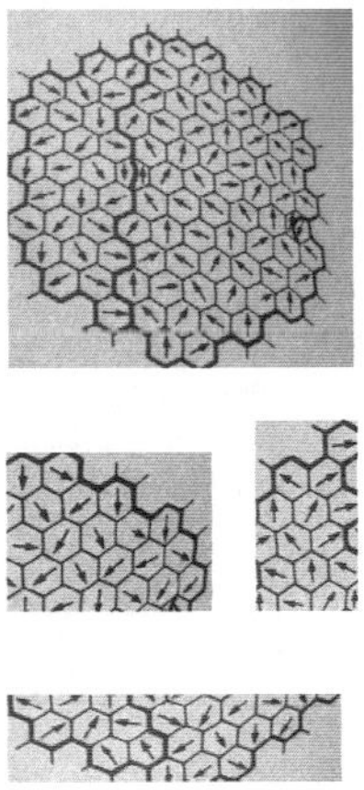

Selective laser melting(SLM) has a cooling rate of 10^5 to 10^7K/sec can Form Fine nano size grain microstructure close to single domain size.

Melt Spinning has cooling rate equivalent or better

Melt spun ribbons generally are blended with polymer to make shapes. SLM provides a possibility to form dense bodies with no polymers enhancing the induction achieved.

$(Nd_{0.8}Ce_{0.2})_{2.4}Fe_{12}Co_2B$ Ribbons

Heyun Li, Yang Liang, Xiaohua Tan,* Hui Xu, Pengfei Hu,* and Kezhi Ren

P2PTech

MAGNETICS 2020

Net Shape 3D Printed NdFeB Permanent Magnet

J. Jaćimović[1*], F. Binda[1], L. G. Herrmann[1], F. Greuter[1], J. Genta[1], M. Calvo[1], T. Tomse[2,3], R. A. Simon[1]

[1] ABB Corporate Research Center, Baden-Daettwil, Switzerland
[2] Department for Nanostructured Materials, Jožef Stefan Institute, 1000 Ljubljana, Slovenia
[3] Jožef Stefan International Postgraduate School, 1000 Ljubljana, Slovenia

P2PTech

MAGNETICS 2020

Visit toABB

(R-L)
Thomas Cristen, Jacim Jacimovic, Sim, Levina Schaerf

P2PTech

MAGNETICS 2020

An ABB Synchronous Reluctance motor. Modified from http://quintecgmbh.com/us/news/161-news-abb-synchronour-reluctance-motor.html

P2PTech

MAGNETICS 2020

SLM for NdFeB Magnets

Spherical powders are used to improve flowability to make a dense powder bed. Commercial MQP-S spherical powder of Nd7.5Pr0.7ZR2.6Ti2.5Co2.5Fe75B8.8 from Magnaquench was used .

The powder size distribution had d50 of 38micron with a flow rate of 3 .33g/cm3 and tap density of 4.67 g/cm3 Which is 61.4%of the full density

As printed magnets had Br of 0.59T,BHmax of 45kJ/m3(5.65MGOe) and grain size of nano scale

J. Jaćimović[1*], F. Binda[1], L. G. Herrmann[1], F. Greuter[1], J. Genta[1], M. Calvo[1], T. Tomse[2,3], R. A. Simon[1]

[1]ABB Corporate Research Center, Baden-Daettwil, Switzerland
[2]Department for Nanostructured Materials, Jožef Stefan Institute, 1000 Ljubljana, Slovenia
[3]Jožef Stefan International Postgraduate School, 1000 Ljubljana, Slovenia

P2PTec

MAGNETICS 2020

SLM Of NdFeB

- **A commercial 3Dprinter was used to produce 3dimensional magnets**
- **A design of 3D object is made by CAD software and sliced in layers to determine the thickness layer deposited on the platform.**
- **Five laser parameters laser power (LP),laser focus(LF),point distance (PD),Exposure time(ET) and hatching distance(HD)**
- **A pulsed NdYAG-Laser with max energy output of 120Watts.**
- **Spot size diameter varies from 15 microns to 30 microns . The movement of laser focus from one point to next is 1to 50 micron defined by PD.**
- **The duration of laser beam 10to 300 microseconds.**
- **LP=1700mA.LF=30micron,PD=30micron,ET 110 microsecond ,LT=20micron,HD=100micron**
- **Grain size printed nano micron,**

J. Jaćimović[1*], F. Binda[1], L. G. Herrmann[1], F. Greuter[1], J. Genta[1], M. Calvo[1], T. Tomse[2,3], R. A. Simon[1]

[1]ABB Corporate Research Center, Baden-Daettwil, Switzerland
[2]Department for Nanostructured Materials, Jožef Stefan Institute, 1000 Ljubljana, Slovenia
[3]Jožef Stefan International Postgraduate School, 1000 Ljubljana, Slovenia

P2PTe(

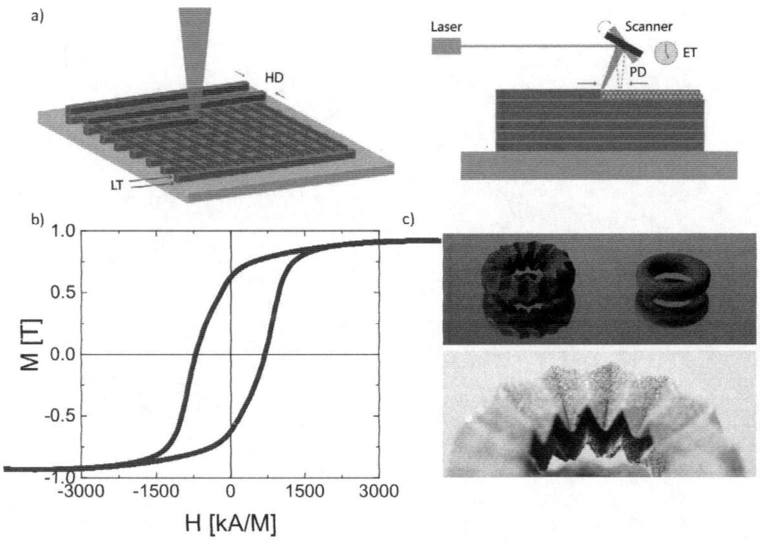

MAGNETICS 2020

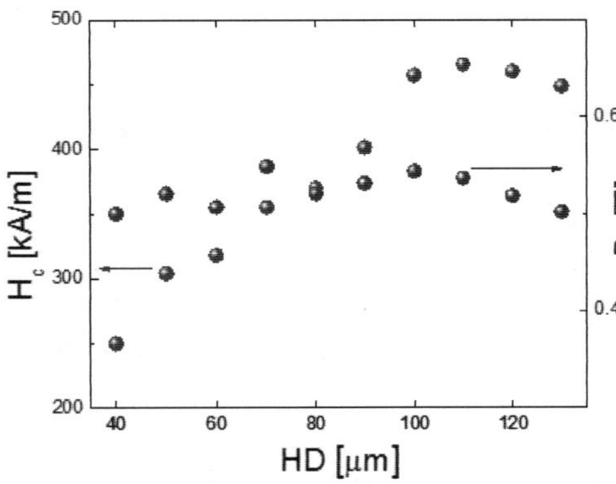

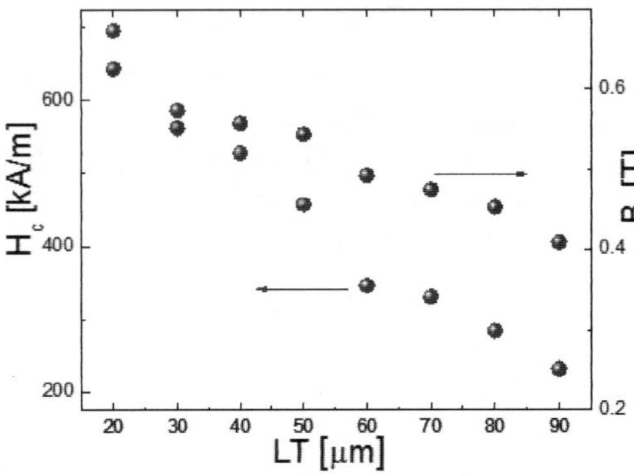

450kA/m= 5643 Oe

700kA/m =8778 Oe

Jacimovic; ABB

P2PTech

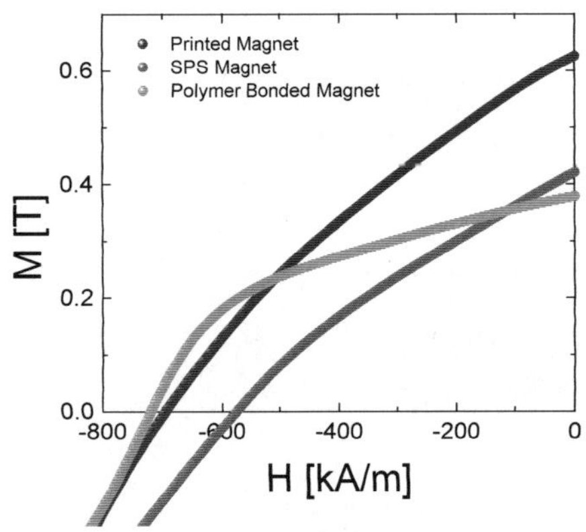

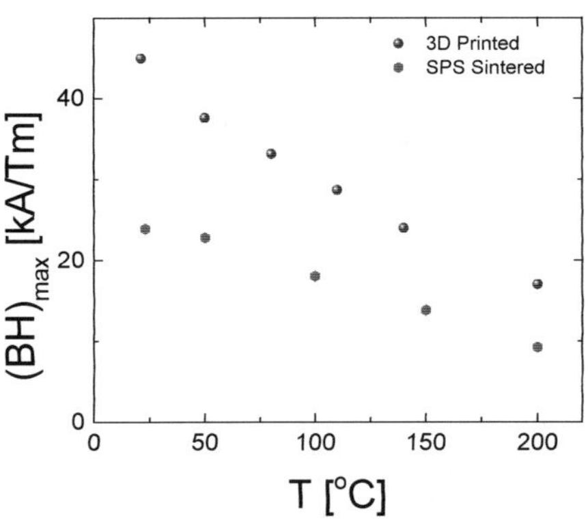

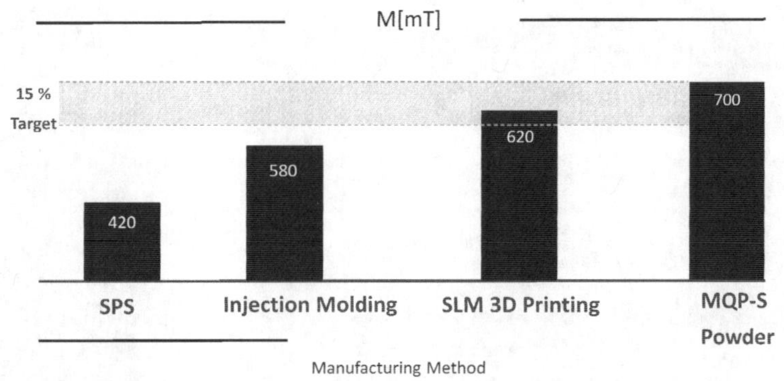

 February 13, 2020 Slide 35

MAGNETICS 2020

Amazing result without magnetizing as printed specimen exhibits zero stray field but when cut ;pieces shows Huge fields as high as 80mT or 800Gauss

P2PTech

MAGNETICS

Selective Laser Melting of Al-Ni-Co permanent magnets

Emma White from Ames laboratory .USA. produced by AM alnico magnets with a remanence of 0.9T and coercivity of 183kA/m

The coercivity is Higher than normal Directional Alnico which generally is about Br of 1.05 to 1.35T and Hc of 55 to 70kA/m

Directional Alnico 8B(Co35%,Ni15%,Cu 4%,Ti5%,Al7%,Fe34%) has Br of 0.87T and coercive force of 127 kA/m

Alnico 5-7 (Al8%,Ni14%,Co24%,Cu3%,bal Fe) which has typical values of Br 1.34 T, coercive force of 59kA/m (740 Oe),BH max of 59.7 kJ/m3((7.5MGOe)

Emma White Data suggest more elongated single domains increasing the coercive force

E. White, A. Kassen, E. Simsek, W. Tang, R. Ott, I. Anderson. Net Shape Processing of Alnico Magnets by Additive Manufacturing. IEEE Transactions on Magnetics, Volume: PP Issue: 99. DOI: 10.1109/TMAG.2017.2711965 (2017)

Elongated single domain particles

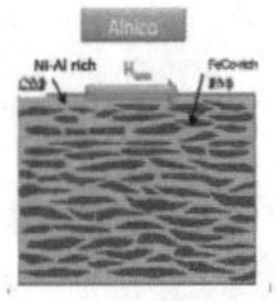

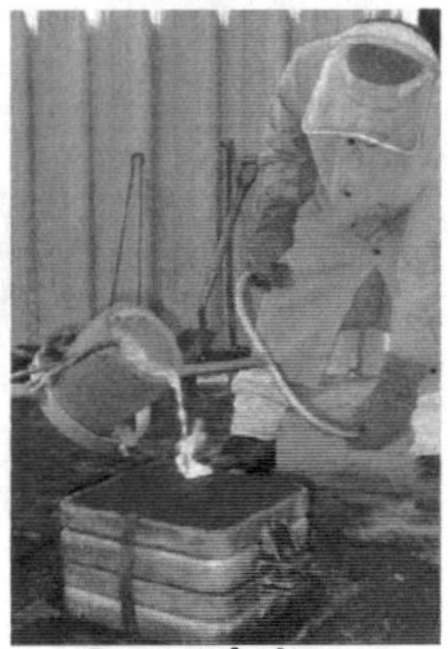

Cast Alnicos process

P2PTech

MAGNETICS 2020

Processing Sequence for MnAlC magnets

- Alloy is cast into billets and warm extruded at about 600C to form the oriented magnetic Tau phase to make anisotropic magnets. energy product of 45kJ/m3(5.65 MGOe). Br of 0.62T Hc of 206kA/m(2588 Oe) are typically produced but has a potential of 127kJ/m(16MGOe)

(A. Ibata and Y. Sakomoto, "Permanent MnAlC Magnets" U.S. Patent 4.648,915, March 1987)

- MnAlC has better properties than Ferrites and raw materials are in abundance

P2PTech

MAGNETICS 2020

MnAlC by AM

. Recently mechanical alloying of MnAl C show that the fine grain powder of € phase can be converted to T magnetic phase by heat treatment

Researchers at Vienna were able to load very fine MnAlC into polymer matrix with a loading of 72% and extruded at 120C to 1. 75mm.diameter wire 12 meters long.

Hc of these filaments are 120KA/m(1500Oe). with a Br of 0.16T. These polymer extruded filaments can be used in binder jetting process for making complex shaped magnets.

- *Ester M. Plamero, Jaavier Ria, Javier de vincente, Julio Camaerero, bjorn Skarman, Hilmar Vidarsson.* "Development of permanent magnet MnAlC/polymer composite and flexible filamnet of bonding and 3dprinting Technologies";Science and Technologgy of Advanced materials,2018,Vol 19.No 1 465-473

P2PTech

MAGNETICS 2020

Binder jet printed magnets of (SmFeN+NdFeB)

Sample	Temperature (K)	H_c (kOe)	B_r (kG)	$(BH)_{max}$ (MGOe)
S1	300	10.8	3.7	2.8
S2	458	11.1	4.7	4.6
S3	468	11.1	6.9	10.2
S4	478	11.0	7.2	11.0

S1=As printed,S2,S3,S4 magnetized at temp at 15KOe field

Kinjal Gandha,Linhg Li,I.C.Niebedim,Brian K.Poat,Vlastimil Kunc, Brian C.Sales, James Bell,M.Prans Paranthaman;"Additve Mnaufacturing of anisotropic hybrid NdFeB-SmFeN nylon composite Bonded magnets;Journal of Magnetism Materials 467,(2018)8-13.

P2PTech

MAGNETICS 2020

Soft Magnetic Materials- select

- For AC applications Resistivity above 120 Micro-Ohm-Cm required to make bulk soft magnetic materials to overcome Eddy current losses

Grade	Composition	Saturation Induction KGauss(Tesla)	Coercive force A/m/(Oe)	Maxmium permeability	Resistivity Micro-Ohm cm
Fe-Si	1%Si	21000	35.2(0.442)	14780	16
	3.0Si	20500	15.2(0.192)	17440	45
	4.8Si	19300	15.9(0.20)	17160	60
	6.4Si	18200	11.7(0.147)	28860	70
DeltaMax	50Ni,balFe	16,000(1.6T)	3.18-12.75(0.04to0.16)	100000	45
Alloy4750	48Ni,Bal Fe	15,500(1.55T)	1.6-7.9(,012-,10)	100000	45
Mu metal	77Ni,5Cu,2Cr,0r4%Mo,balFe	7500(.75T)	0.8-2.4(.01-.03)	100000	60
Supermendur	49Co,2V,balFe	24000(2.4T)	16(0.2)	92000	40
Finemet	1Cu,3Nb,13.5Si,9B,73.5Fe	12400(1.24T)	0.5(0.06)	10000	~50 to 130
2714A(Metglas)	85Co,3Ni,plus Glass former	5700(0.57T)	---	100000	142
2826MB(Metglas)	38Ni,4Mo,18B,40Fe	8800(0.88)	0.4	10000	142
2605SA1(Metglas)	84Fe,Si,Mn,B,C	15600(1.56T)	2.4	35000(as cast)	130

P2PTech

MAGNETICS 2020

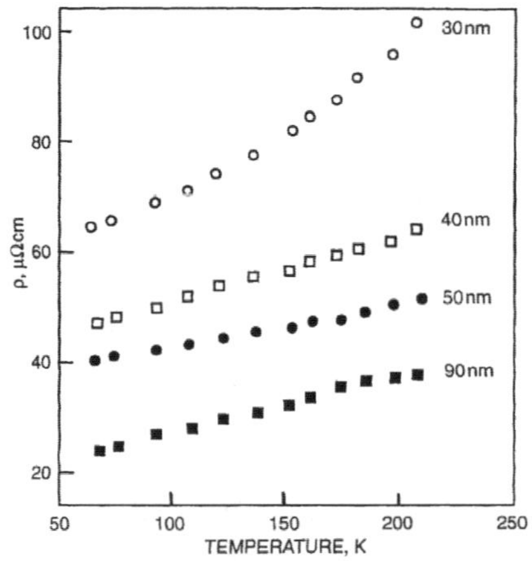

13 Variation of electrical resistivity with temperature for nanocrystalline Fe–Cu–Si–B alloys (after Ref. 167)

Nanocrystalline materials

C.Suryanarayana; "nano Crystalline Materials" International Materials Review,Jan 1995

P2PTech

Grain size controls the resistivity

Processing metallic glasses by selective laser melting

Simon Pauly[1], Lukas Löber[1,2,*], Romy Petters[1,*], Mihai Stoica[1], Sergio Scudino[1], Uta Kühn[1] and Jürgen Eckert[1,2]

Materials Today • Volume 16, Numbers 1/2 • January/February 2013

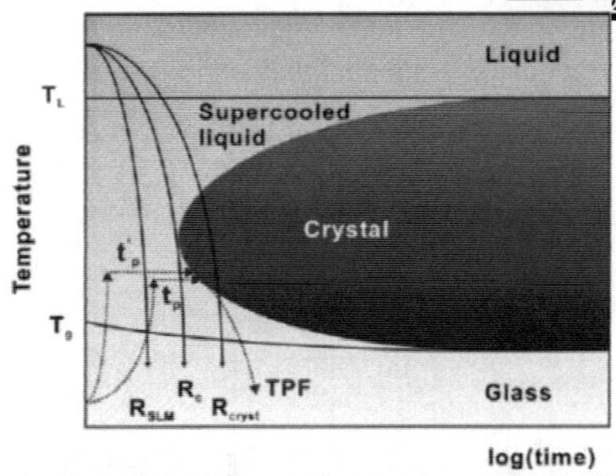

FIGURE 1

Schematic CCT diagram for a metallic glass former. Vitrification occurs when the melt is cooled at rates higher than the critical cooling rate, R_c. At lower cooling rates, R_{cryst} for example, the crystalline 'nose' is crossed and the melt partially or fully crystallizes. This is generally avoided during SLM as it has high intrinsic cooling rates, R_{SLM}. In the course of thermoplastic forming (TPF) the glass is heated into its supercooled liquid region and brought into the desired shape in a maximum time, t_p. Subsequently, the supercooled liquid has to be cooled to room temperature at sufficiently high rates. When the heating step is finished in an extremely short time

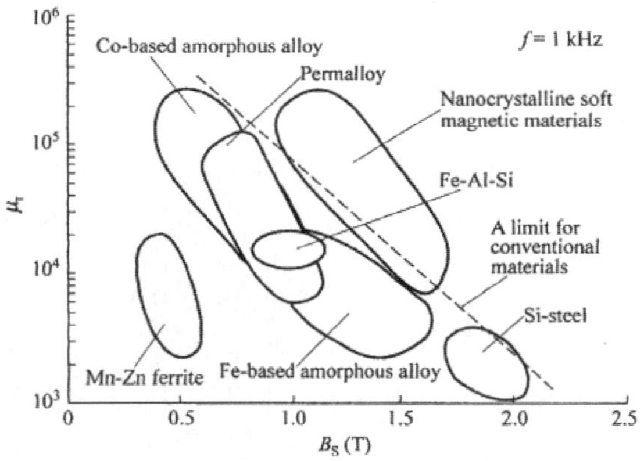

Figure 4. 1 Relationship between relative permeability μ_r and saturation magnetic induction B_S for typical soft magnetic materials.

4 Nanocrystalline Soft Magnetic Materials and Their Applications

Yoshihito Yoshizawa

Yoshihito Yoshizawa "Nano crystalline Soft magnetic Materials and Their applications" Handbook of Advanced Magnetic Materials pp 1452-1486 (2006)

MAGNETICS 2020

J. Appl. Phys. **115**, 17A319 (2014)

High speed electric motors based on high performance novel soft magnets

J. M. Silveyra,[1] A. M. Leary,[2,a)] V. DeGeorge,[2] S. Simizu,[3] and M. E. McHenry[2]

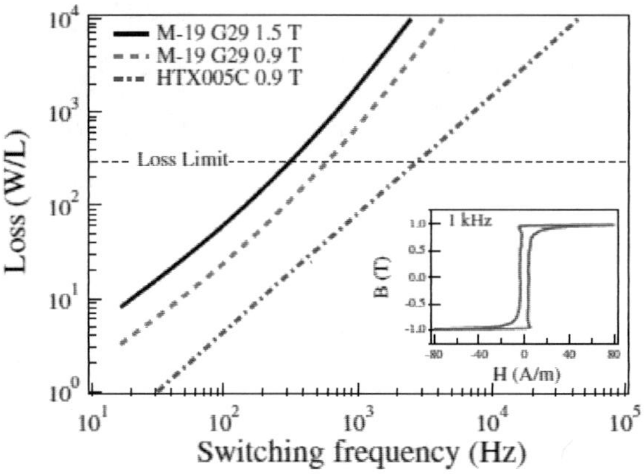

FIG. 1. Comparison of iron loss for M-19 G29 (B_P = 1.5 and 0.9 T) and HTX-005C (B_P = 0.9 T) vs. f. Horizontal dashed line shows a 300 W/L iron loss limit of air-cooled machines. Inset: hysteresis loop of HTX-005C at 1 kHz.

P2PTech

MAGNETICS 2020

- Suitable printer parameters for processing Fe-Co powder were first searched based on the literature and practical test.
  - The aim here was to maximise the density of the parts.
- Besides the topology optimized rotors of a switched reluctance machine, various test specimens for the magnetic, electrical, mechanical and structural characterisation were prepared.

NAFEMS VTT

3D printed rotor for a switchod reluctance machine. Outer dimensions of the rotor are approximately 3 cm x 4.5 cm.

www.nafems.org

P2PTech

MAGNETICS 2020

Conclusions

- **Brief overview of Additive manufacturing is presented highlighting benefits and short coming.**
- **3D Printing Additive manufacturing is a new tool available for making permanent magnets and soft magnetic material for small volume production .**
- **Variety of designs are possible removing the constraint from current manufacturing methods**
- **NdFeB and Rare earth free MnAlC magnets by AM show potential and needs further research**
- **Melt spun rare earth magnets can be replaced by SLM of rare earth alloy powders**

P2PTech

A Technology Roadmap To Anisotropic NdFeB Magnet Advancements

Sep 2019

韵升集团
YUNSHENG GROUP

Road Map of Magnet Development

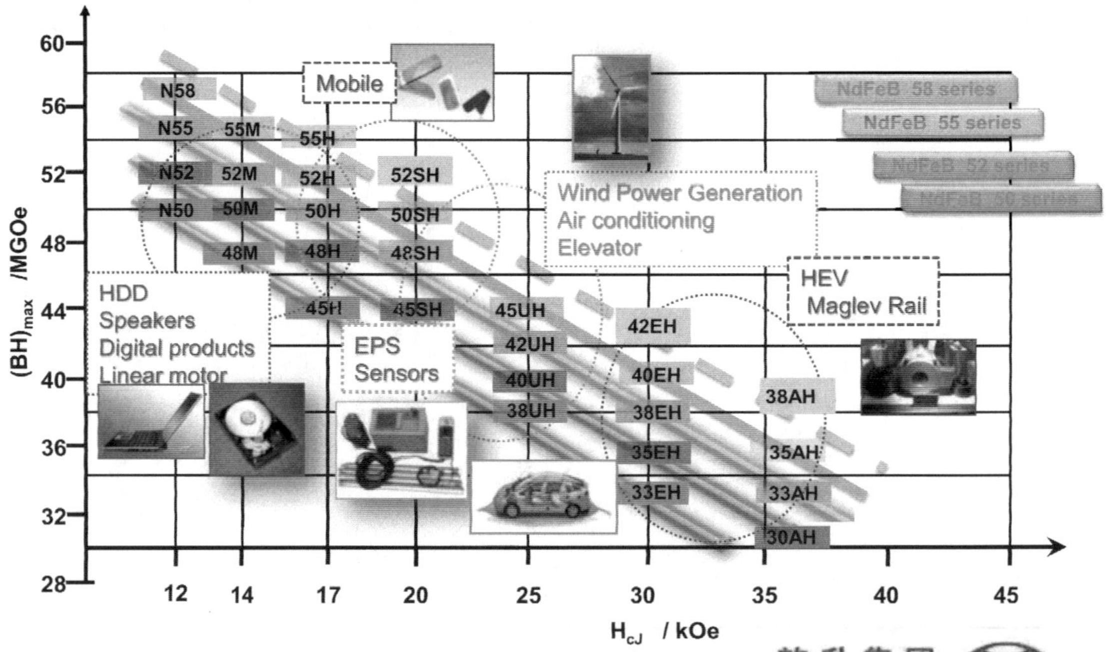

韵升集团
YUNSHENG GROUP

Content

1. HRE Free & Less HRE Technology

1.1 Grain Refining

1.2 Dual (Double) alloy

1.3 Grain Boundary Diffusion

2. Low Cost Technology (using Ce material replacing Nd)

3. New Pressing Technology

3.1 Near Net-shape

3.2 Multi-pole Ring

韵升集团 YUNSHENG GROUP

HRE Free & Less HRE Technology

Micro-structure Optimization

- Grain Refining
- Grain Size Consistence

Micro-component Optimization

- Double Alloy
- Grain Boundary Diffusion

韵升集团 YUNSHENG GROUP

1.1 Grain Refining - Theory

The relationship of grain particle size to Hcj

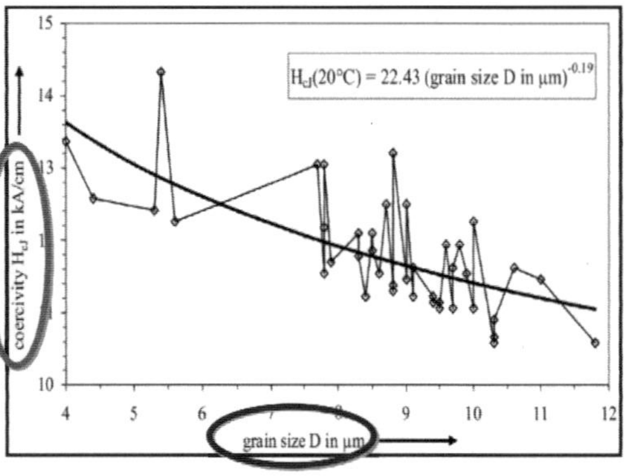

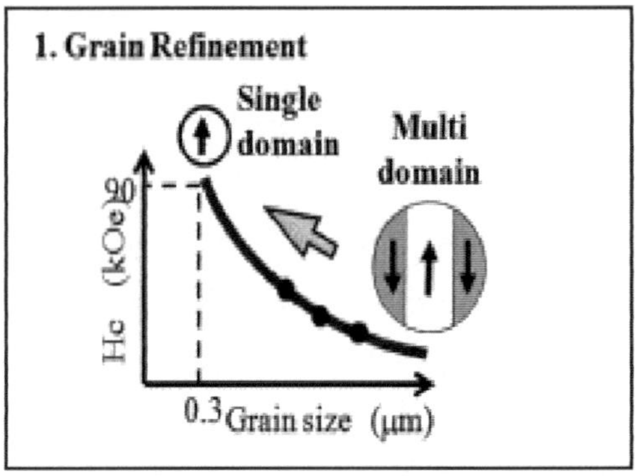

Smaller Grain Size → Better Domain Orientation → Better Microstructure Consistency → Higher flux& better soaking rate

韵升集团 YUNSHENG GROUP

1.1 Grain Refining - Relative process improvement

Strip Casting
- Improve strip casting technology to get more regular and compact dendritic crystal in casting sheet

Jet Milling
- Refining powder size with less large particle

Sintering
- Optimize sintering temperature to prevent grain from over-grow.

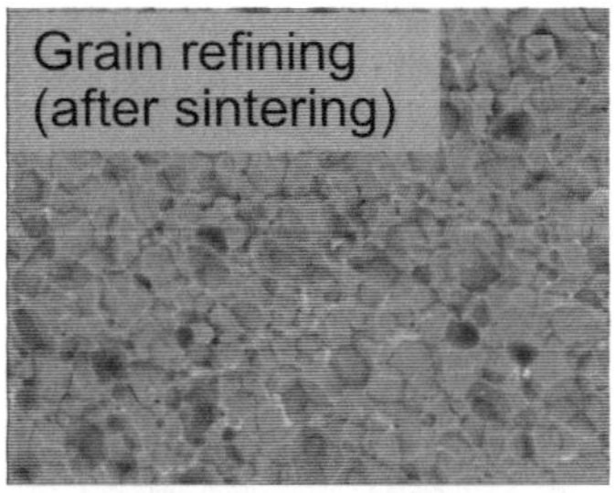

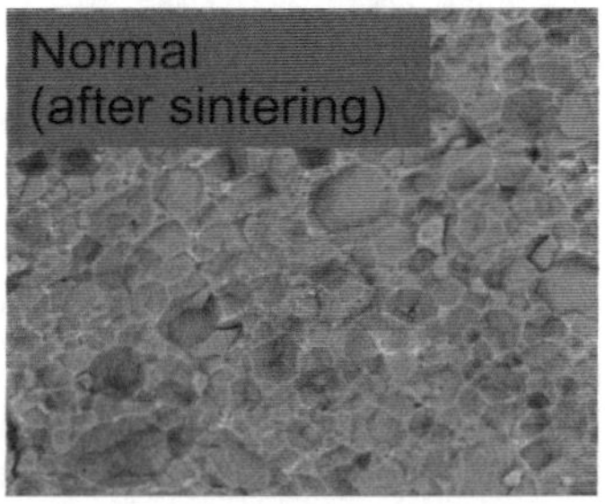

韵升集团 YUNSHENG GROUP

1.1 Grain Refining – High Performance

Optimizing microstructure of casting strip

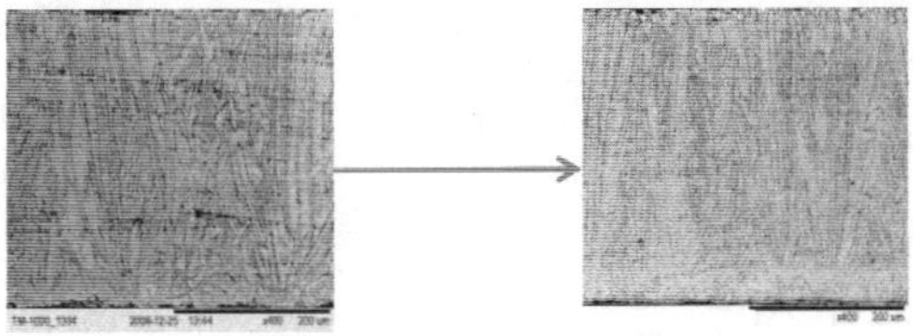

55M (no heavy rare earth)
B_r=14.7kGs
H_{cj}=14.4kOe
$(BH)_{max}$=52.06MGO**e**

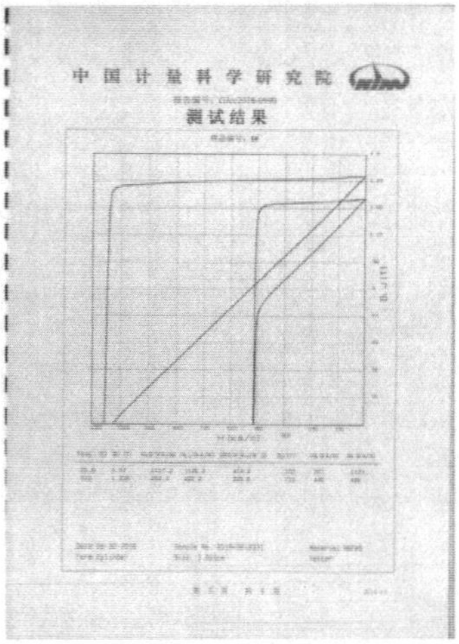

Optimizing particle size distribution

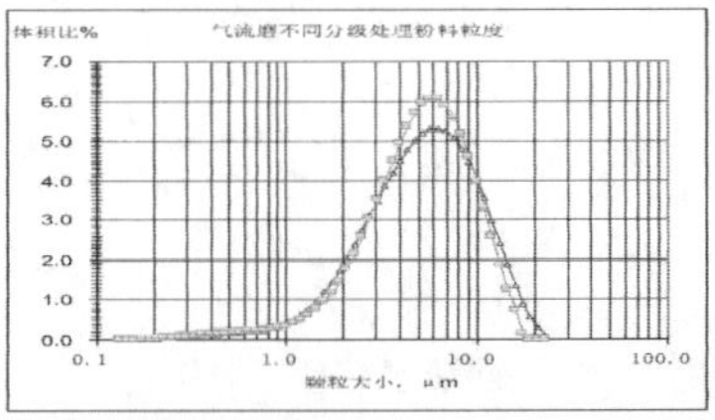

Optimizing microstructure of grain

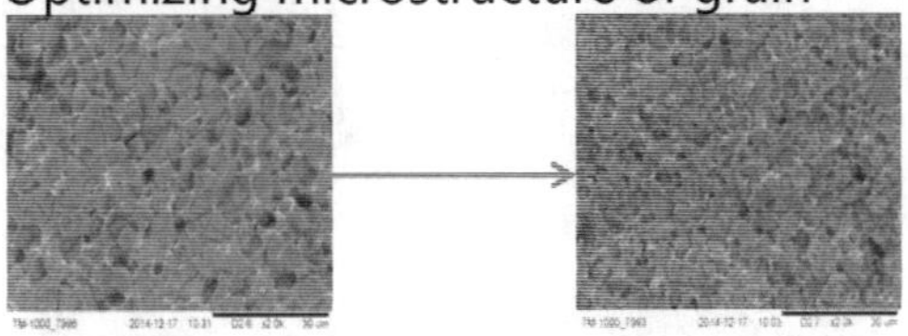

韵升集团
YUNSHENG GROUP

1.1 Grain Refining – Scope of Application

GR technology can be used for all magnets, 50H HRE FREE is currently under research.

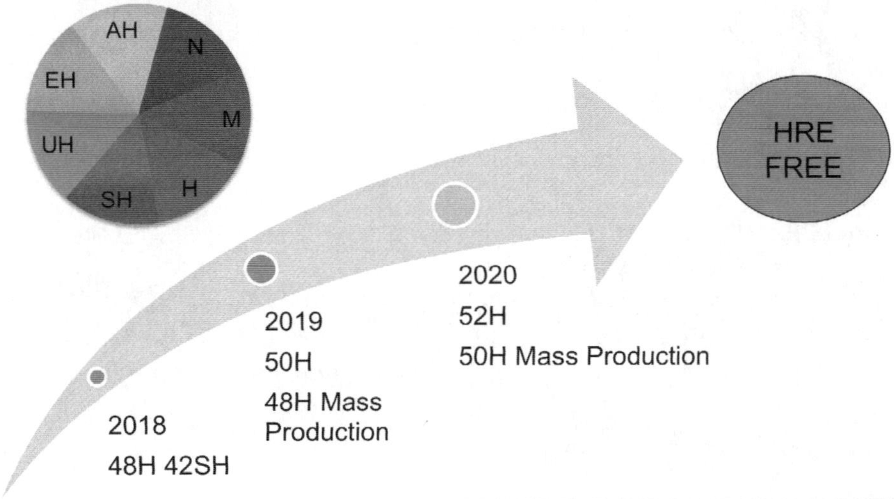

韵升集团
YUNSHENG GROUP

1.1 Grain Refining – Status

Before 2015

- Previous technology particle size 3.0um ~ 3.5um

End 2017

- Mass Production Particle size 2.6um ~ 3.2um with Less HRE, further refining particle size.

韵升集团 YUNSHENG GROUP

1.3 Double Alloy - Theory

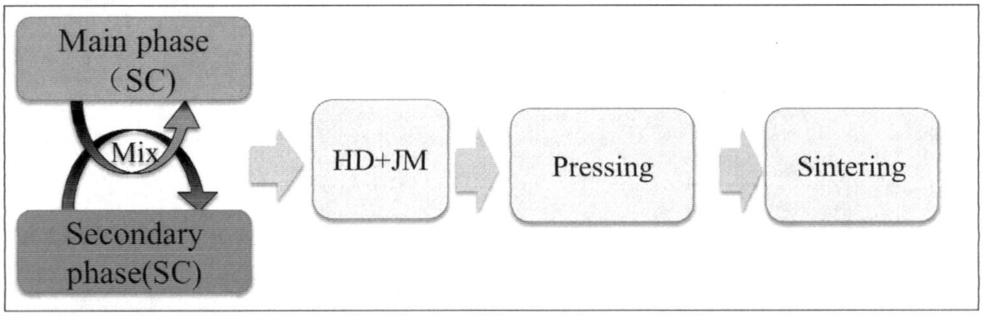

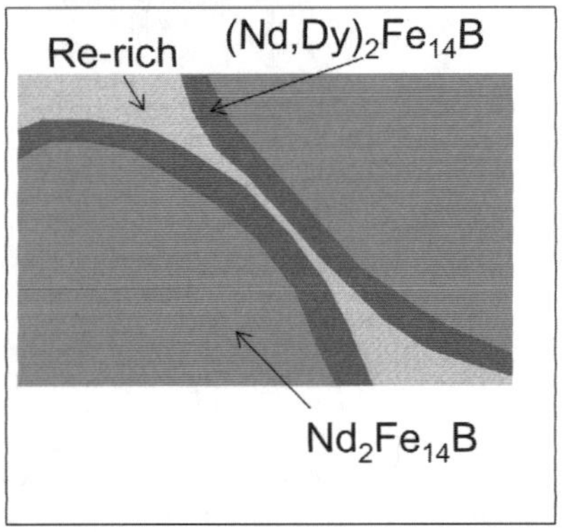

The HREE as Dy will be distributed in grain boundary, forming $(Nd,Dy)_2Fe_{14}B$ phase, enhancing the magneto-crystalline anisotropy and coercivity.

韵升集团 YUNSHENG GROUP

1.3 Double Alloy – Performance

Use double alloy technology, 48SH material can reach Br≥13.8kGs and Hcj≥21kOe but Tb ≤ 1%.

Year	Re%	Dy%	Tb%	Br /kGs	Hcj/kOe
2017	31.26	1.1	1	13.58	21.2
2018	30.975	0.7	1	13.88	21.77
2019	30.975	0.7	0.7	13.84	21.36

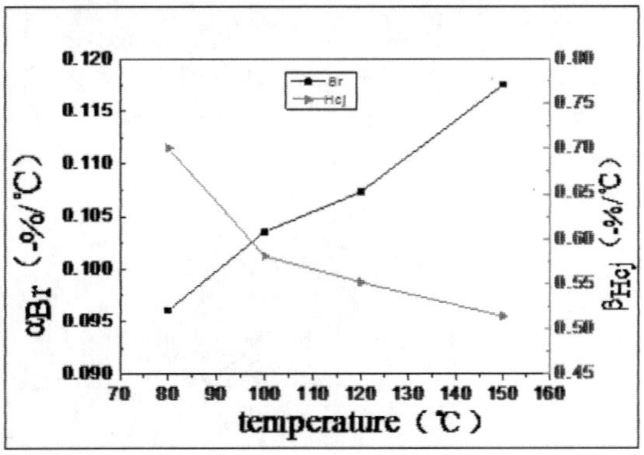

韵升集团 YUNSHENG GROUP

1.3 Double Alloy – Scope of Application

Double alloy technology is used on high grade material to save HRE and get better performance.

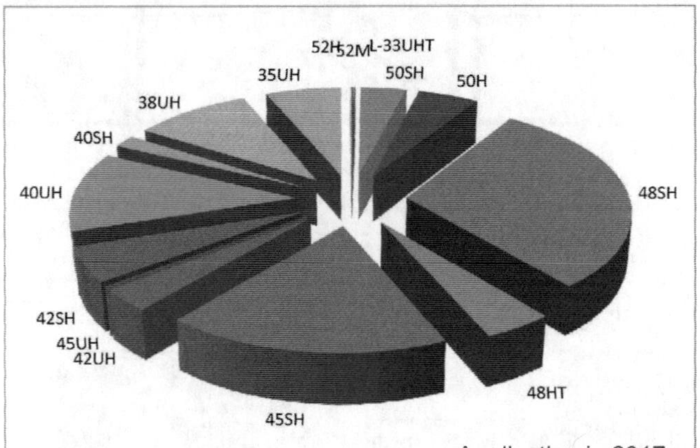

Application in 2017

韵升集团 YUNSHENG GROUP

1.3 Double Alloy – Status

In 2017

- More than 1400T blocks were produced by double alloy technology.

In 2019

- More than 3000T blocks were produced by double alloy technology.

韵升集团
YUNSHENG GROUP

1.2 Grain Boundary Diffusion - Theory

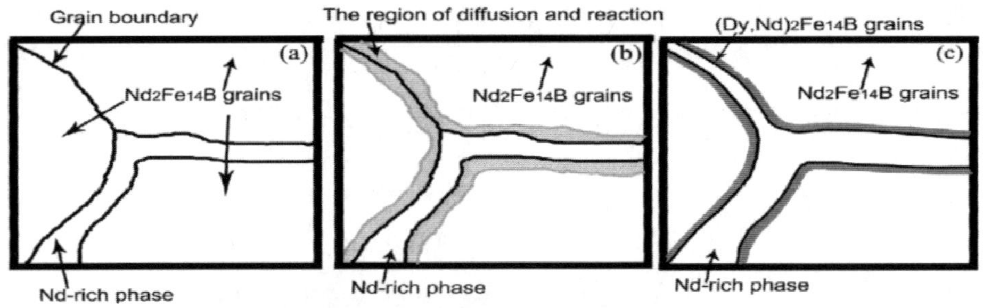

By grain boundary diffusion process, very small Dy was diffused to grain boundary, the coercivity was greatly improved, at the same time, the remanence was rarely decreased. This kind of process need new procession and equipment, and only for thin slice magnets.

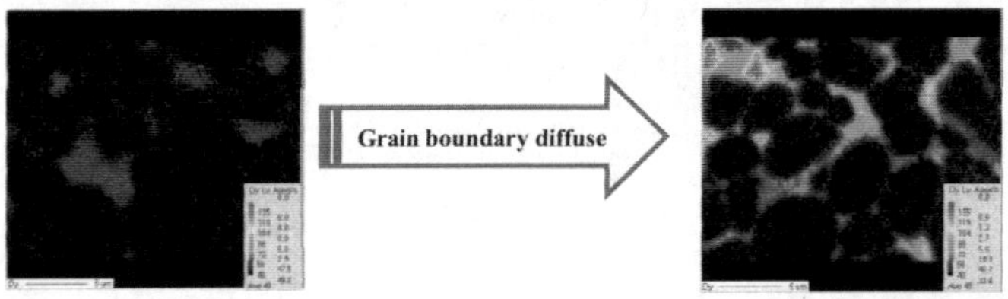

韵升集团
YUNSHENG GROUP

1.2 Grain Boundary Diffusion – Process Flow

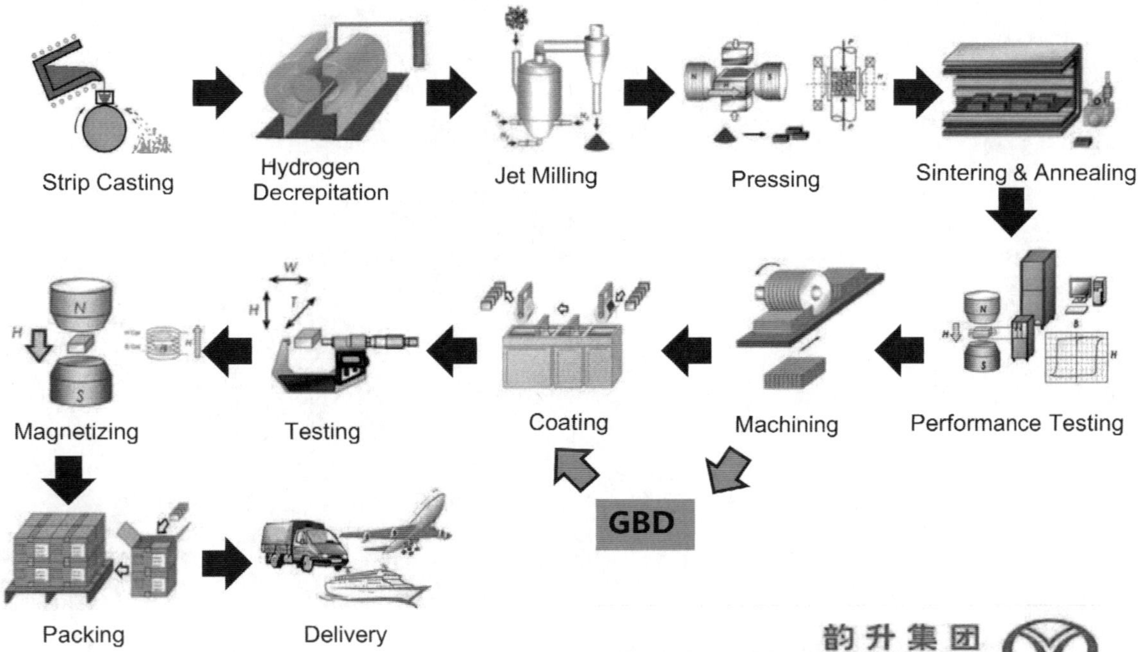

韵升集团 YUNSHENG GROUP

1.2 Grain Boundary Diffusion - Performance

GBD technology can achieve grades which cannot be reached by normal processes.

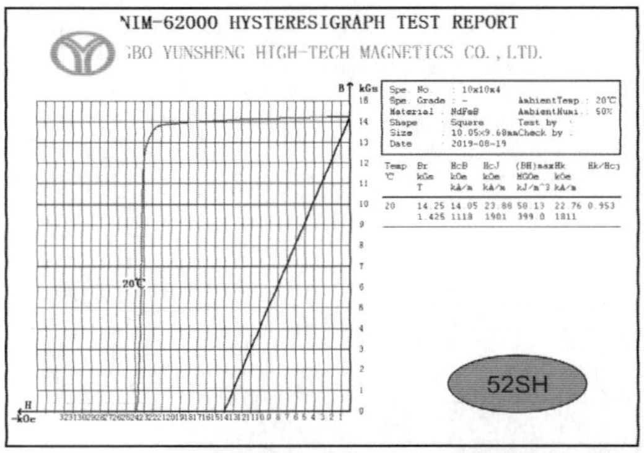

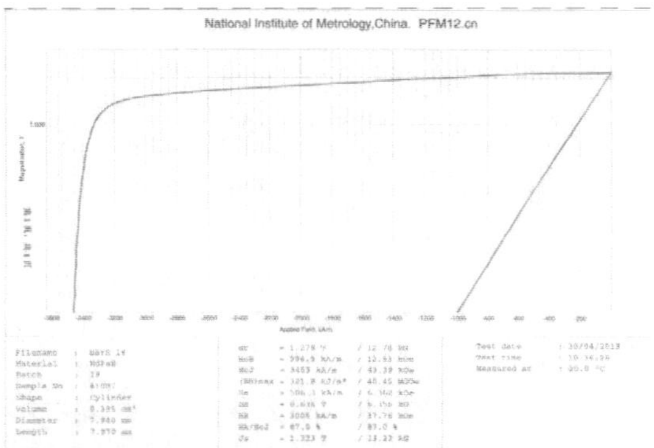

Grade	Br / kGs	H_{cj} / kOe	(BH)max / MGOe
52SH	14.25	23.88	50.13
/	12.78	43.39	40.45

韵升集团 YUNSHENG GROUP

1.2 Grain Boundary Diffusion – Scope of Application

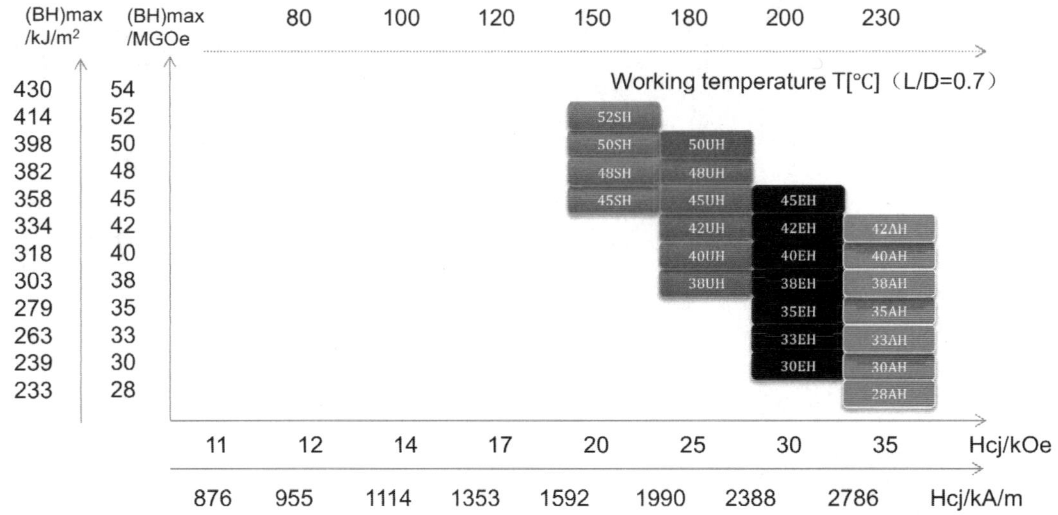

韵升集团 YUNSHENG GROUP

1.2 Grain Boundary Diffusion – Status

End 2019

- Ramp up capacity of 500T/Year

End 2020

- Ramp up the daily capacity to 800T/Year

韵升集团 YUNSHENG GROUP

1.2 Grain Boundary Diffusion – Patent Statement

Yunsheng always valued and respected intellectual property rights. Currently, most of Grain Boundary Diffusion technology are patent protected.

After years of research, our material scientists, have succeeded in finding new diffusion media and diffusion methodologies, which avoid the infringement of any existing Patents.

- Applied 8 domestic invention patents, including 4 authorized patents.
- Applied 2 PCT patents, apply for entry into the USA and EU, and have been accepted by USA.

No.	Chinese patent		Germany patent		American patent	
	Reference Number	state	Reference Number	state	Patent Number	state
1	CN201310301718.X	Granted	-	-	-	-
2	CN201310308670.5	Granted	-	-	-	-
3	CN201410320955.5	Granted	-	-	-	-
4	CN201510003209.8	In progress	-	-	-	-
5	CN201510894807.9	In progress	-	-	-	-
6	CN201510997488.4	Granted	11 2016 005 950.7	In progress	US15742032	In progress
7	CN201510995271.X	Granted	11 2016 005 949.3	In progress	US15742531	In progress
8	CN201610080584.7	In progress	-	-		-
9	CN201711416008.6	In progress	-	-	-	-
10	CN201711417664.8	In progress	-	-	-	-

韵升集团 YUNSHENG GROUP

2. Low Cost Technology (Less Nd) Introduction

RE	Js/T	H_A/kA·m^{-1}
La	1.38	2000
Ce	1.17	3600
Pr	1.56	5840
Nd	1.61	5600

R&D investigations have led to the study of the addition of Ce in Nd-Fe-B. Ce, can reduce the cost of some low grade material, and meet the customer's requirements.

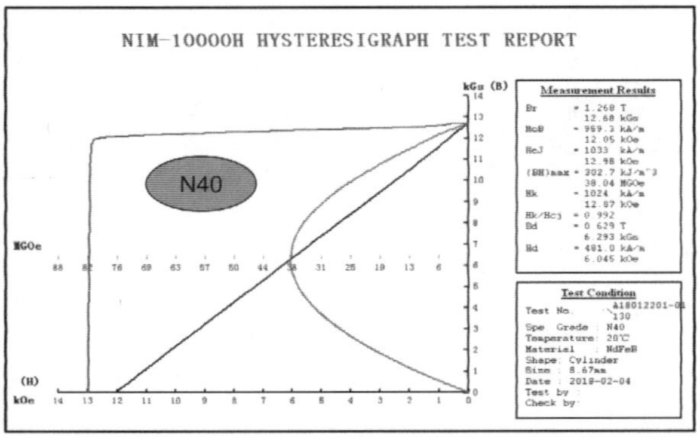

6.5% Ce instead of PrNd
save 5.5% cost down

韵升集团 YUNSHENG GROUP

2. Low Cost Technology (Less Nd) Introduction

NdFeB vs Ce NdFeB

		NdFeB	Ce NdFeB	Remarks
Commonality	Magnetic performance	Both can meet customer specifications		
	Application Performance	Similar		
	Process of material preparation, machining, plating	Same		
Differences	Recipe	The main R.E. element is PrNd	Partial PrNd is replaced by Ce	(1) The price of Ce is about 10% of PrNd (2) The price of Ce is relatively stable
	Cost	High	Low	

韵升集团 YUNSHENG GROUP

2. Low Cost Technology (Less Nd) Introduction

Ce % of replacement vs Finished Magnet Cost Down

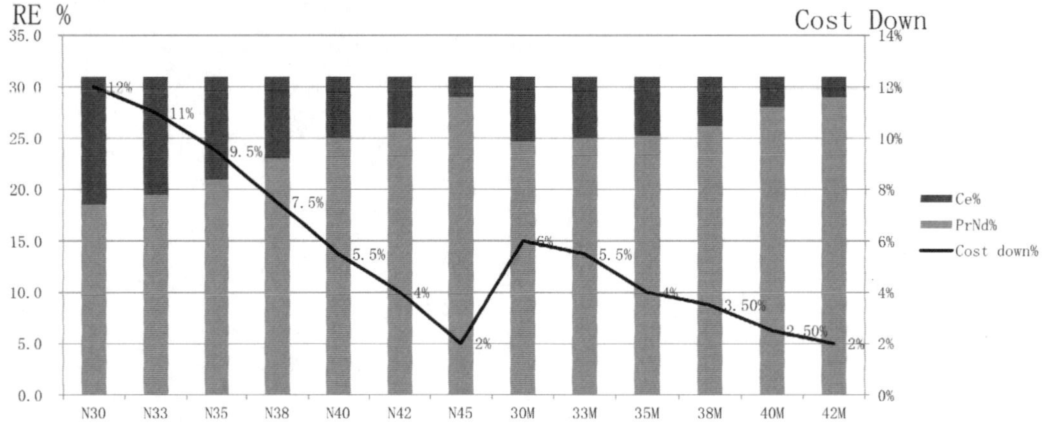

韵升集团 YUNSHENG GROUP

3.1 Near Net-shape Pressing- Theory

Independent design process and equipment:
Full automation, the product directly into sintering process after compaction.

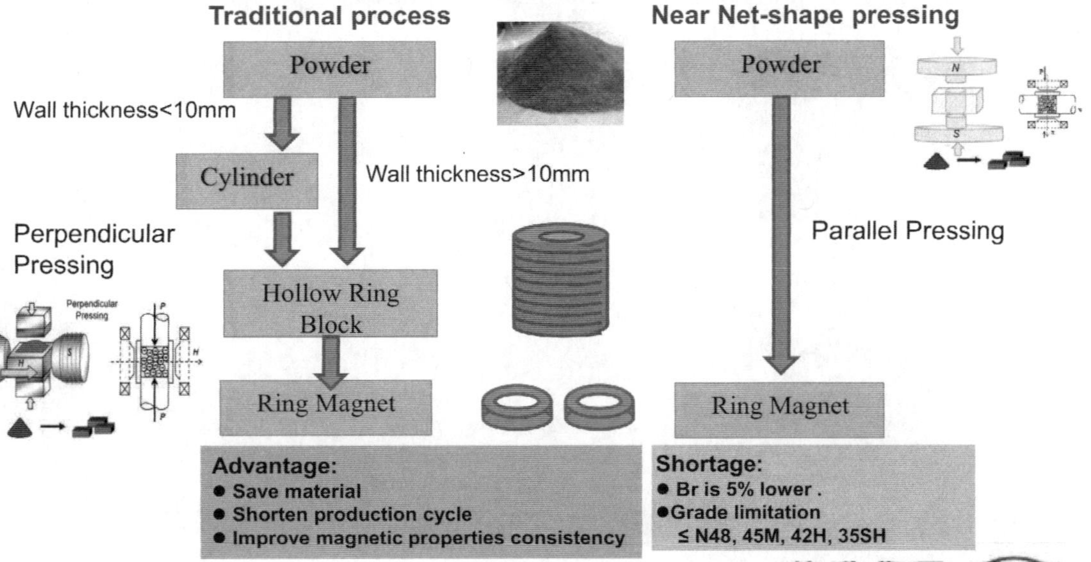

韵升集团 YUNSHENG GROUP

3.1 Near Net-shape Pressing– Status

End 2017

- Establish daily capacity of 3000pcs
- 1 pressing out of 2 magnet

End 2019

- Ramp up the daily capacity to 6000pcs
- Research 1 pressing out of 4 magnets and will twice the capacity

韵升集团 YUNSHENG GROUP

3.2 Multi-polar Ring Magnet - Theory

Use special coil and mold of compaction machine to make Multi-polar ring molding magnets to instead of assembling magnetic ring.

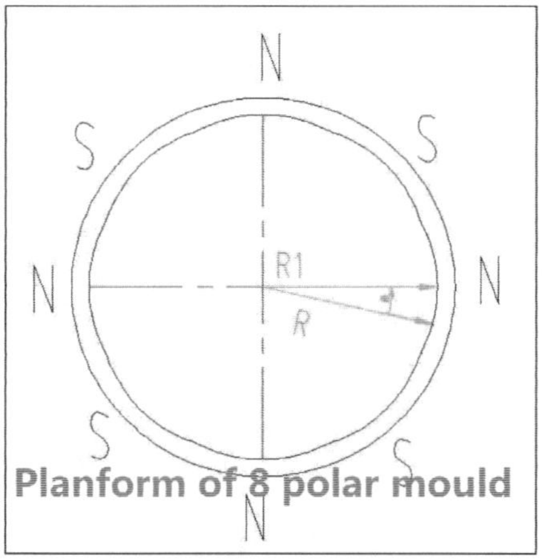

Planform of 8 polar mould

Advantage: Save material, shorten production cycle and high flux density.

韵升集团
YUNSHENG GROUP

Comparison between multi-pole ring and radial ring

Item	Radial ring	Multi-pole Ring
Orientation	See pic (a)	See pic (b)
Pole	pole number is flexible / achievable	Pole number fixed at pressing
Wave	Trapezoid wave	Sine wave
Flux Density	Low	High

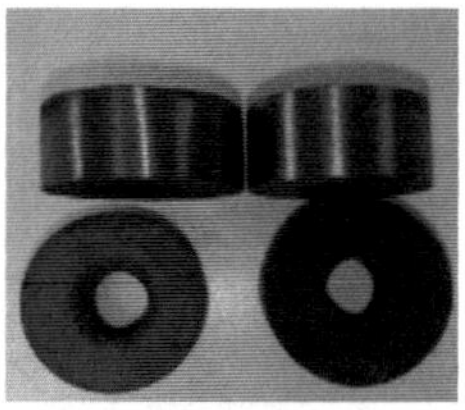

8 poles ring
(D31×D16×12mm)

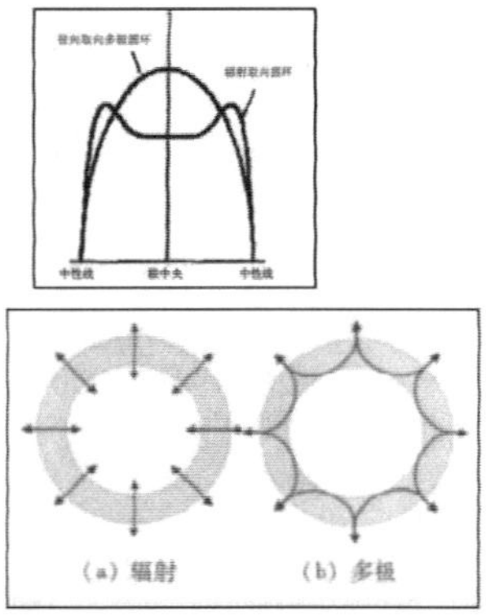

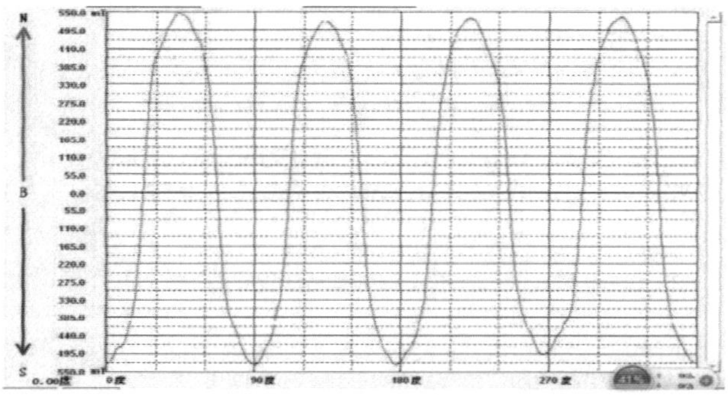

Surface flux wave form of the 8 poles ring

韵升集团
YUNSHENG GROUP

3.2 Multi-polar Ring Magnet - Status

Machine

- 20T new compaction machine
- 8 polar mould

Capability

- D31×D16×12mm
- Finished sample in Aug. 2018

韵升集团
YUNSHENG GROUP

- **Thank you for your attention!**

韵升集团
YUNSHENG GROUP

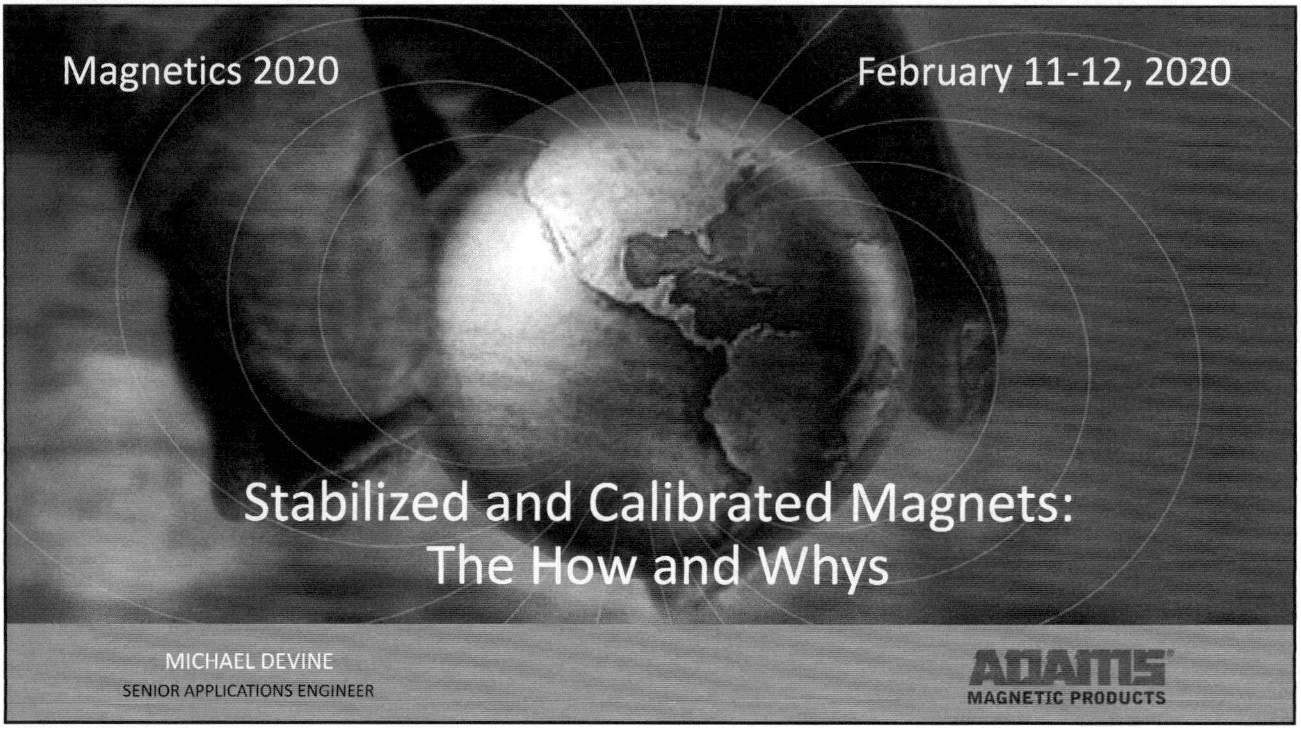
Magnetics 2020
February 11-12, 2020
Stabilized and Calibrated Magnets:
The How and Whys
MICHAEL DEVINE
SENIOR APPLICATIONS ENGINEER
ADAMS
MAGNETIC PRODUCTS

Sometimes there is a disconnect between expectations and reality in magnet performance

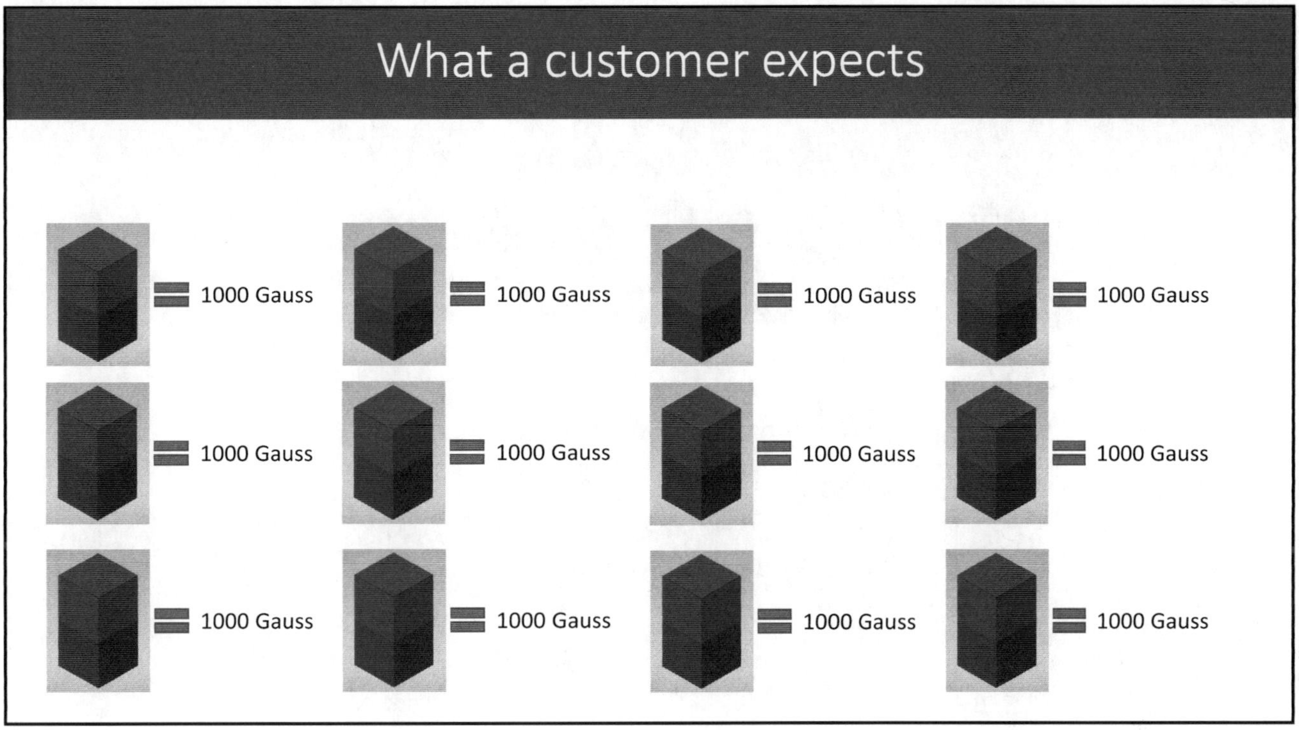
What a customer expects
1000 Gauss
1000 Gauss
1000 Gauss
1000 Gauss
1000 Gauss
1000 Gauss
1000 Gauss
1000 Gauss
1000 Gauss
1000 Gauss
1000 Gauss
1000 Gauss

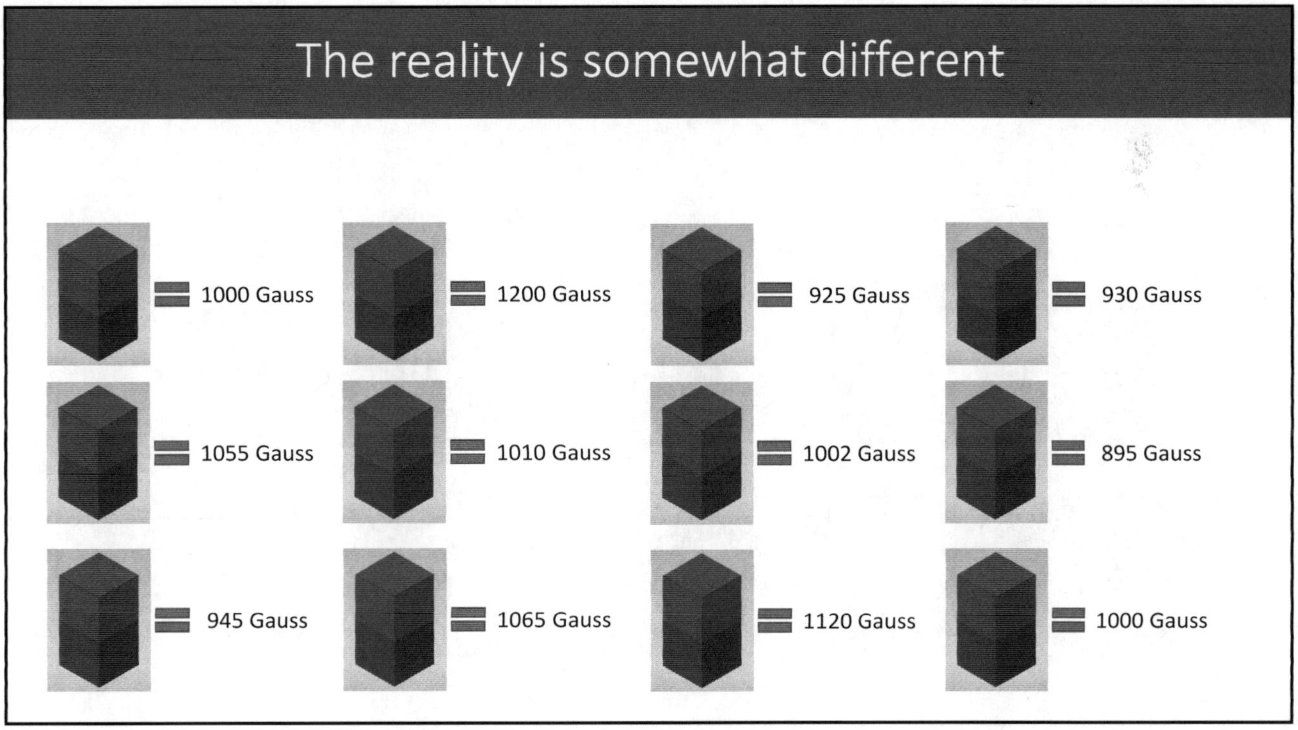
The reality is somewhat different
1000 Gauss
1200 Gauss
925 Gauss
930 Gauss
1055 Gauss
1010 Gauss
1002 Gauss
895 Gauss
945 Gauss
1065 Gauss
1120 Gauss
1000 Gauss

Some applications call for tight requirements

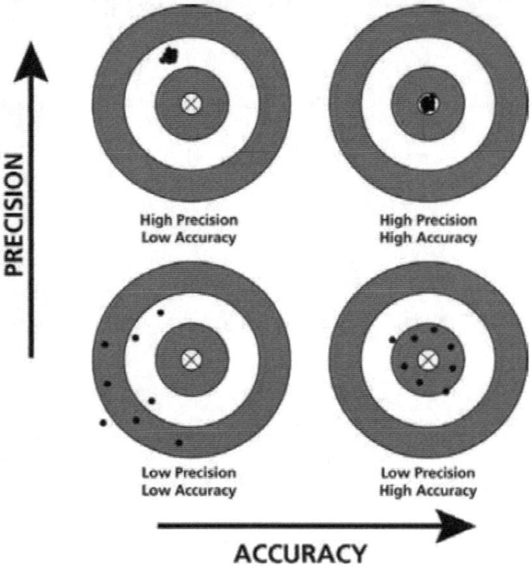

Factors that affect magnet output

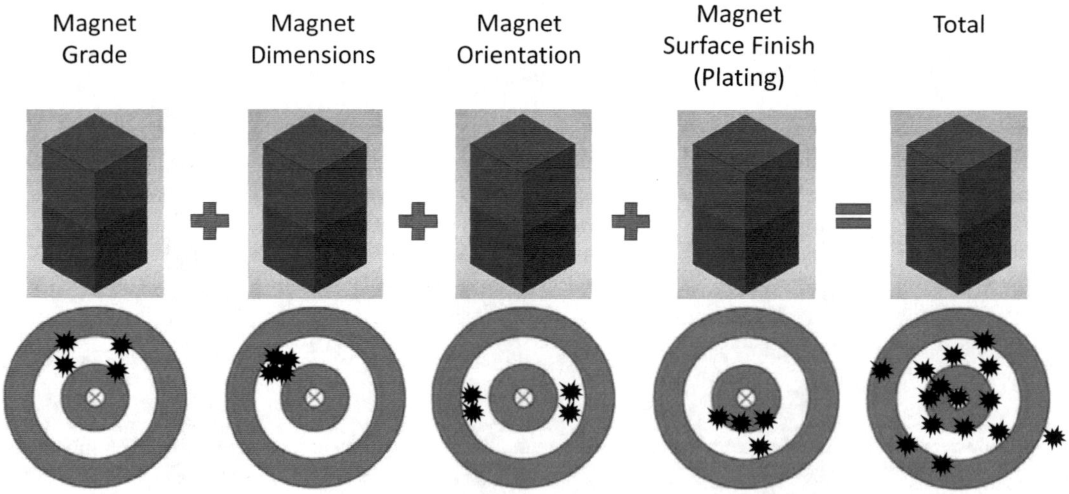

Some applications require consistency

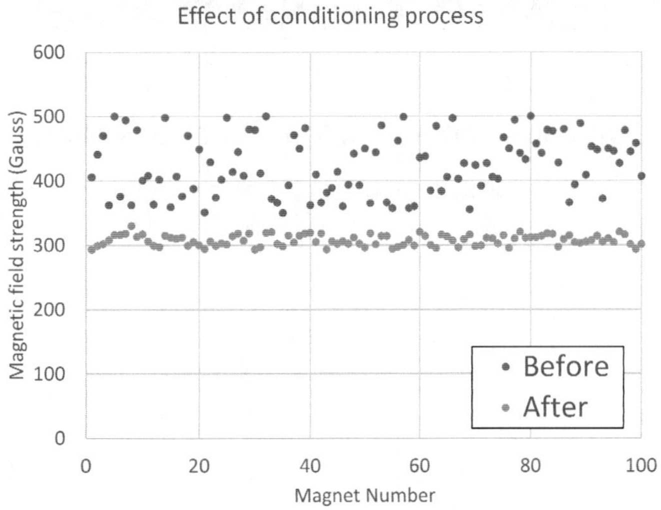

Applications requiring tight specifications

- Robotics/Automation
- Traveling Wave Tubes
- Quadrupoles
- High uniformity dipoles
- Reed switches
- Safety critical systems

Goldilocks: Not too strong, not too weak

Robotics / Automation

- Magnetic positioning for Robotics /Actuator
- Flexible magnetic strip – Accuracy depends on magnetic waveform

AS5304/AS5306 - Detailed Description

Figure 13:
Quadrature A / B and Index Output

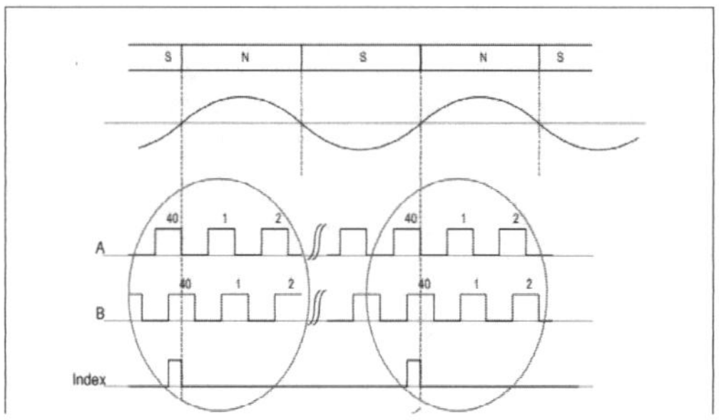

Traveling Wave Tube

To properly direct the beams, each magnet must be tightly controlled

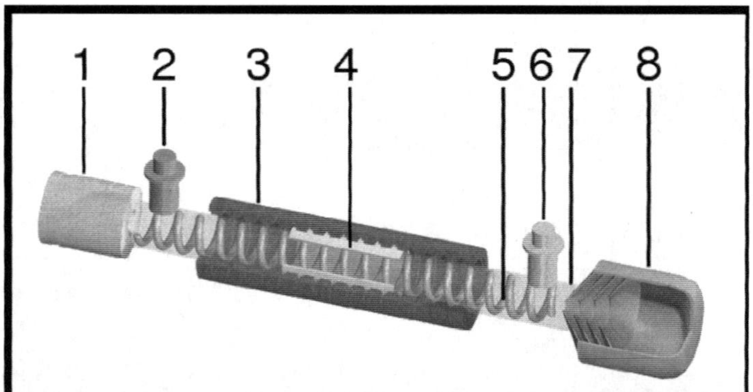

Cutaway view of a helix TWT. (1) Electron gun; (2) RF input; (3) Magnets; (4) Attenuator; (5) Helix coil; (6) RF output; (7) Vacuum tube; (8) Collector

(From Wikipedia)

Reed switches

Pull In / Drop Off values can be tight

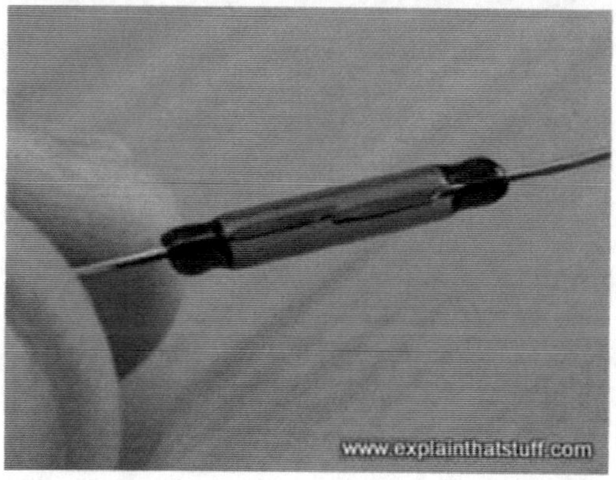

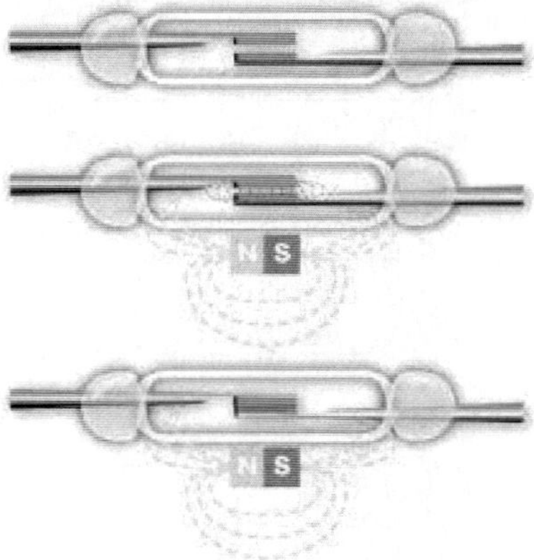

Out of scope of most magnetic standards

- MMPA: Only on the magnetic grade
- Most spec out minimums

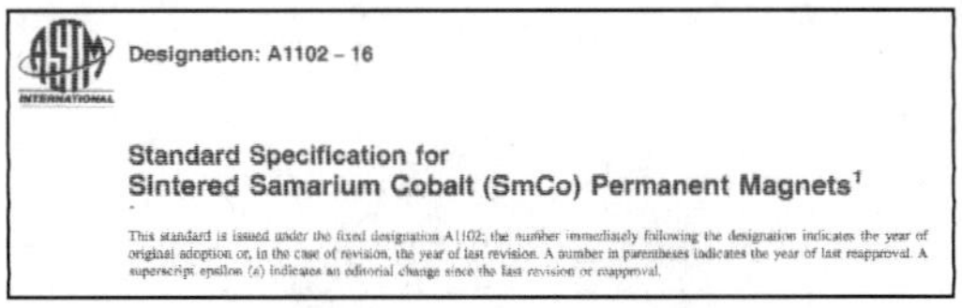

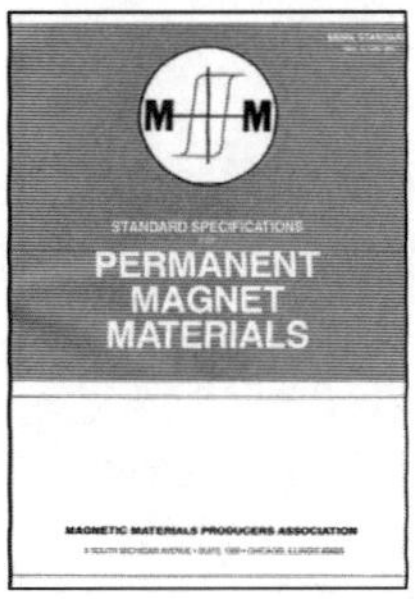

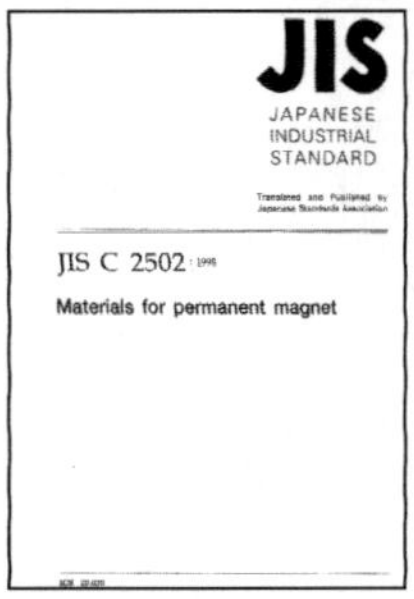

Alnico

- Usually stabilization is in addition to initial knockdown
- Most common method is magnetic stabilization
- Ringing demagnetizer – Hold magnet outside of device
- Watch out for time lag
- Handle carefully after processing!

ADAMS MAGNETIC PRODUCTS

Ceramic / Hard Ferrite

- Most common method is magnetic stabilization
- Watch out for self demagnetization at low temperatures

ADAMS MAGNETIC PRODUCTS

Samarium Cobalt

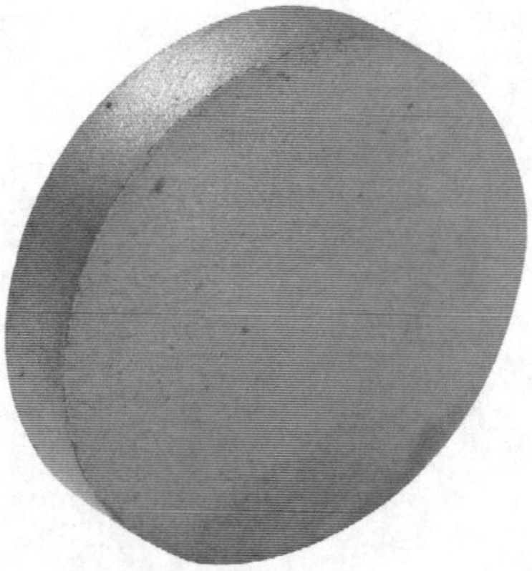

- Thermal stabilization
- Magnetic stabilization

ADAMS MAGNETIC PRODUCTS

Neodymium Iron Boron

- Thermal stabilization
- Magnetic stabilization

ADAMS MAGNETIC PRODUCTS

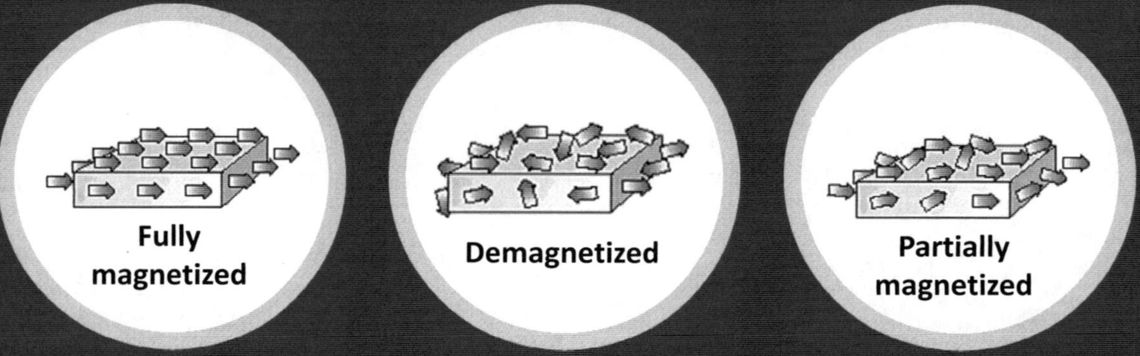

What's happening to the magnet

How much is too much?

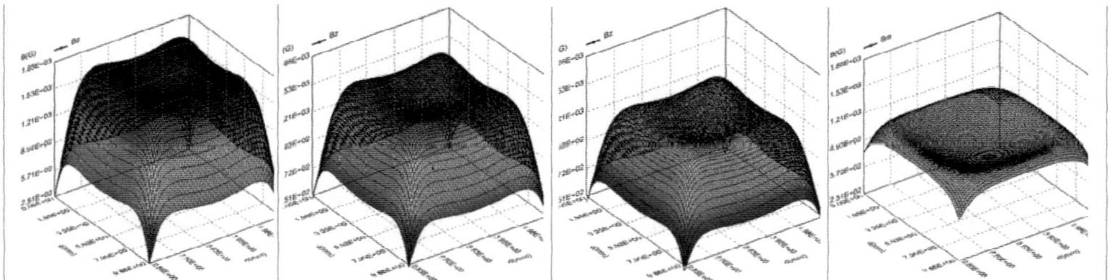

100% | 75% | 50% | 25%

Alnico	No weaker than 70% of fully magnetized condition
Hard Ferrite	No weaker than 50% of fully magnetized condition
SmCo	No weaker than 25% of fully magnetized condition
NdFeB	No weaker than 50% of fully magnetized condition

How it's done: Equipment

Magnetically

- Electromagnet or Solenoid
- Measuring equipment
- Test fixture

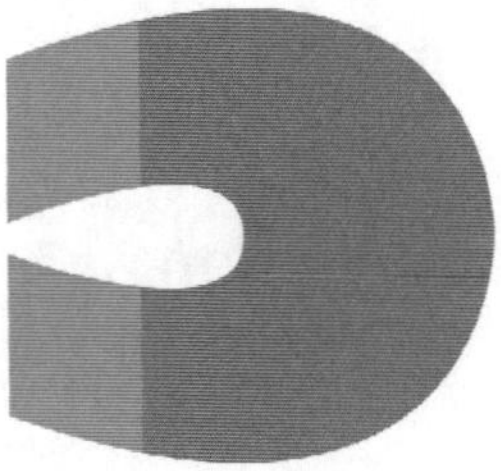

Thermally

- Thermal source
- Measuring equipment
- Test fixture

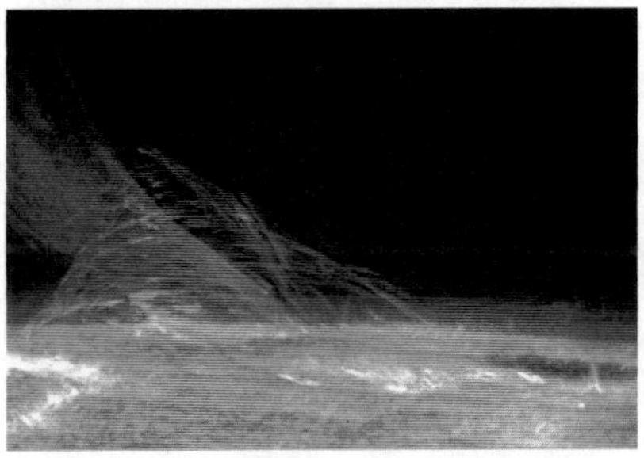

Magnetic methods

- Strong permanent magnet – not my favorite
- Ringing Demagnetizer
- Electromagnet
- Solenoid coil – be careful to fixture part, repulsion forces can be hazardous

Things to keep in mind

- Alnico can drift over time. Recommend testing a few minutes after conditioning
- Magnet must be held securely at center of solenoid. Any ‘jumping’ is wasted energy
- If possible, build the measurement capability into the fixture holding the magnet. The less handling, the better.
- Electromagnets / Solenoids get weaker as they warm up
- Capacitive discharge magnetizing systems are not precision instruments

Thermal methods

- Furnace
- Vacuum furnace
- Magnets must be separated – No stacks

Things to watch out for

- Stacks of magnets behave differently than individual magnets
  - Magnets on ends of stack weaken more than magnets in middle
  - Varying coercivity also contributes to varying knockdown
- The effects are not cumulative – One thermal exposure to 200°C will provide 'insurance' against later excursions to sub-200°C

Magnets must be separated

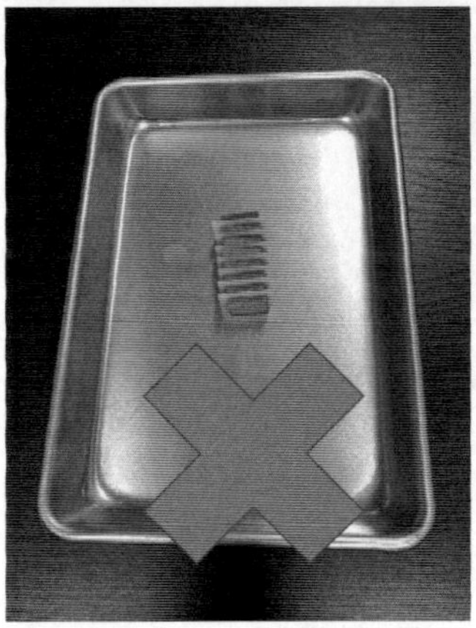

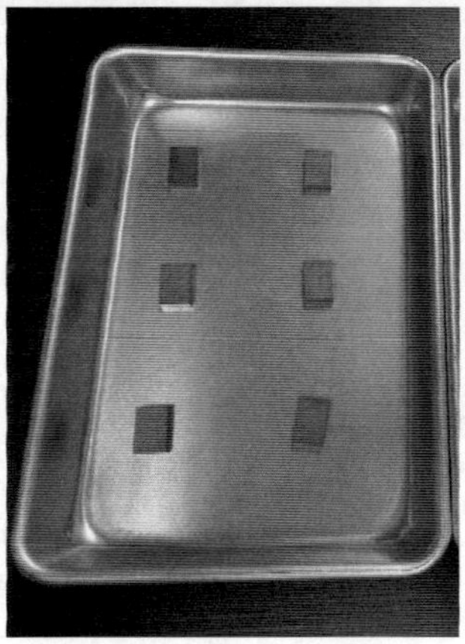

Why can't a stack of magnets be used?

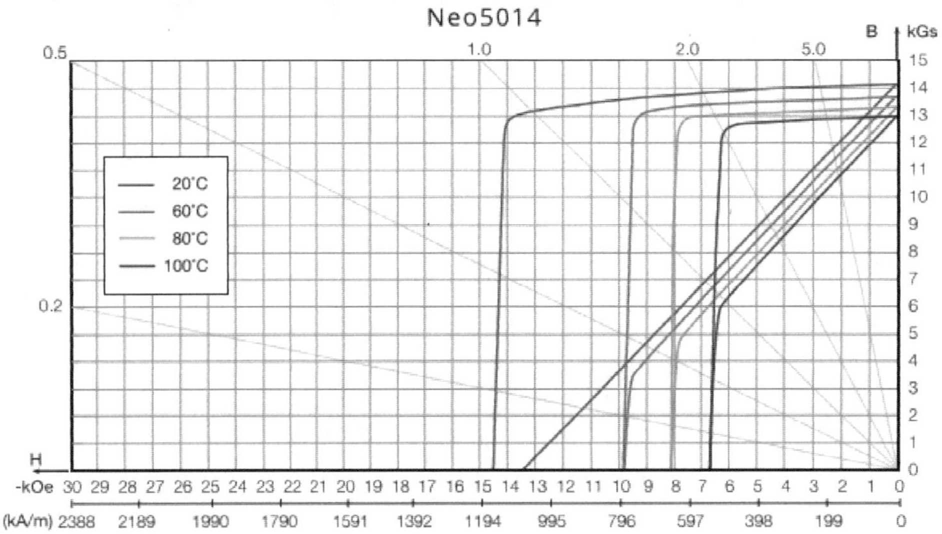

Permeance coefficient of a stack is higher than that of an individual magnet.

Some automated measuring systems out there

Need to account for measuring equipment

- Accuracy for Gauss/Tesla-meter: ½% to 3%
- Typical accuracy for Search / Helmholtz Coil & Fluxmeter: 1% to 2%

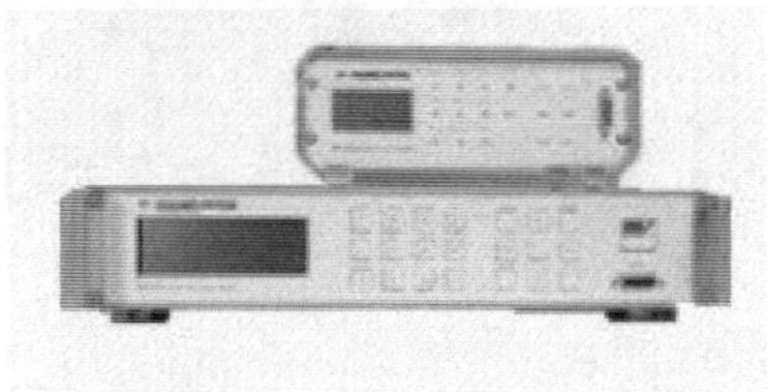

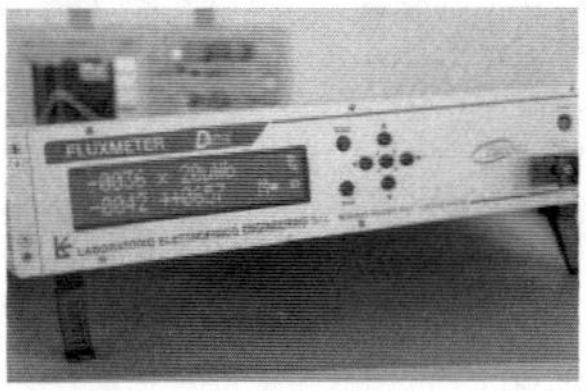

Sensing area on Hall probes

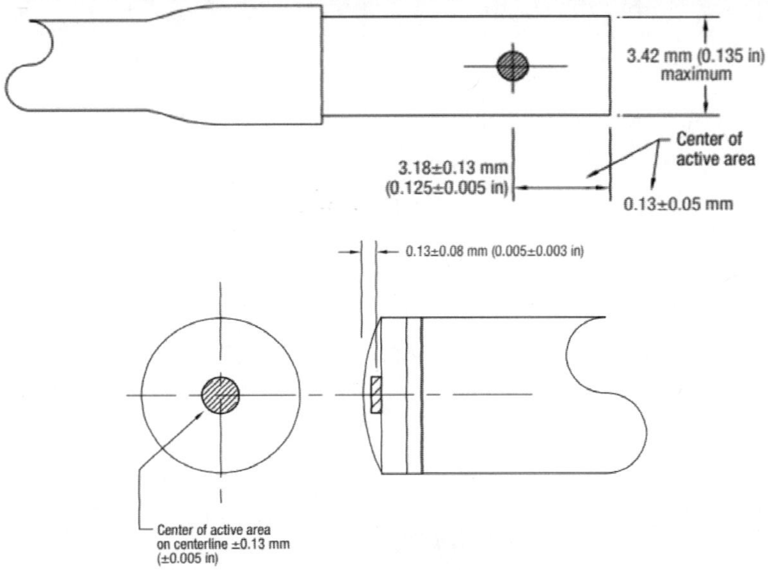

www.lakeshore.com

Fixture designs

Questions?

Thank you!

ADAMS
MAGNETIC PRODUCTS

The Growing Demand for
Permanent Magnets in Transportation

Steve Constantinides
Magnetics & Materials LLC

Magnetics 2020, February 11, 2020

MAGNETICS 2020

World Population by Region

Population in millions

Region	Population 2015	World Share	Forecast 2050	World Share	Net Change
Asia	4 420	59.9%	5 257	53.8%	837
Africa	1 194	16.2%	2 528	25.9%	1 334
Europe	741	10.0%	716	7.3%	-25
Latin Amer./Caribbean	632	8.6%	780	8.0%	148
North America	356	4.8%	435	4.5%	79
Oceania	40	0.5%	57	0.6%	17
World	**7 383**		**9 772**		**2 389**

United Nations Probabilistic Population Projection, 2017 Revision; Median Prediction Interval

Transportation: It hasn't always been gas or diesel...

Riker electric, 1897

Source: https://www.curbed.com/2017/9/22/16346892/electric-car-history-fritchle; One of the many Fritchle electric cars manufactured in the early 20th century. 30003403, History Colorado

Stanley Steamer

Davidson armored cars, c.1900
Source: https://en.wikipedia.org/wiki/Davidson_Automobile_Battery_armored_car

https://www.greencarreports.com/news/1061795_1914-detroit-electric-pretty-spry-for-a-century-old-video

Modes of Transportation

- Electric bicycles
  - Primarily in Asia but growing globally
  - Annual neo magnet usage in 2015 = 8,250 rising to 11,000 tpa by 2020 and then gradual tapering to 2050 as they are replaced with enclosed vehicles and public transport
- Cars and small trucks (LDV – light duty vehicles)
  - Hybrid and electric in early growth phase
  - Total neo magnet usage in 2015 = 3,850 rising to 18,025 tpa in 2020 with continuing increase through 2050
- Large (commercial-scale) trucks: limited activity at present
- Railroads: urban, some long distance
- Airplanes: Electric plane development is just "getting off the ground"
- Ships: Some military uses of electric drives but limited commercial use to-date

Mahindra Treo Electric Truck priced at Rs. 2.14 Lac.

Photo by George Chernilevsky, 8 Feb 2012. Electric locomotive Škoda ChS4-109 with new metal car body after heavy locomotive overhaul. This locomotive was made in 10.1969. The Moscow — Odessa train in Vinnytsia railway station.

Sweden inaugurates first electric road for heavy transport vehicles
The experiment is based on the government's goal of energy efficiency and a fossil fuel-free vehicle fleet by 2030, and will contribute to strengthening Sweden's competitiveness.

The Acronyms

Common	Alternative	
ICE		**I**nternal **C**ombustion **E**ngine
LDV		**L**ight **D**uty **V**ehicles (cars, SUVs, pickup trucks)
EV		**E**lectrically driven **V**ehicle
BEV	BV	**B**attery-powered, **E**lectrically driven **V**ehicle
HEV	HV	**H**ybrid **E**lectric **V**ehicle
PHEV	PHV	**P**lug-in **H**ybrid **E**lectrically driven **V**ehicle
FCEV	FCV	**F**uel **C**ell **E**lectrically driven **V**ehicle

Drive Type versus Vehicle Size

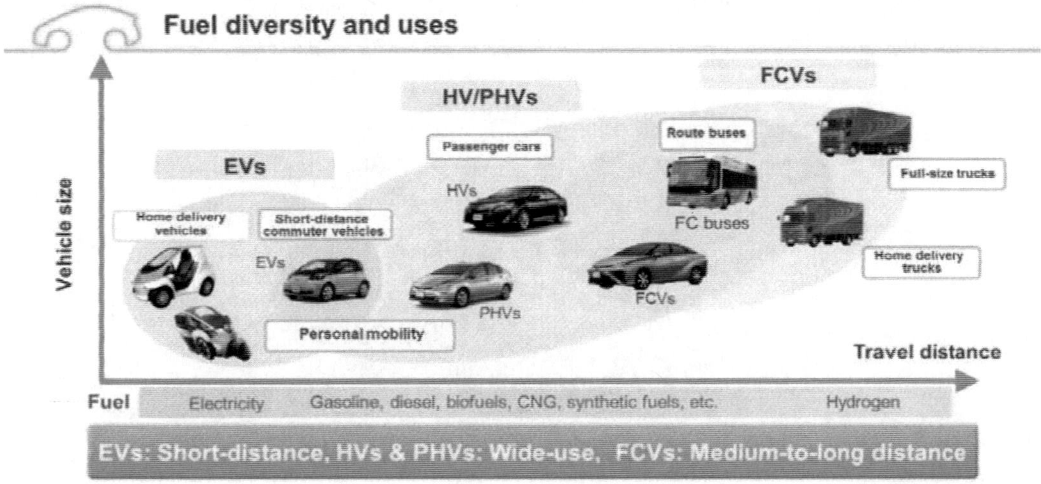

Source: Toyota Motor Corp

Vehicle Drive Type

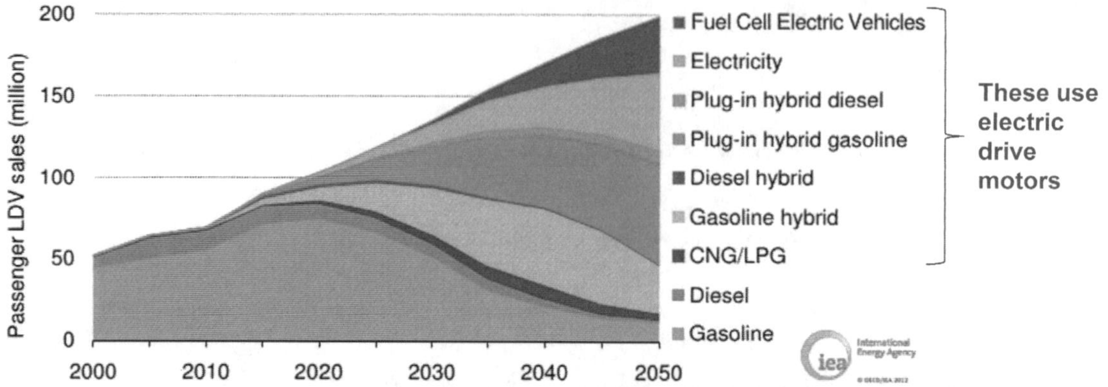

Slide 7 | © *Magnetics & Materials LLC*

MAGNETICS 2020

Global Sales of Plug-In LDVs

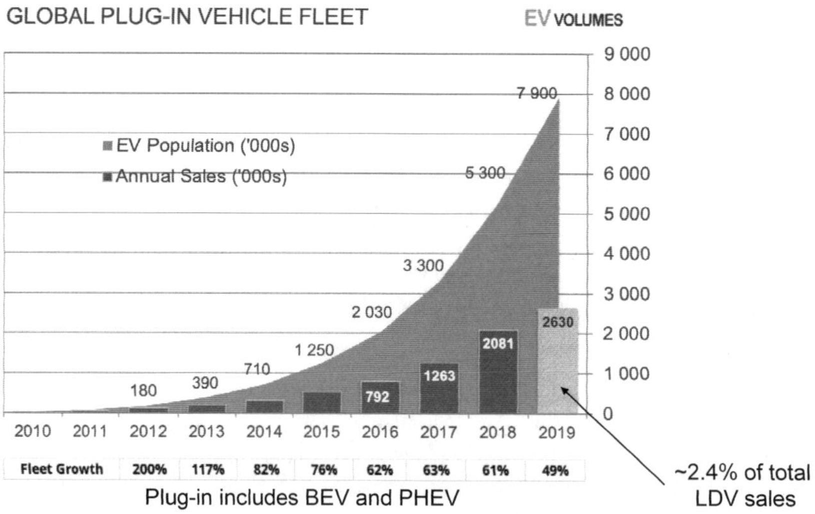

Plug-in includes BEV and PHEV

Source: www.ev-volumes.com/country/total-world-plug-in-vehicle-volumes/

Slide 8 | © *Magnetics & Materials LLC*

MAGNETICS 2020

Automotive market

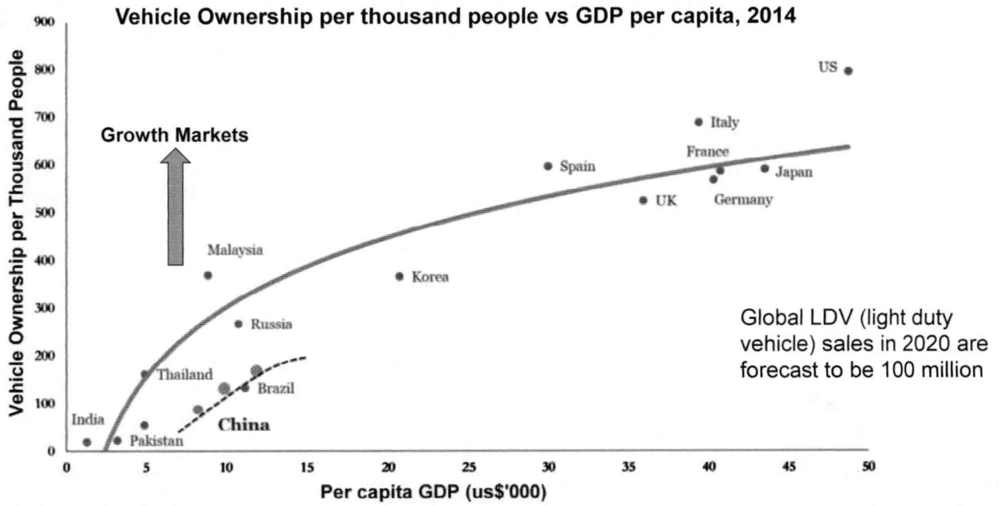

Source: PwC Autofacts, PwC analysis

Magnet Requirements for LDVs

Current actual; future hypothetical. Annual, new production; magnet requirements for only for traction drive motor.

	Total Market, millions		BEV & PHEV, %		BEV & PHEV, #		Magnets Req'd, tons		TREO Req'd
Year	USA	Global	USA	Global	USA	Global	USA	Global	Global
2015	17.4	88.0	2.9%	3.5%	0.5	3.1	505	3,080	6,740
2020	16.9	103.0	8.5%	14.0%	1.4	14.4	1,437	14,420	31,560
2025	16.8	113.0	17.0%	25.0%	2.9	28.3	2,856	28,250	61,840
2030	16.7	119.0	25.0%	28.0%	4.2	33.3	4,175	33,320	72,930
2035	16.5	122.0	30.0%	30.0%	5.0	36.6	4,950	36,600	80,110
2040	16.5	**125.0**	35.0%	35.0%	5.8	43.8	5,775	43,750	95,760
2045	16.3	130.0	40.0%	40.0%	6.5	52.0	6,520	52,000	113,820
2050	16.0	132.0	50.0%	50.0%	8.0	66.0	8,000	66,000	144,470

Vehicle quantities shown in millions
Average kg NdFeB magnets per traction drive system = 1.0
Extreme case in **2040**:

All cars are some form of EV = 125,000,000 vehicles
Average 1.0 kg magnet per vehicle traction drive motor = 125,000 tons of magnets
125,000 tons of NdFeB magnets requires 273,600 tons of total REO

Flying Cars – a Sampling

Aston Martin's Volante Vision Concept aircraft seats three and can operate in autonomous mode. (Source: Aston Martin)

Opener's single-seat eVTOL BlackFly can fly 25 miles at 62 mph. (Source: Opener)

Ehang 184 drone can carry a passenger (Source: Opener)

AirSpaceX unveiled its latest prototype, Mobi-One, at the North American International Auto Show in early 2018. Like its closest rivals, the electric aircraft is designed to carry two to four passengers and is capable of vertical take-off and landing

More at: https://www.dailymail.co.uk/sciencetech/article-5957893/Rolls-Royce-unveils-flying-taxi.html

The concept uses gas turbine technology to power an electric battery and the wings are able to rotate 90 degrees. As well as a taxi, the vehicle could also be deployed for personal, cargo and military use, said Rolls-Royce: The forward wing rotates 90 degrees to enable vertical takeoff and landing. (Source: Rolls-Royce)

Ragone Chart for Batteries

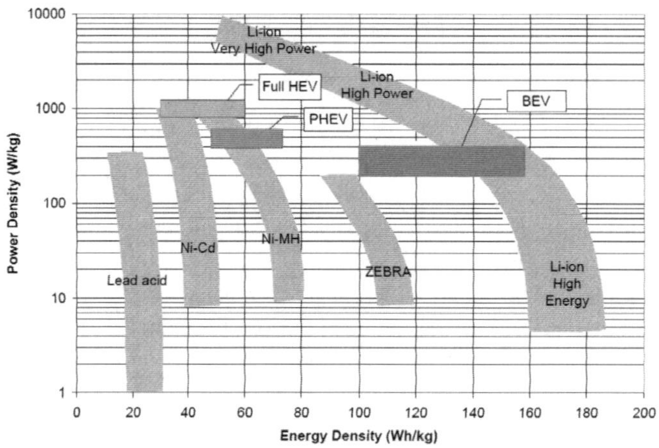

Battery Considerations
- Size
- Weight
- Total energy contained
- Rate at which power can be delivered
- Number of charge cycles
- Deep charge capability
- Performance over wide ambient range
- "Memory"
- Chemical stability
- Manufacturability
- Cost-performance ratio
- No toxic content
- Recyclability

Status and Prospects for Zero Emissions Vehicle Technology: Report of the ARB Independent Expert Panel 2007, Fritz R. Kalhammer, Bruce M. Kopf, David H. Swan, Vernon P. Roan, Michael P. Walsh, Chairman, April 13, 2007

Importance of Battery Energy Density: Weight

VW Lupo 3L 1.2 TDI car	Diesel ICE Weight		Battery Electric Weight	
	kg	lbs	kg	lbs
Vehicle chassis minus power train	595	1312	595	1312
Powertrain				
engine + gearbox + drive shafts	180	397	85	187
cooling (radiator, hoses, coolant, etc.)	10	22	7	15
exhaust	15	33		
power electronics (inverter, charger, DC-DC conv.)			20	44
fuel tank + cooler + filter	9	20		
diesel (7 L)	6	13		
Battery pack kWh: front 8.3, center 7.7, rear 11			273	602
Total for Powertrain	245	540	435	959
Curb weight	840	1852	1030	2271

26% of curb weight

Figure 1. As you can see, drivetrain of an ICE is 29% of overall weight, but in the BEV is 42%, with the battery 26.5% of overall weight in this tiny diesel car converted to all electric. Source: Besselink, I.J.M., et al. 2010. Design of an efficient, low weight battery electric vehicle based on a VW Lupo 3L. 25th World Battery, Hybrid and Fuel Cell Electric Vehicle Symposium & Exhibition.

Source: Posted April 28, 2015 on http://energyskeptic.com/2015/electric-vehicle-overview/

EV Commodity Requirements

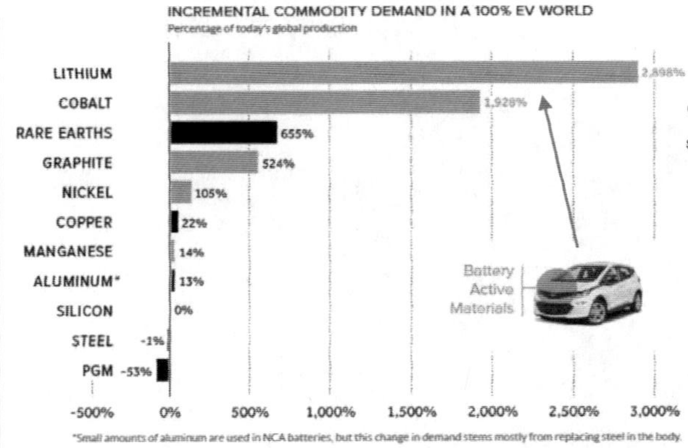

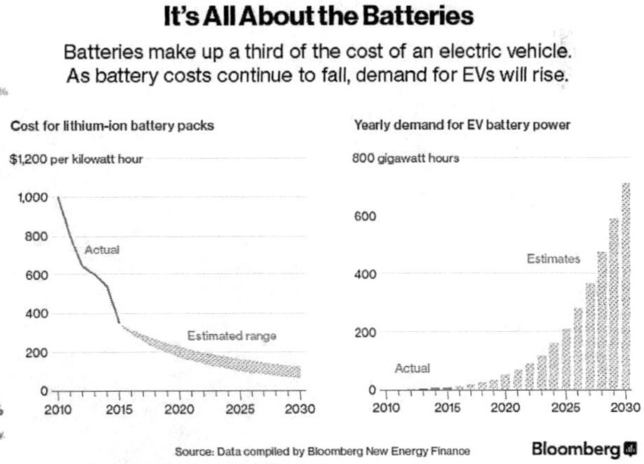

Incremental Commodity Demand in a 100 percent EV World - UBS – 2017
Also see page 74 of: http://www.advantagelithium.com/_resources/pdf/UBS-Article.pdf

Technology drives cost down; Demand drives price up!

World electricity production by energy source, 2017

Global production of electricity by coal, oil, natural gas, and biofuels is 66.8% of total.

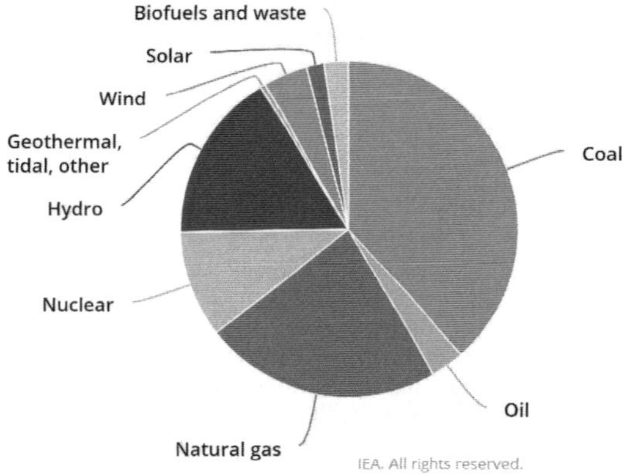

https://www.iea.org/statistics/electricity/

The conversion from ICE to EV will require concurrent transformation of electric power generation from fossil fuel to more sustainable and less polluting sources of energy.

The dirty human cartoon by Marian Kamensky at Artivism

Examples of PMs in Automotive: Combination of REPM and Ferrite

Application Guide (Automotive)

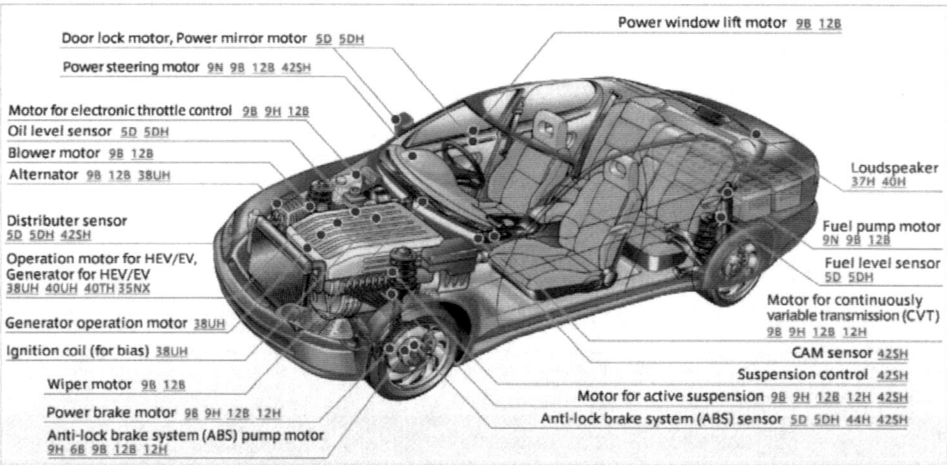

Source: TDK, https://product.tdk.com/info/en/products/magnet/technote/ap_automotive.html Magnet grades are shown in blue

Change in PM Usage

Typical applications and magnet types

- Devices associated with the internal combustion engine are eliminated
- Devices associated with the platform continue (e.g., windshield wipers)
- Devices associated with the traction drive and charging systems are added

APPLICATION	ICE, HEV, PHEV REPM	ICE, HEV, PHEV Ferrite	BEV, FCEV REPM	BEV, FCEV Ferrite
ABS Pump Motor		•		•
ABS Sensor		•		•
Alternator (12 V	•	•	•	•
CAM Sensor	•			
CVT		•		
Distributor Sensor	•	•		
Door Lock Motor		•		•
Electronic Brakes		•		•
Electronic Throttle Control Motor		•		
Engine Cooling Fan		•		
EV Traction Drive Motor			•	•
Exhaust Gas Recirculation Valve	•	•		
Fuel Level Sensor		•		
Fuel Pump Motor		•		
EV & HEV Generator		•		•
HVAC Blower Motor		•		•
Ignition Coil Bias	•			
Loudspeaker	•		•	
Mirror Adjust Motor	•	•	•	•
Oil Level Sensor		•		
Power Brake Motor		•		•
Power Steering Motor	•	•	•	•
Seat Positioning Motor	•	•	•	•
Engine Starter Motor		•		
Suspension Control	•		•	
Suspension Motor	•	•	•	•
Variable Valve Actuator		•		
Water Pump	•	•		
Window Lift Motor		•		•
Windshield Wiper Motor		•		•

Source: Hitachi, TDK, GM publications

Traction Drive: Why use permanent magnets?

Typical torque versus RPM for 2010 Toyota Prius

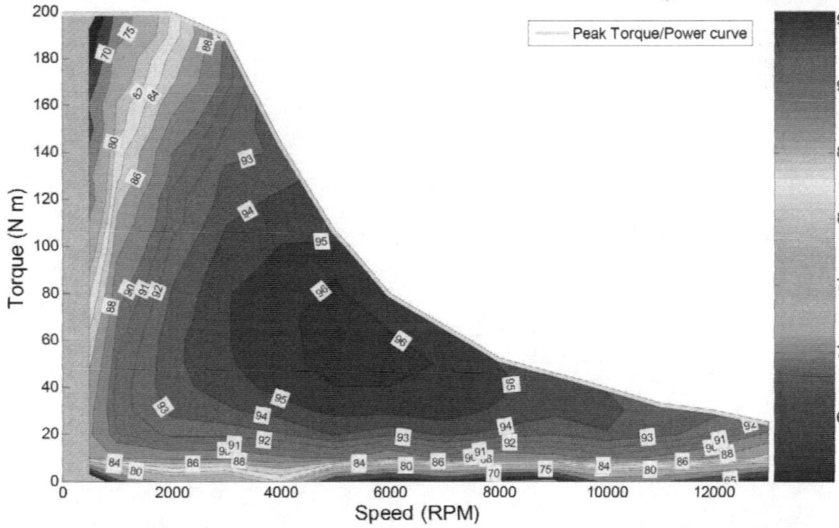

Evaluation of the 2010 Toyota Prius Hybrid Synergy Drive System; T. Burress et al, ORNL, March 2011

PM versus Induction Motor Torque Curves

"Typically, most of the manufacturers use synchronous motors, but whether it is a permanent magnet or electromagnet strongly influences the performance," said Viswanathan.

"Tesla... made a significant change with its Model 3 in its decision to use a permanent-magnet electric motor instead of the AC induction motor it has used so far. The key difference is that AC induction motors have to use electricity to generate the magnetic currents inside the motor, which cause the rotor to spin, whereas a permanent magnet motor doesn't require that additional current since its magnets... are always "on." This all means that the Model 3's motor is more efficient and thus better for smaller and lighter cars, but not ideal for high-performance cars, since an AC induction motor can produce greater power."

Secrets of Electric Cars and Their Motors: It's not all about the battery; E. Adams, January 9, 2018

IM = Induction Motor
IPM = Internal Permanent Magnet Motor

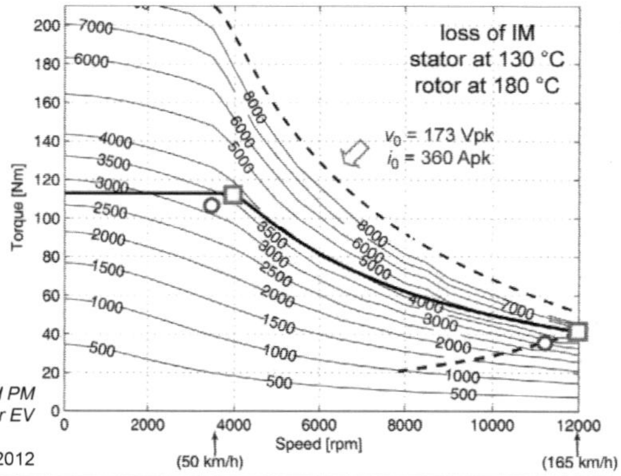

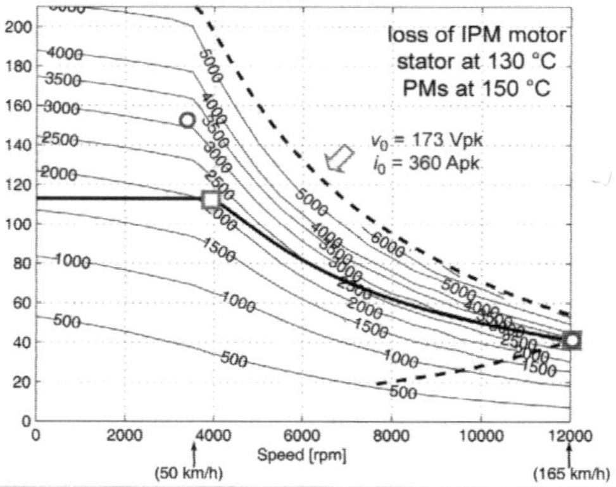

Source:
Comparison of Induction and PM synchronous motor drives for EV application including design examples; Pellegrino et al - 2012

Permanent Magnet Alternatives

- Second quadrant normal curves (B vs H)
- Red dot is at point of maximum energy product

Best combination of
- Energy density
- Resistance to demag
- Material availability

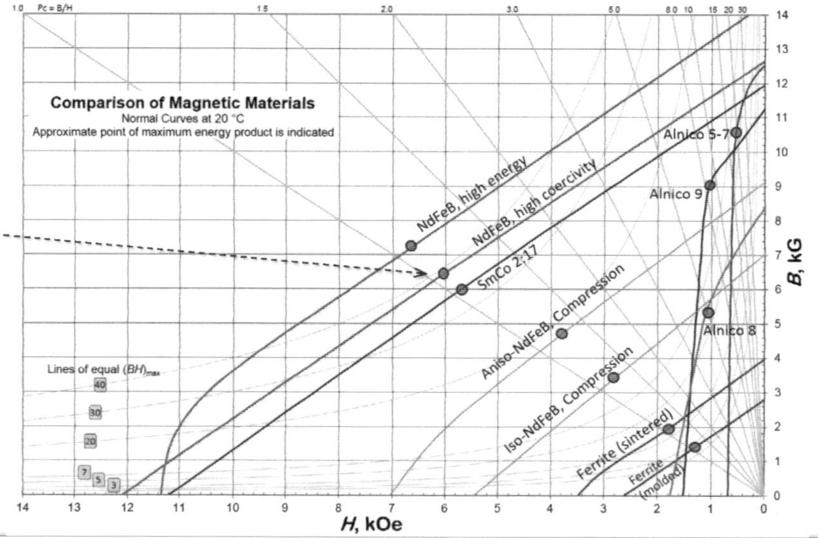

Global Sales of Permanent Magnets (metric tons)

Material	2010	2020	2030	2040	2050
NdFeB	*100,000	190,000	250,000	325,000	400,000
SmCo	2,310	4,000	4,500	5,000	5,500
SmFeN	400	1,100	1,300	1,500	1,800
Ferrite	567,000	820,000	900,000	950,000	1,000,000
Alnico	5,555	6,500	6,750	7,000	7,250
Other	300	350	400	450	500
Totals	675,565	1,021,950	1,162,950	1,263,950	1,365,050

*Due to the surge in black market REOs between 2003 and 2010 coupled with the rapid expansion of manufacturing capacity within China, NdFeB production in 2010 is only approximate.

Sources: Multiple including Benecki, Clagett, Ormerod, Trout, Kingsnorth; JL Mag; HPMG; Yang Luo; Wang et al; numerous other industry sources.

ASTM International – Permanent Magnet Standards

- A1054: Sintered Ferrite Permanent Magnets
- A1070: Cast and Sintered Alnico Permanent Magnets
- A1101: Sintered and Fully Dense Neodymium Iron Boron (NdFeB) Permanent Magnets
- A1102: Sintered Samarium Cobalt (SmCo) Permanent Magnets

www.astm.org

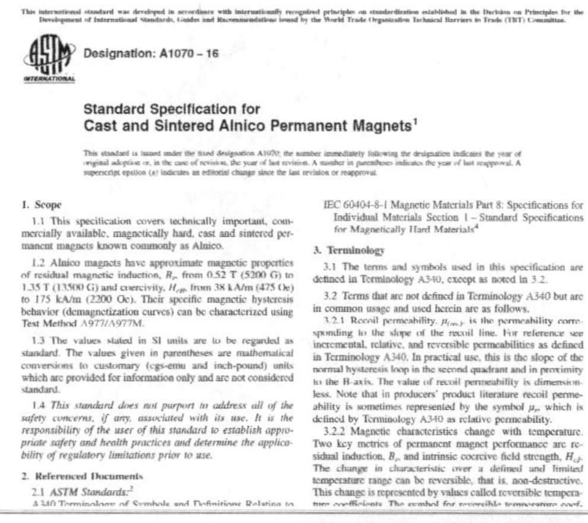

This international standard was developed in accordance with internationally recognized principles on standardization established in the Decision on Principles for the Development of International Standards, Guides and Recommendations issued by the World Trade Organization Technical Barriers to Trade (TBT) Committee.

Designation: A1070 – 16

Standard Specification for Cast and Sintered Alnico Permanent Magnets[1]

This standard is issued under the fixed designation A1070; the number immediately following the designation indicates the year of original adoption or, in the case of revision, the year of last revision. A number in parentheses indicates the year of last reapproval. A superscript epsilon (ε) indicates an editorial change since the last revision or reapproval.

1. Scope

1.1 This specification covers technically important, commercially available, magnetically hard, cast and sintered permanent magnets known commonly as Alnico.

1.2 Alnico magnets have approximate magnetic properties of residual magnetic induction, B_r, from 0.52 T (5200 G) to 1.35 T (13500 G) and coercivity, H_{cB}, from 38 kA/m (475 Oe) to 175 kA/m (2200 Oe). Their specific magnetic hysteresis behavior (demagnetization curves) can be characterized using Test Method A977/A977M.

1.3 The values stated in SI units are to be regarded as standard. The values given in parentheses are mathematical conversions to customary (cgs-emu and inch-pound) units which are provided for information only and are not considered standard.

1.4 *This standard does not purport to address all of the safety concerns, if any, associated with its use. It is the responsibility of the user of this standard to establish appropriate safety and health practices and determine the applicability of regulatory limitations prior to use.*

2. Referenced Documents

2.1 *ASTM Standards:*[2]

A340 Terminology of Symbols and Definitions Relating to

IEC 60404-8-1 Magnetic Materials Part 8: Specifications for Individual Materials Section 1 – Standard Specifications for Magnetically Hard Materials[4]

3. Terminology

3.1 The terms and symbols used in this specification are defined in Terminology A340, except as noted in 3.2.

3.2 Terms that are not defined in Terminology A340 but are in common usage and used herein are as follows.

3.2.1 Recoil permeability, $\mu_{(rec)}$, is the permeability corresponding to the slope of the recoil line. For reference see incremental, relative, and reversible permeabilities as defined in Terminology A340. In practical use, this is the slope of the normal hysteresis loop in the second quadrant and in proximity to the B-axis. The value of recoil permeability is dimensionless. Note that in producers' product literature recoil permeability is sometimes represented by the symbol μ_r, which is defined by Terminology A340 as relative permeability.

3.2.2 Magnetic characteristics change with temperature. Two key metrics of permanent magnet performance are residual induction, B_r, and intrinsic coercive field strength, H_{cJ}. The change in characteristic over a defined and limited temperature range can be reversible, that is, non-destructive. This change is represented by values called reversible temperature coefficients. The symbol for reversible temperature coef-

MMPA PMG-88 Re-write

Permanent Magnet Guide and Reference

- Symbols, Terminology and Glossary
- Basic physics of permanent magnetic materials
- Design Relationships and Figures of Merit
- Measuring
- Magnetizing and Demagnetizing
- Stabilizing, Calibrating and Handling
- Specifications, Standards, and Communications
- Permanent Magnet Materials
- Bonded Magnets
- Bibliography

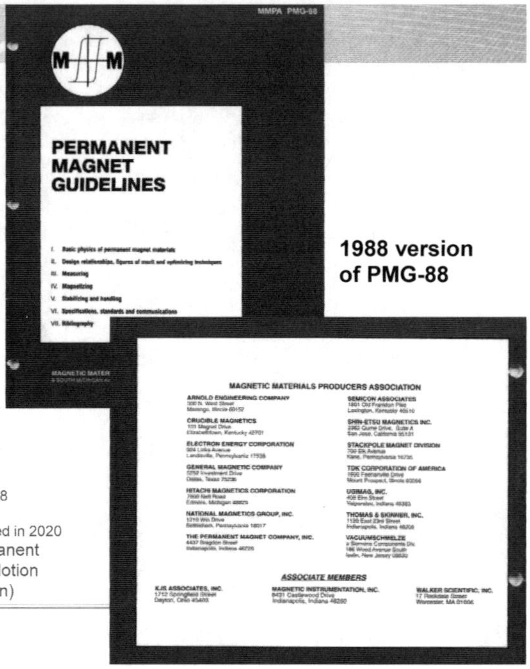

1988 version of PMG-88

- First published from 1967
- Rewritten by R.J. Parker in 1988
- Last printing 1998
- Re-written Guide to be published in 2020

To be published by the Permanent Magnet Division of MCMA (Motion Control and Motor Association)

Steve Constantinides
Magnetics & Materials LLC
4785 County Road 33
Honeoye, NY 14471
www.magmatllc.com

Honeoye Lake in the Finger Lakes region of New York State

- Education in Materials Science
- Four years Military
- 12 years with Corning Inc. (Glass Works)
- 3 years with tungsten carbide manufacturer (GTE)
- 4 years with Crucible Magnetics (Crumax)
- 25 years with Arnold Magnetic Technologies
- 3 years as independent consultant-contractor

End-of-Shaft Magnets for Angular Position Measurements

- *Very short overview over injection molded magnets*
- *Types of magnet - sensor configurations*
- *Comparison of magnetization schemes for two pole systems*
- *Pin magnets and magnet-shaft interaction*
- *Quick glance on design methods*
- *Magnet-sensor misalignments*
- *Stray field compensating sensors and related magnets*

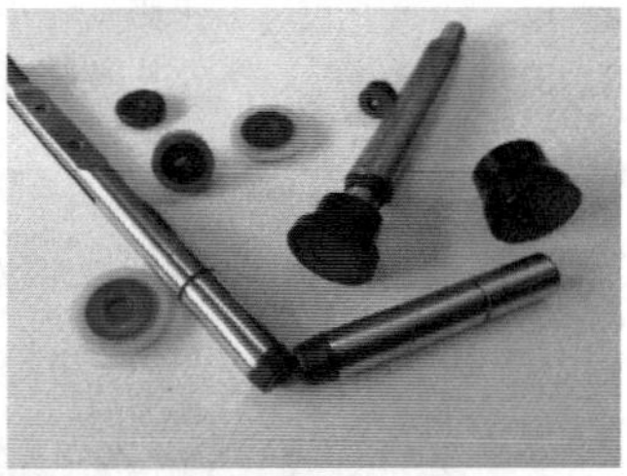

Injection Molded Magnets: Applications/Overview

Applications:
- **Field sources for sensors**
- **PM for electrical machines**
- Magnetic couplings
- Magnetic bearings
- …

Advantages
- **Complicated shapes**
- **High variety of field distributions**
- **Easy combinability with mechanical parts**

A preferable solution also for end-of-shaft sensors !

Injection Molded Magnets: Manufacturing

Conventional injection molding machines, high grade of automatization

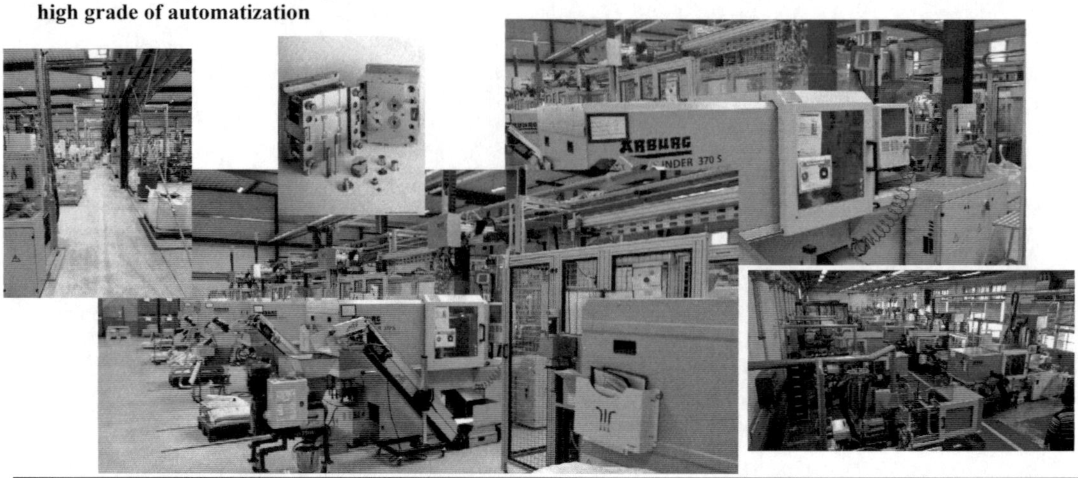

Magnet-Sensor Configurations

direct

indirect

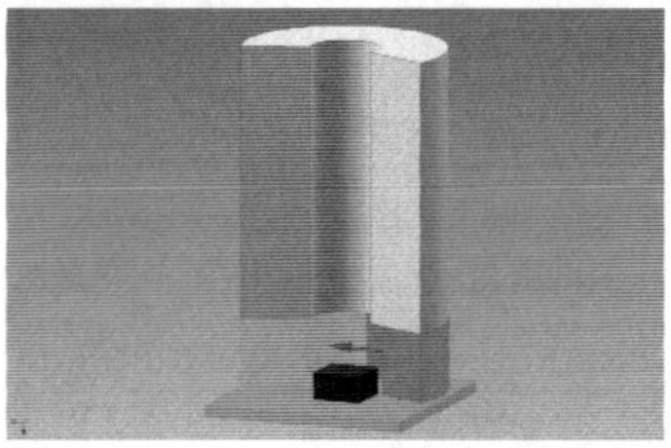

diving

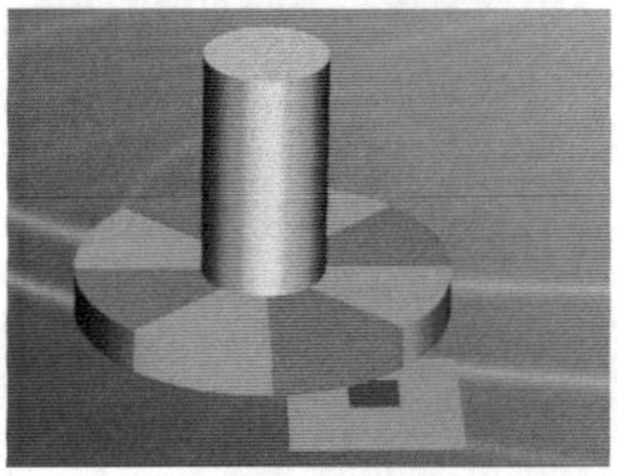

multipolar

A Few Definitions for Two Pole Magnets

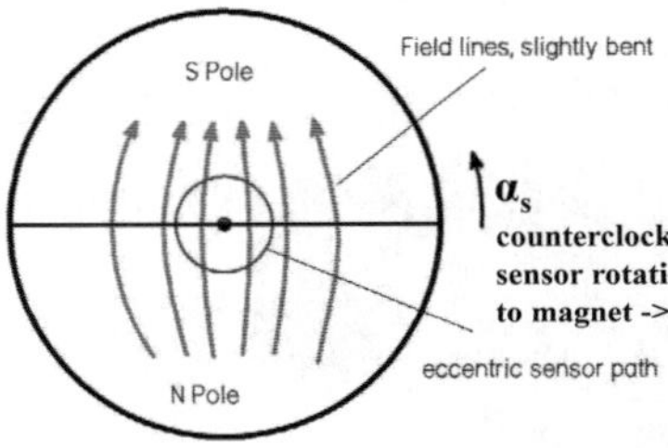

α_s
counterclockwise
sensor rotation relative
to magnet -> magnet clockwise

☆ $\alpha_{rot} = \mathrm{atan2}(\frac{B_{rad}}{B_{tan}})$

Measured angle of field rotation

$\alpha_{err} = \alpha_{rot} - \alpha_s$

Angular error of sensor at sensor position α_s

$\alpha_{dev} = \mathrm{atan2}(\frac{B_y}{B_x}) - 90°$

Angular deviation from homogeneity

Angle of system rotation follows the angle of field α_{rot}.
Can be calculated by using radial and tangential field components by B_{rad} and B_{tan} of Hall sensors or by AMR, GMR TMR angle sensors

Angular error α_{err} is reflected with opposite sign by deviation α_{dev} of field from homogeneity $\alpha_{err} = -\alpha_{dev}$

u_r, u_t -> unit vectors of field components e.g. in 2D Hall sensor

Due to system tolerances at 2-pole systems there can be a maximum eccentricity of sensor path relative to the center of rotation
=>
Slightly bent field lines lead to deviations of field angles => angular error

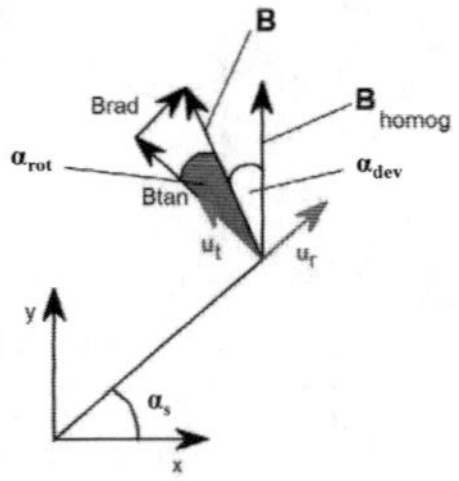

$$B_{xy} = \sqrt{B_{rad}^2 + B_{tan}^2}$$

Vector sum on eccentric path, may vary with position on path

$$B = B_0$$

Field on rotational center, is constant (when magnetized accurately)

☆ Angles of field rotation are temperature independent !

Another Glance on What Happens

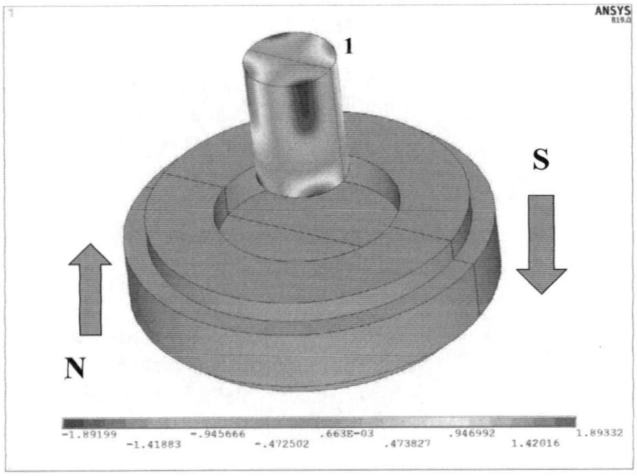

It can be observed that:

- **maximum errors occur at increased radial position**
- **error extrema are located around 45° from the transition zone**
- **at specific axial distances angular errors can approach zero**
- **Angular deviations change sign with rotation of sensor**

Diameter magnet 8mm
Diameter sensor space 2mm

Sensor magnet with two pole axial magnetization with angular deviation in sensor space

Sorts of Magnetization (Magnetically Decoupled from Shaft)

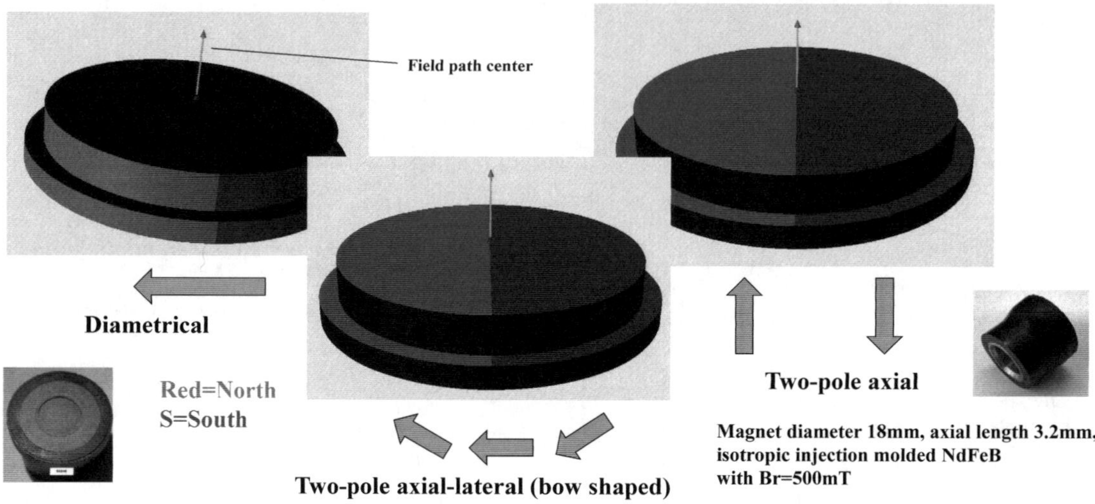

Sorts of Magnetization - Comparison of Field Strength at Sensor Side

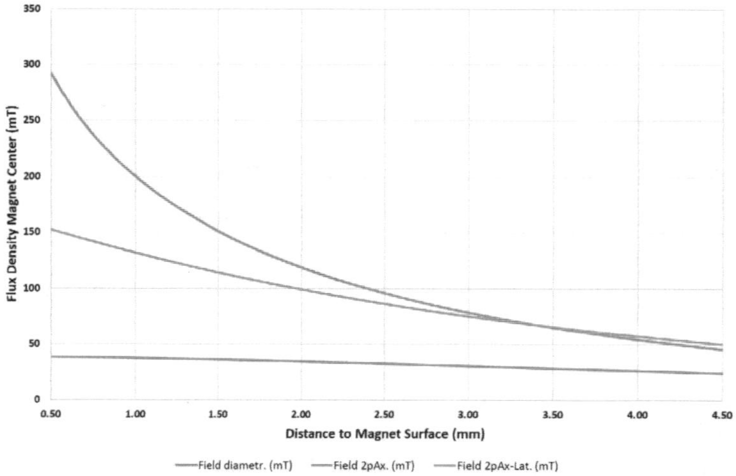

- **Very large fields with 2-pole axial magnetization, substitution with cost effective ferrite possible**
- **Intermediate field strength with bow shaped magnetization**
- **Lowest values with diametrical magnetization, hard to substitute with ferrite but slow decrease**

Sorts of Magnetization - Comparison of Field Strength at Other Locations

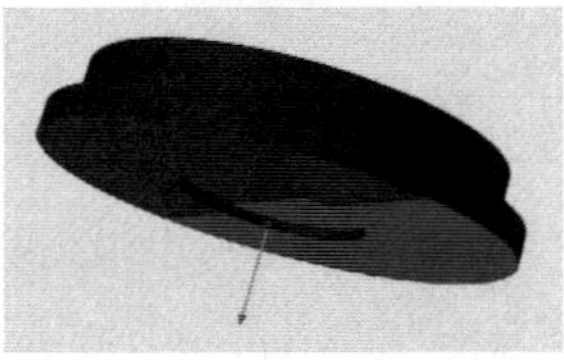

Linear path at bottom side

Stray fields of bow shaped magnetization are lowest at center. Rigid axial magnetization shows largest fields here.

At large radii stray fields below magnets are low for both sorts of axial magnetization. But high for diametrical magnetization.

Decision what to use is system dependent.

Circular path a few mm remote from bottom side

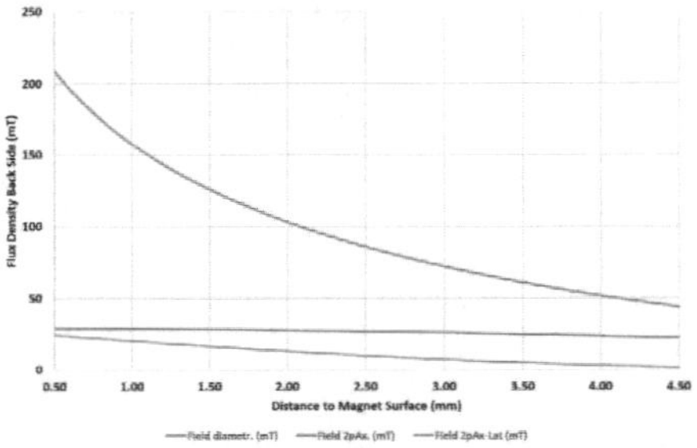

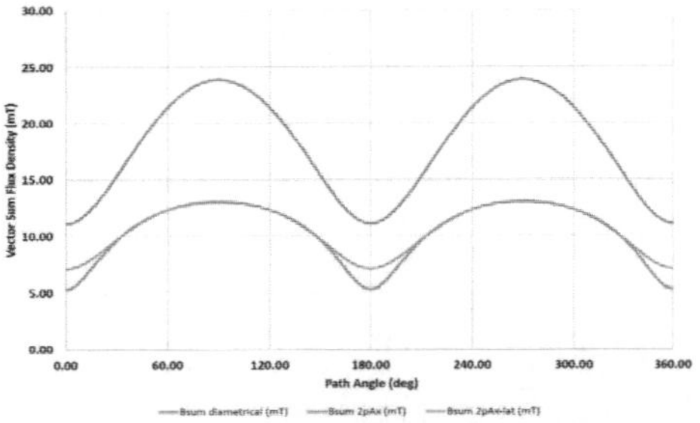

Angular Error Calculation at Maximum Eccentricity

Circular path at maximum eccentricity 1.3mm, distance 2.0mm here

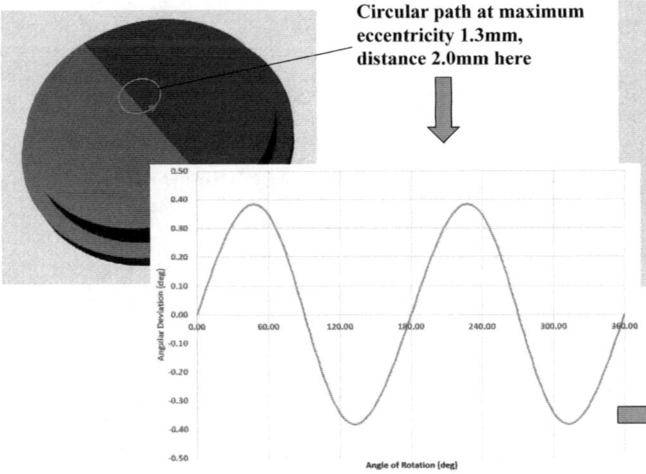

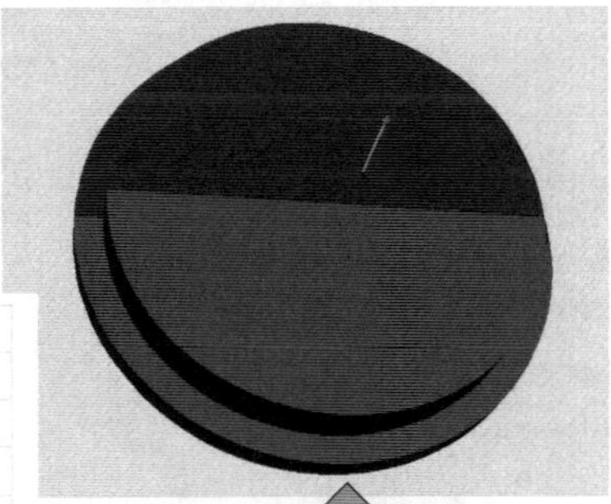

As maximum errors appear at 45°+i·90°, the following maximum error calculations were done at r=1.3mm, φ=45° on a linear path.

Angular Deviations at Maximum Eccentricity

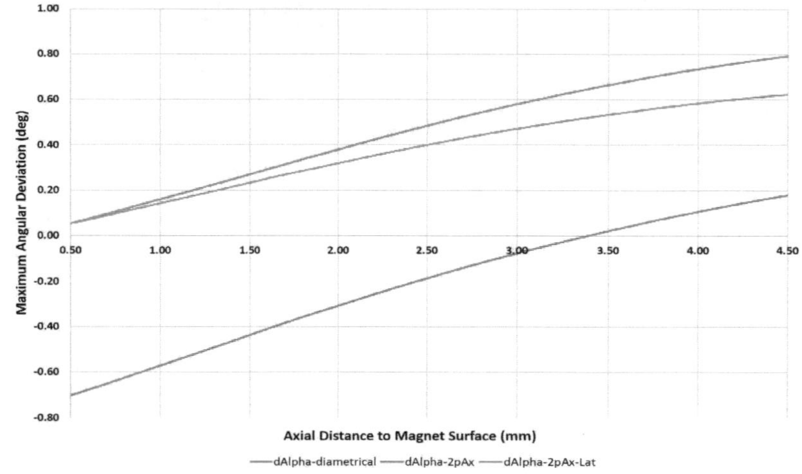

Axial- lateral magnetization shows the smallest span of angular deviation over distance.

Diametrical magnetization reveals zero crossing, which means bent of field distortion changes direction. This can be used to minimize errors when placing sensor locations near those zones.

Optimizing the Location of Direction Changes of Angular Deviation to Reduce Angular Errors

Introduction of a depression of diameter 7mm and depth 0.5mm for all sorts of magnetization

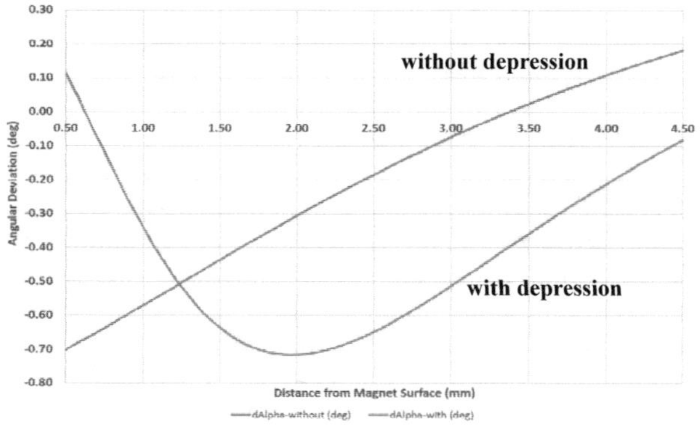

For diametrical magnetization this seems to be inadequate

Optimizing the Location of Direction Changes of Angular Deviation to Reduce Angular Errors

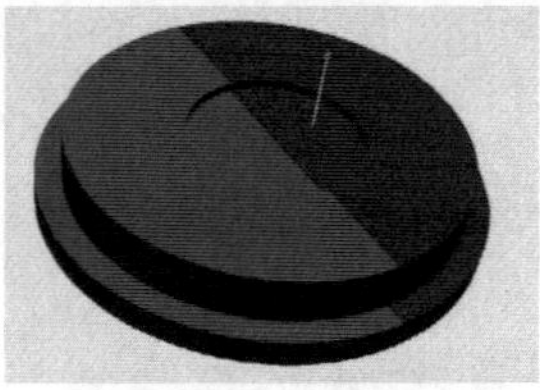

works well for both sorts of axial magnetization

Two pole axial-rigid

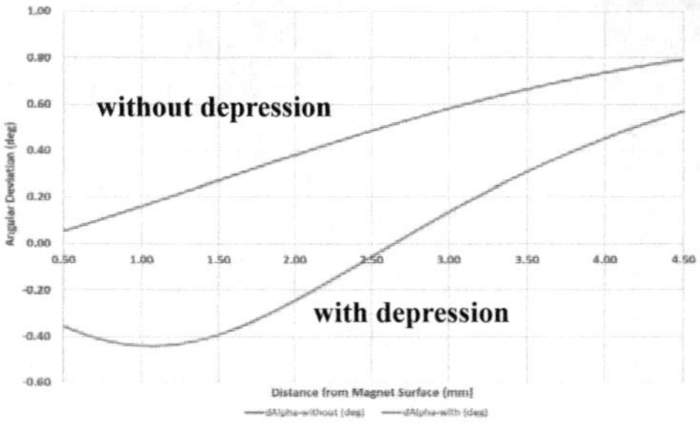

Two pole axial-lateral (bow shaped)

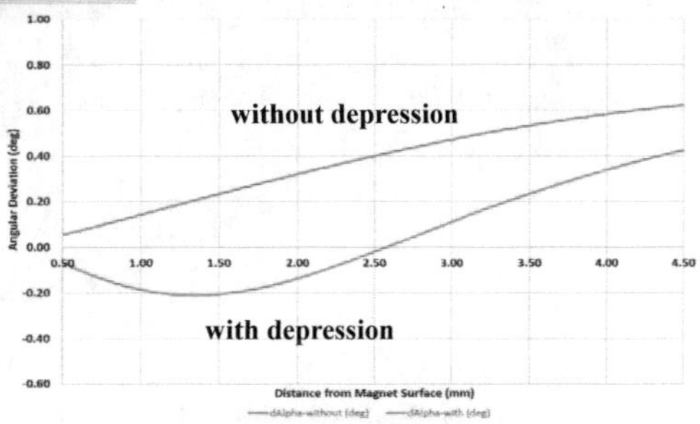

Summary for Magnetization Schemes

Pro
Con

Diametrical magnetization shows lowest distance variation of B

Diametrical magnetization shows the largest stray fields

Axial and axial-lateral magnetization have low stray fields

Axial and axial-lateral magnetization may show too large B values at small distances

Axial and axial-lateral magnetizations can be tweaked to nearly zero angular errors by geometric features like depressions on sensor face **(also valid for diametrical magnetization at different geometries than shown here)**

Axial and axial-lateral magnetization can suffer from sensor misalignments, diametrical magnetization does not !

Coupling to Shaft by Pin

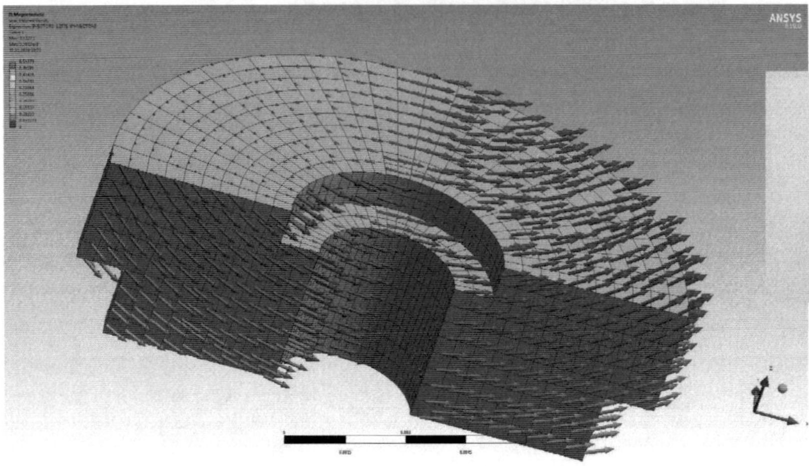

Axial lateral polarization of pin magnet

Coupling to Shaft by Pin

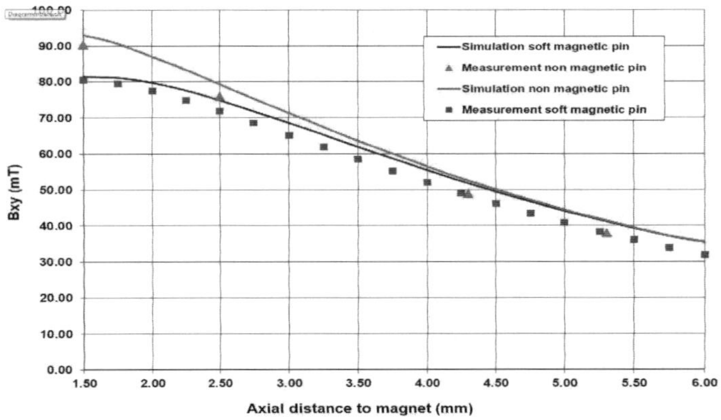

The soft magnetic shaft has some impact on field strength near magnet face which seems to be more or less marginal.

But impact on angular error is large, see next slide !

Pin magnet with bow shaped magnetization. Field B_{xy} in disc plane at 45°.
Eccentricity from center of rotation 1mm.
Comparison of results for non magnetic and soft magnetic shaft

Coupling to Shaft by Pin

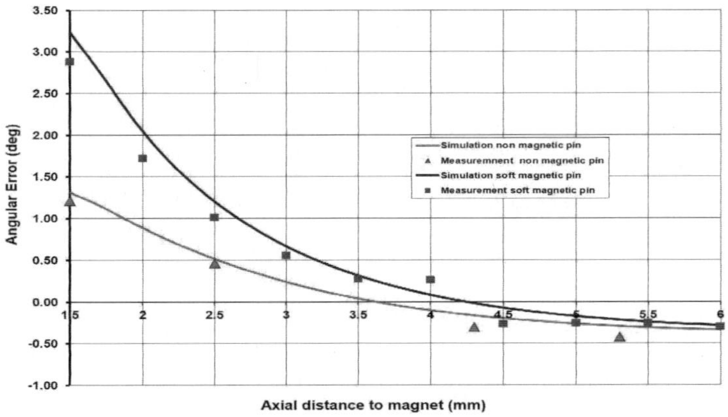

The directional distortion of field near the shaft leads to a very large angular error !

Pin magnet with bow shaped magnetization. Angular error in disc plane at 45°.
Eccentricity from center of rotation = 1mm.
Comparison of results for non magnetic and soft magnetic shaft

A Few Words about Design Methods Used so Far: Analytical

General Solution of Poisson equation with boundaries at infinity:

$$\vec{H}(\vec{r}) = \frac{1}{4\pi}\oint_A \frac{(\vec{M}\cdot\vec{n}')(\vec{r}-\vec{r}')}{\left|\vec{r}-\vec{r}'\right|^3}dA' - \frac{1}{4\pi}\int_V \frac{(\vec{\nabla}'\cdot\vec{M})(\vec{r}-\vec{r}')}{\left|\vec{r}-\vec{r}'\right|^3}dV'$$

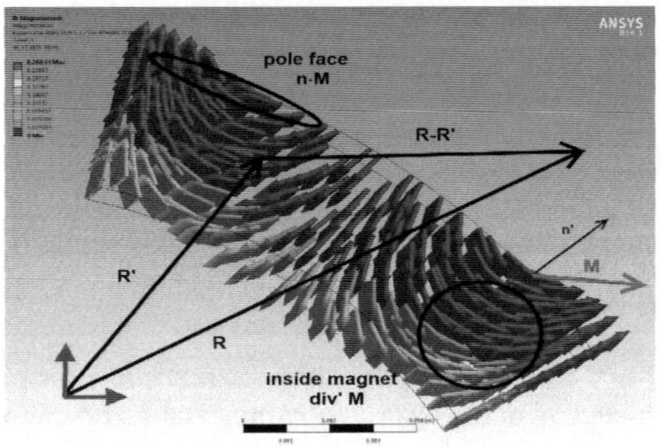

Adequate formula for distribution of magnetization is needed !

Even the most complicated magnetic structures only need the solution of face and volume integrals, but the handling of soft magnetic parts near magnets is limited.

A Few Words about Design Methods Used so Far: FEM

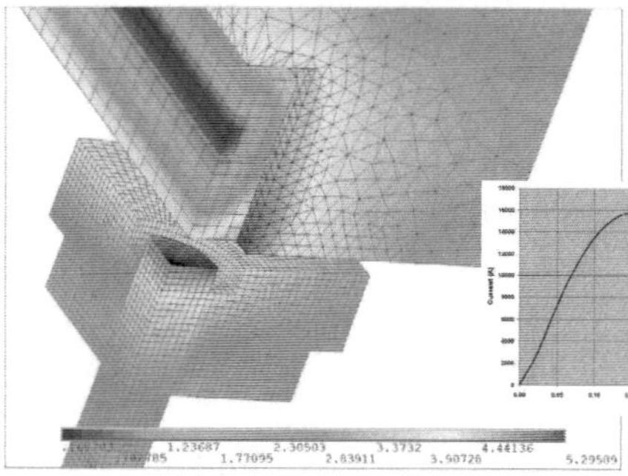

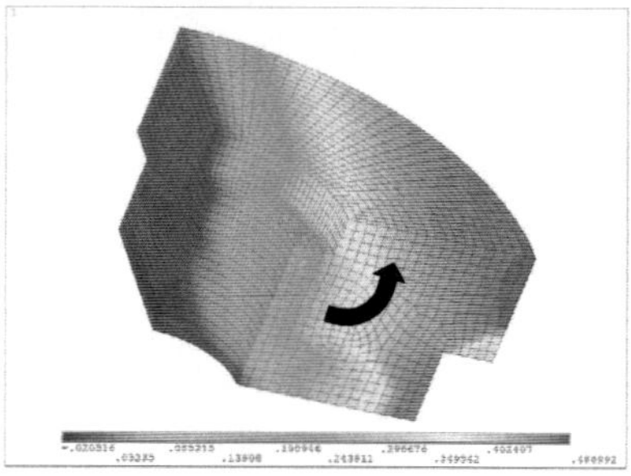

Magnet (magnetostatic)

Pulse magnetizing coil
(time transient)

Magnetizing Field H'

Calculation of B_r and μ_r from hysteresis-model

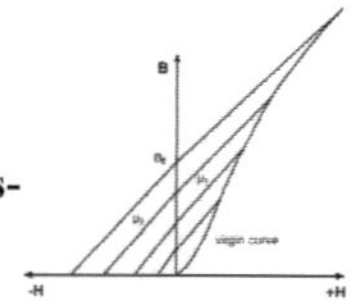

For in mold magnetization of Ferrites: Magnetostatic approach instead of pulse magnetization

A Few Words about Design Methods Used so Far:

Deviations from Measurements:

	Diametrical Mag.	2 Pole Axial Mag.	2 Pole Axial-Lateral
FEM	ΔB ~ a few mT $\Delta\alpha \sim 0.1°$ *	ΔB ~ a few mT $\Delta\alpha \sim 0.1°$ *	ΔB ~ a few mT $\Delta\alpha$ a few 0.1° *
Analytical	ΔB a few mT $\Delta\alpha \sim 0.1°$	ΔB a few mT $\Delta\alpha \sim 0.1°$	Estimate possible only, as modeling depends on magnetizing unit which may vary

**appropriate element shape, size and potential formulation assumed*

Table valid for isotropic magnets. For in mold oriented quality of prediction can decrease at least for $\Delta\alpha$ due to flow and cooling effects.

Another impact onto accuracy can be a misalignment of sensor axes by assembling tolerances. Small tilts can lead to effects like doubling angular errors => see next slide.

Sensor Misalignments

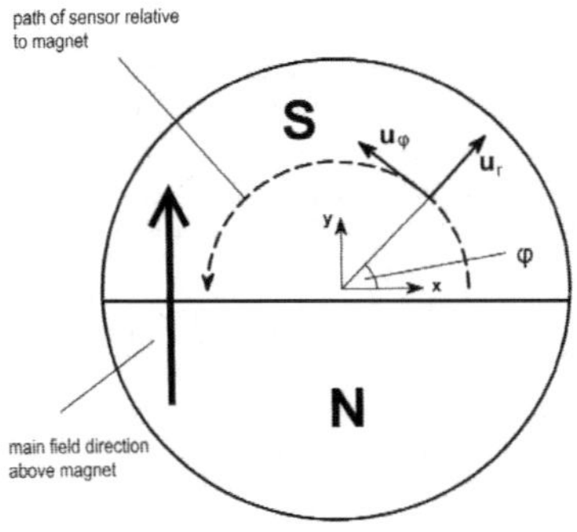

Schematic sketch

φ : angle of relative rotation about the magnet axis, to be measured

γ : angle of sensor tilt around radial axis u_r

α : angle of sensor tilt around tangential axis u_φ

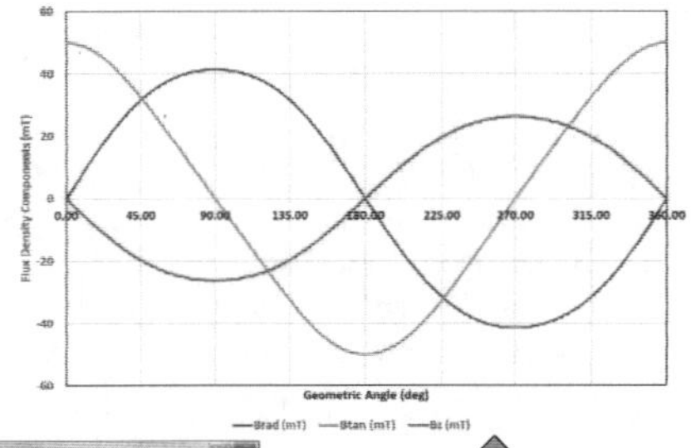

Field components on circular path of sensor

Analytical calculation of simple disc with 2 pole axial magnetization

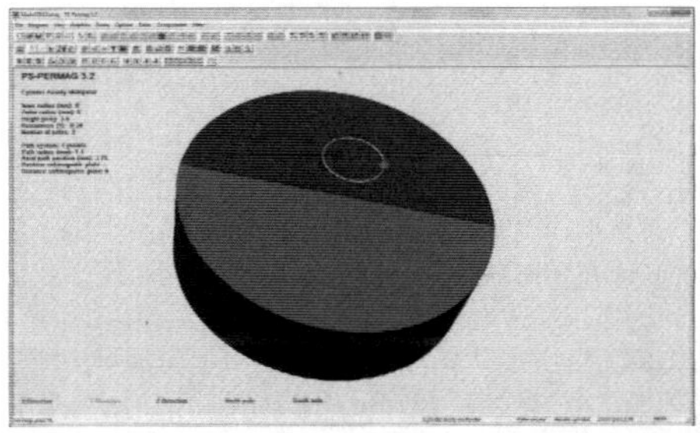

Sensor Misalignments

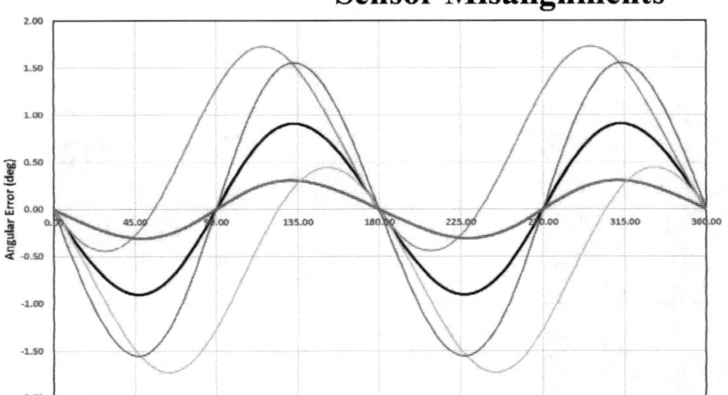

error (γ,α)

Angular error and its change by rotation of +-2° around radial and tangential sensor axis.

Misalignments can lead to large errors in angle measurement as well as in judgement of magnet quality.

Reason is the axial component of field => diametrically magnetized magnets are less sensitive as B_z is small there.

Controlled rotations of sensor into the right direction can be used to reduce angular errors, see the red curve.

no tilt

$$\alpha_{err} = -\alpha_{dev} = \mathrm{atan2}(\frac{Br}{B\varphi}) - \alpha_s$$

tilt about u_r

$$\alpha_{err} = -\alpha_{dev} \approx \mathrm{atan2}(\frac{Br}{B\varphi + Bz \cdot \sin\gamma}) - \alpha_s$$

tilt about u

$$\alpha_{err} = -\alpha_{dev} \approx \mathrm{atan2}(\frac{Br - Bz \cdot \sin\alpha}{B\varphi}) - \alpha_s$$

External-Field-Compensation

In automotive industry a maximum external field of 5mT has currently been established, which must not impact on the performance of magnetic sensors !

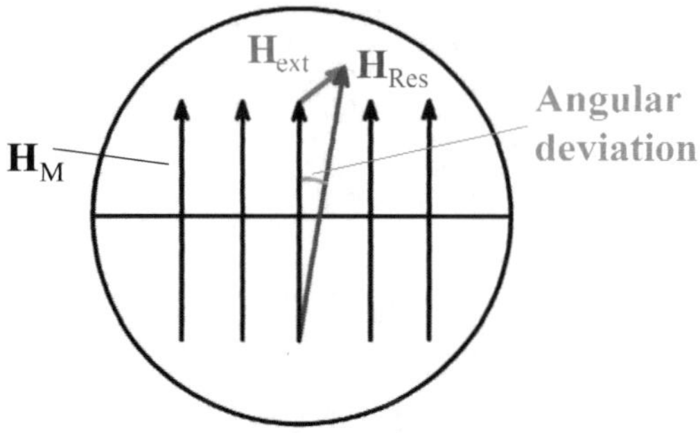

Angular deviations from external fields result from simple vector addition in most cases.

E.g. from permanent magnetic fields around 20mT and a perpendicular external field of 5mT an angular deviation of 14° results !

Solutions:

Shielding by soft magnetic housings. Disadvantages are: Costs, space consumption, imperfections…..

External field compensating sensors. Are slowly establishing during the last 10 years, but cannot cover all demands for accuracy and general applicability yet.

External-Field-Compensating Sensors – Practical Example

MLX90371 – Triaxis® Position Processor from Melexis

Four pole permanent magnet in brass holder

Sensor chip

Permanent magnets to provide external field at sensor location

External-Field-Compensating Sensors – Practical Example

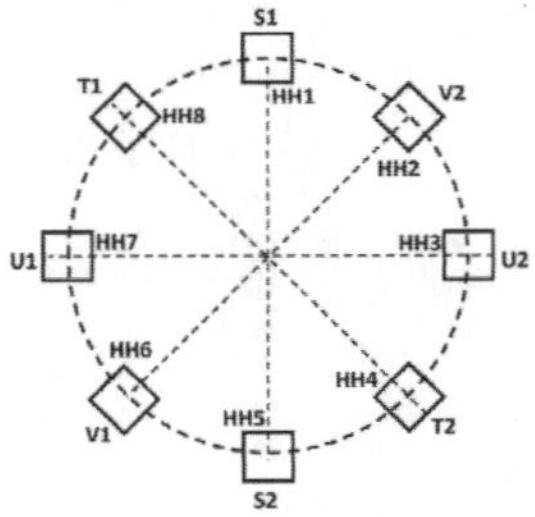

(C.Schott, S.Huber: "Arrangement, Method and Sensor for Measuring an Absolute Angular Position Using a Multipole Magnet" WO 2014/029885A1, Melexis Technologies NV)

Array of 8 Hall sensors near center of rotation of a 4 pole magnet with axial magnetization. Diameter of circle < 1mm. Use of radial and tangential field components of magnet.

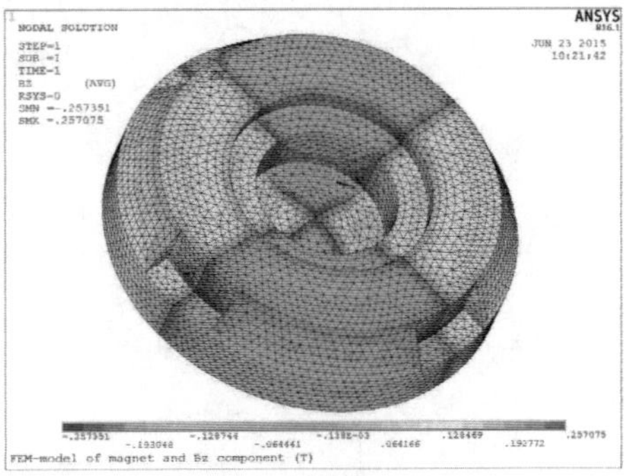

Diameter of used magnet 14mm, effective diameter of sensor < 1mm

$F_{Sin}=(S_1+S_2)-(U_1+U_2)$

$F_{Cos}=(T_1+T_2)-(V_1+V_2)$

$\varphi=0.5\cdot \mathrm{atan2}(F_{sin}/F_{cos})$

As sensor pairs like S1 and S2 have opposite signs of field components in each element, values subtract => gradient sensor principle, i.e. differences of fields are measured.
=> Cancelling of external field components (when sufficiently homogenous).

External-Field-Compensating Sensors – Practical Example

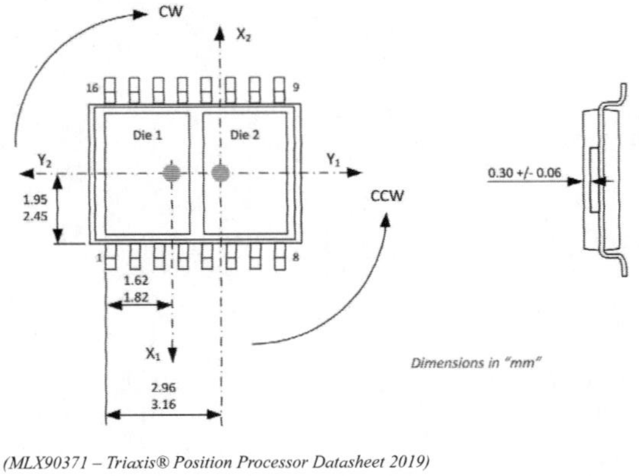

(MLX90371 – Triaxis® Position Processor Datasheet 2019)

Use of both dies for measuring at center or rotation r=0mm (die 1) and at r=1.3mm (die 2).

Position of die 2 reflects typical eccentricities caused by system tolerances

Angular errors at 0mT external field
< > average value per interval

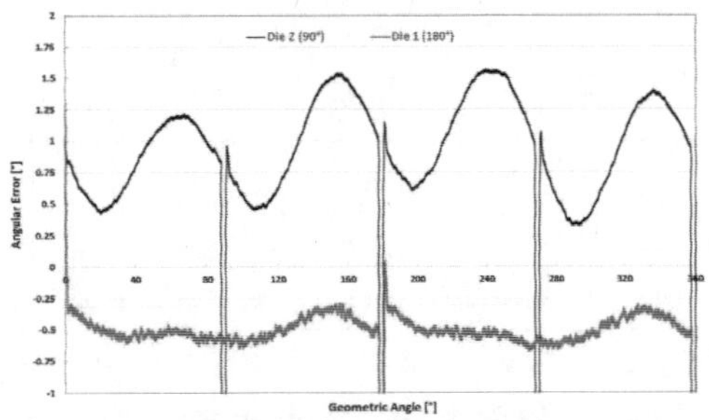

$\langle AE_1pp\rangle=0.37°$ $\langle AE_2pp\rangle=1.24°$

External-Field-Compensating Sensors – Practical Example

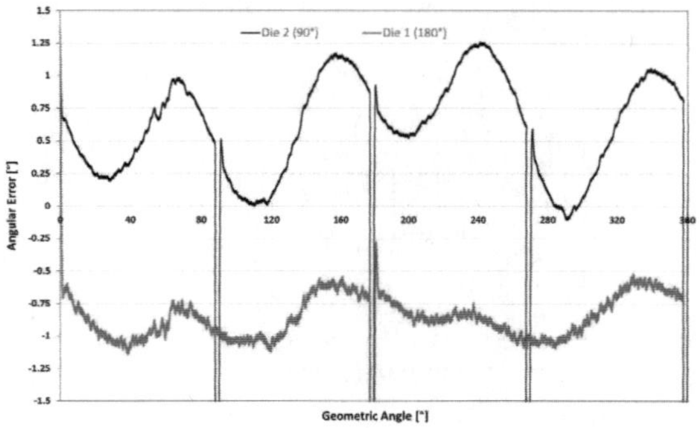

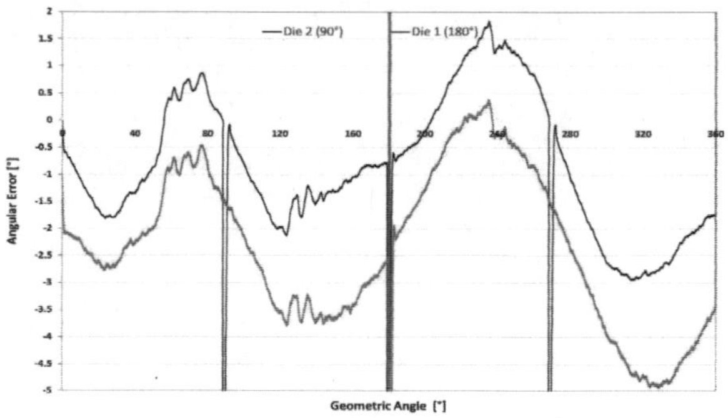

Angular errors at 10mT external field

<AE_1pp>=0.57° **<AE_2pp>=1.37°**

Not much larger than without external field!

Angular errors at 25mT external field

<AE_1pp>=5.33° **<AE_2pp>=4.79°**

Very large angular errors !

External-Field-Compensating Sensors – Practical Example

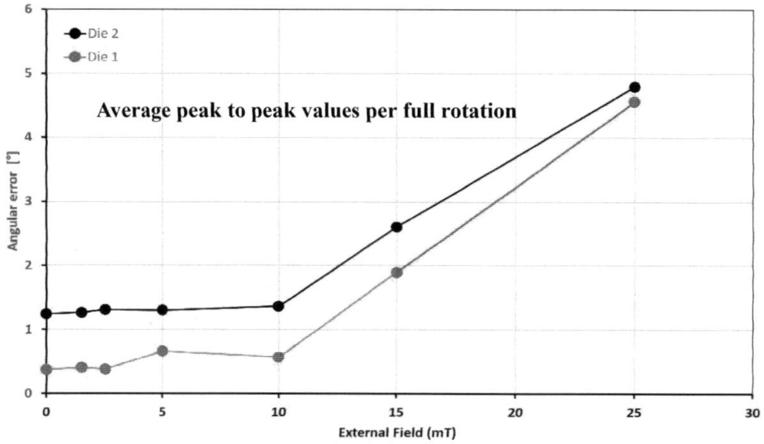

=> Sensor compensates sufficiently low external fields pretty well

A New External-Field-Compensating Sensor

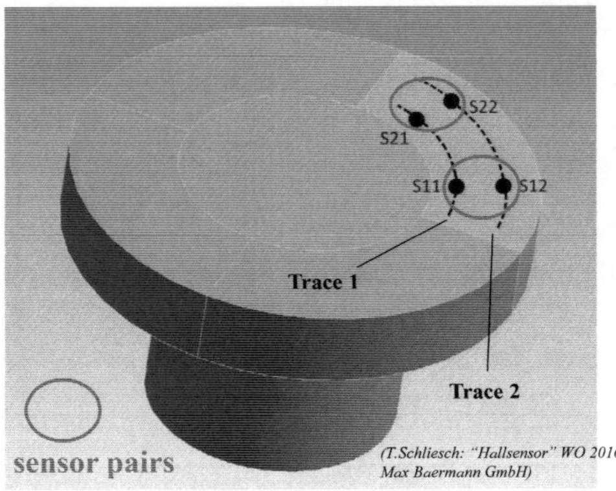

Two sensor pairs above 4-pole ring magnet with axial-lateral magnetization, using the gradient principle. Both pairs assembled with 45° phase difference to harvest the sine and cosine signal of the radial field components here.

Use of the field differences between trace 2 and 1 instead of classical principle of using one sensor only

$F_{Sin}=S_{12}-S_{11}$
$F_{Cos}=S_{22}-S_{21}$

$\varphi=\mathrm{atan2}(F_{sin}/F_{cos})$

Without external field

$F_{sin}(H_e)=(S_{12}+H_e)-(S_{11}+H_e)=F_{Sin}$
$F_{cos}(H_e)=(S_{22}+H_e)-(S_{21}+H_e)=F_{Cos}$

$\varphi=\mathrm{atan2}(F_{sin}/F_{cos})$

With external field, result is the same

Sensor principle can be used both for end-of-shaft as well as on-shaft sensor systems. Precondition is that sensor fits above head face of the magnet ring.

A New External-Field-Compensating Sensor

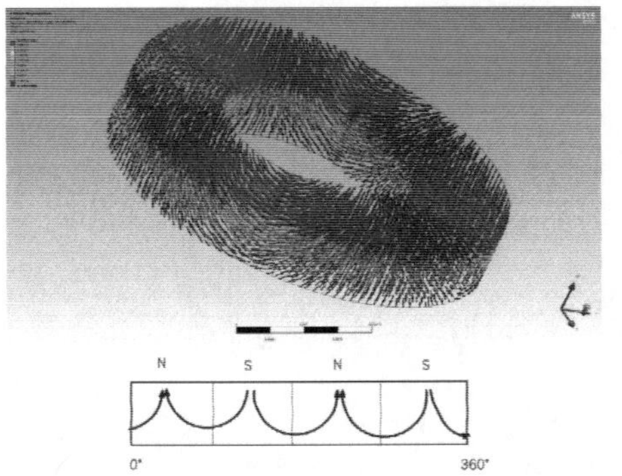

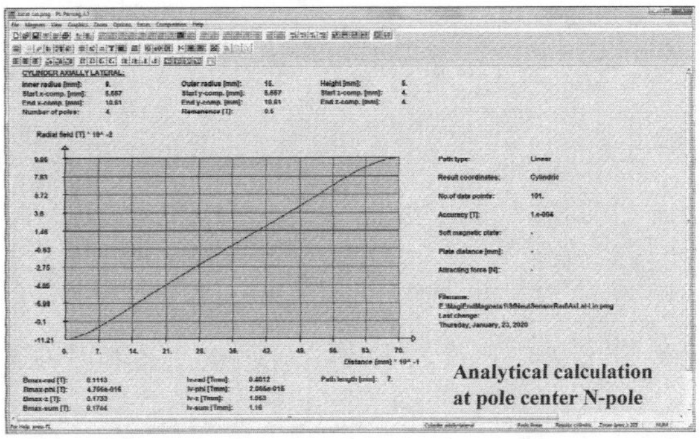

Axial-lateral magnetization of the above scheme provides radial field components with a high linearity in radial direction. This has following advantages:

- **Sufficiently large differences between two traces lead to good signal quality of the signal pairs**
- **Low sensitive against magnet-sensor movement in radial direction**

Injection molded NdFeb magnet, inner diameter 16mm, outer diameter 30mm axial length 5mm, sensor distance 1.5mm

A New External-Field-Compensating Sensor

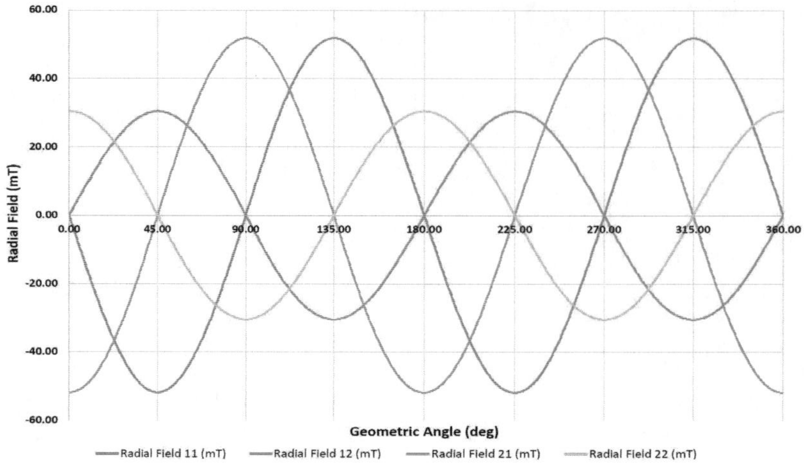

Fields of single sensor elements Trace 1 r=10mm, Trace 2 r=12.5mm

A New External-Field-Compensating Sensor

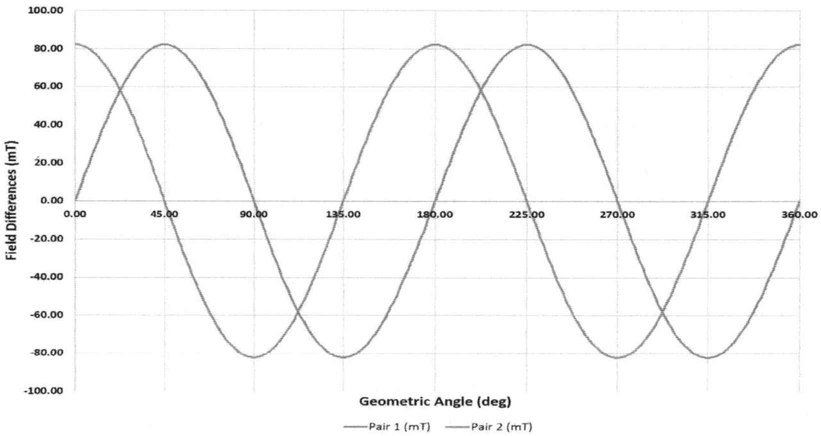

Output of sensor pairs with and without external field, i.e. full compensation takes place. Due to the steepness of radial field component as well as by the relatively large distance of single sensors of 2.5mm, signals are fairly strong.

A New External-Field-Compensating Sensor

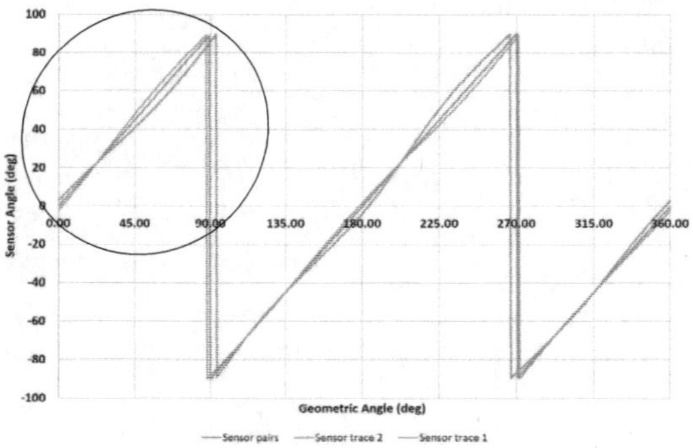

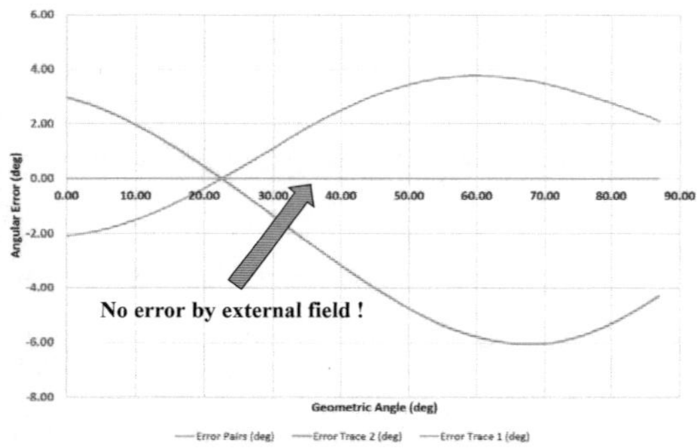

Sensor angle of sensor pairs in comparison to single sensors on trace 1 and 2. External field of strength 5mT at 45°. Without compensation errors up to 4° and 6° result, which are far above the usually allowed deviations of a few 0.1° up to 1°, see e.g. above.

Sensor is currently built up by a German research institute together with MB for practical testing.

End-of-Shaft Magnets for Angular Position Measurements

Thank you for your attention !

MagnetoDynamics LLC

Consultancy in Magnetics

Magnets in EV/HEV traction motors. Designs and state of the art manufacturing

Dr James F Bell

Consultant

MagnetoDynamics LLC.

MagnetoDynamics LLC

Consultancy in Magnetics

Presentation Summary

- A few motor basics
- Examples of magnets in EV/HEV traction motors
- EV/HEV traction motor magnet consumption
- State of the art manufacture of EV magnets

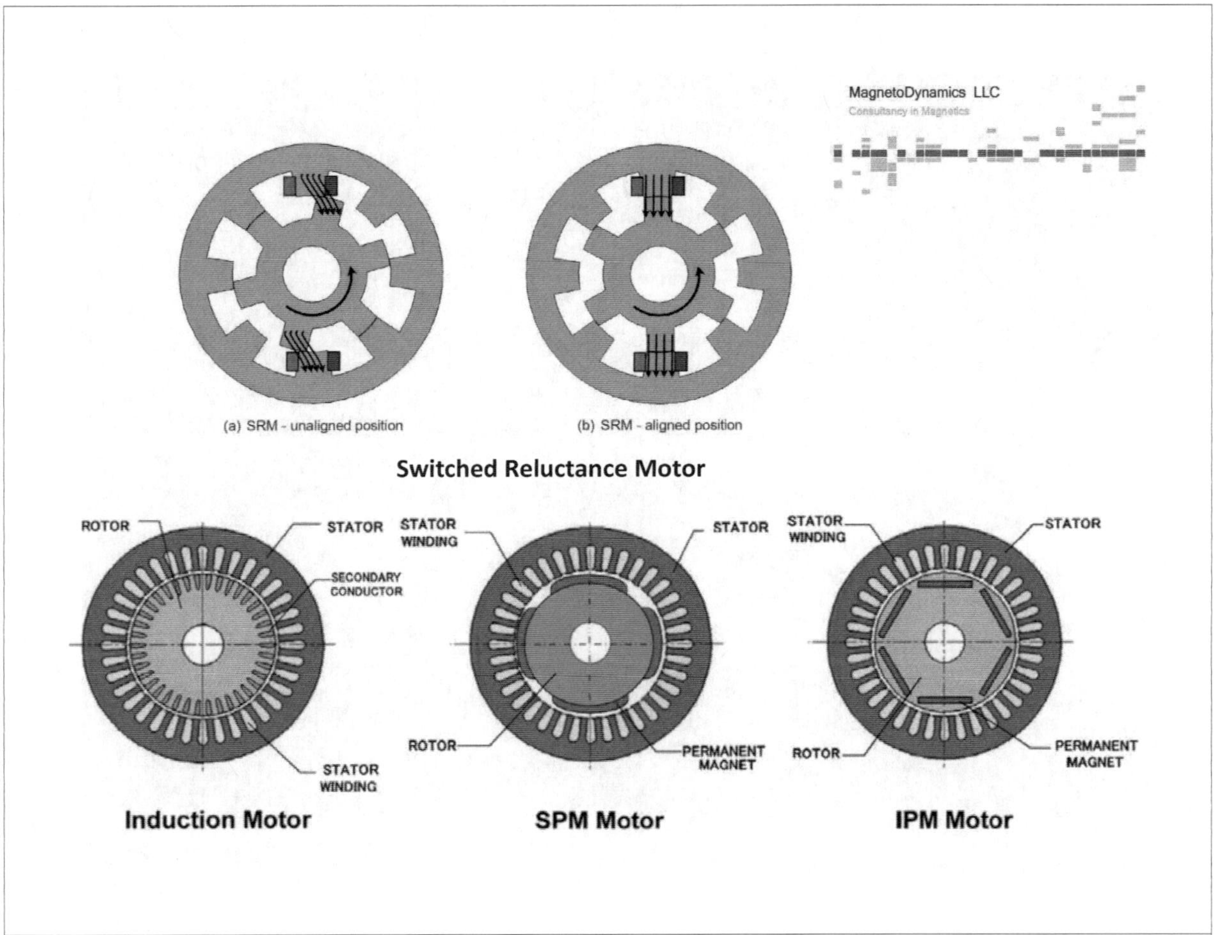
MagnetoDynamics LLC
Consultancy in Magnetics
(a) SRM - unaligned position
(b) SRM - aligned position
Switched Reluctance Motor
ROTOR
STATOR
SECONDARY CONDUCTOR
STATOR WINDING
STATOR WINDING
STATOR
ROTOR
PERMANENT MAGNET
STATOR WINDING
STATOR
ROTOR
PERMANENT MAGNET
Induction Motor
SPM Motor
IPM Motor

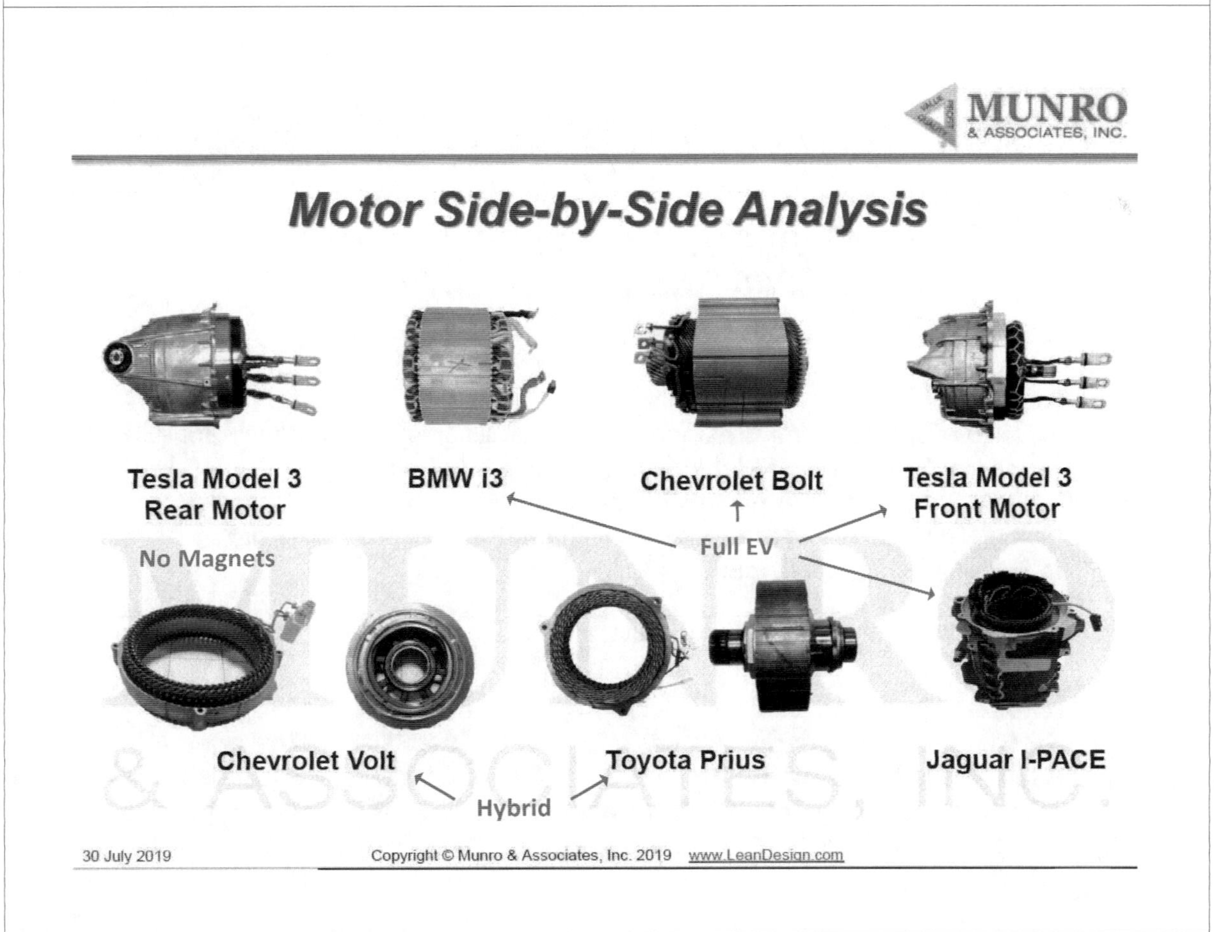
MUNRO & ASSOCIATES, INC.
Motor Side-by-Side Analysis
Tesla Model 3 Rear Motor
BMW i3
Chevrolet Bolt
Tesla Model 3 Front Motor
Full EV
No Magnets
Chevrolet Volt
Toyota Prius
Jaguar I-PACE
Hybrid
30 July 2019
Copyright © Munro & Associates, Inc. 2019 www.LeanDesign.com

Commercial Alert !

MUNRO & ASSOCIATES, INC.

Tesla 3 Teardown and Benchmarking Study

1

Tesla Model 3 Benchmark Report

$1,000,000 Analysis for $87,000

Purchasers of this ~2400 page report will receive the following:

a. Component Fit Finish Quality Assessment (FFQ) and Ride & Drive Report
b. Zone Eye Catching Features and Quick Cost Estimate Report with Zone Summary Costed Bill of Material and associated photos.
c. Vehicle Executive Summary with Consolidated Eye Catching Features
d. Complete Vehicle Summary CBOM with photos, weights and most materials and suppliers identified

Individual Zone Reports are Available for Those Only Interested in Specific Vehicle Areas

o **Zone 1**	Body and Chassis	**$31,000 USD**	500 Pages
o **Zone 2**	Controlling Electronics	**$37,000 USD**	374 Pages
o **Zone 3**	Interiors and Safety	**$31,000 USD**	621 Pages
o **Zone 4**	Powertrain and Battery Pack	**$43,000 USD**	448 Pages

Side-by-Side Comparison

MUNRO & ASSOCIATES, INC.

MOTOR SPECIFICATIONS							
Parameters	Tesla Model 3 Rear	BMW I3	Chevrolet Bolt	Jaguar I-Pace	Tesla Model 3 Front	Chevrolet Volt	Toyota Prius
Motor Type	PM	PM	PM	PM	Induction	PM	PM
Total Motor Weight (kg)	41.46	35.47	33.76	38.03	27.99	13.35	15.79
STATOR							
Total Weight (kg)	24.2	20.58	17.63	23.05	16.49	7.6	11.48
Stack Configuration	Glued and pressed	Formed depressions and laser welded	Formed depressions and laser welded	Formed depressions and laser welded	Formed depressions and pressed	Formed depressions and laser welded	Formed depressions and laser welded
Laminate OD/ID (mm)	232 / 151.4	242 / 180	242 / 140.6	203.3 / 137.5	232 / 135	287 / 204	228 / 142.5
Laminate Thickness (mm)	0.25	0.23	0.25	0.27	0.25	0.27	0.25
Lamination Count	536	636	466	611	263	119	240
Winding Configuration	Winding Laced	Winding Laced	Hairpin	Hairpin	Winding Laced	Hairpin	Hairpin
Winding Material	Copper	Copper	Copper	Copper	Copper	Copper	Copper
Insulation Configuration	2-piece	2-piece	2-piece	2-piece	2-piece	2-piece	1-piece
ROTOR							
Total Weight (kg)	17.24	14.84	16.13	14.97	11.5	5.75	4.31
Stack Configuration	Glued and pressed	Formed depressions and pressed	Formed depressions and pressed	Formed depressions and pressed	Formed depressions and pressed	Formed depressions and pressed	Formed depressions and pressed
Laminate OD/ID (mm)	149.8 / 70	178 / 60	139.50 / 49.95	136.5 / 55	133.95 / 41.95	201.7 / 130	126 / 47
Laminate Thickness (mm)	0.25	0.3	0.25	0.27	0.25	0.27	0.25
Lamination Count	540	468	470	613	272	128	174
Number of Poles	6	12	8	8	N/A	12	10
Magnet Configuration	Single V	Two-pattern, Parallel	Double V	Three-pattern, Parallel	N/A	Semi-Circular	Single V
Magnet Material	NdFeB	NdFeB	NdFeB	NdFeB	N/A	Ferrite	NdFeB
Total Magnets	192 (48 assemblies)	144	256	196	N/A	216	40
Total Magnet Weight (kg)	1.79	2.01	1.57	2.16	N/A	0.69	0.42
Number of Rotor Bars / Material	N/A	N/A	N/A	N/A	70 / Copper	N/A	N/A
Total Copper Weight (kg)	N/A	N/A	N/A	N/A	4.47	N/A	N/A

30 July 2019 www.LeanDesign.com 4

MUNRO & ASSOCIATES, INC.

Stator Specs.

Total Weight (kg)
Stack Configuration
Laminate OD/ID (mm)
Laminate Thickness (mm)
Lamination Count
Winding Configuration
Winding Material
Insulation Configuration

Rotor Specs.

Total Weight (kg)
Stack Configuration
Laminate OD/ID (mm)
Laminate Thickness (mm)
Lamination Count
Number of Poles
Magnet Configuration
Magnet Material
Total Magnets
Total Magnet Weight (kg)
Number of Rotor Bars / Material
Total Copper Weight (kg)

Side-by-Side Comparison

MUNRO & ASSOCIATES, INC.

Battery Electric Vehicles (BEV)

	2017 Tesla Model 3 Rear Motor	2014 BMW i3 Extended Range	2017 Chevrolet Bolt EV	2019 Jaguar I-Pace	2018 Tesla Model 3 Front Motor
	Long Range 4dr Sedan	Extended Range 4dr Hatchback	Premier 4dr Hatchback	EV400 90kWh AWD	Premium Long Range 4dr Sedan
Drivetrain	RWD, Rear Motor	RWD, Rear Motor	FWD, Front Motor	AWD	AWD
Power	346* HP	170 HP	200 HP	394 HP	N/A HP
Torque	389* lb-ft	184 lb-ft	266 lb-ft	512 lb-ft	N/A lb-ft
Motor Type	Permanent-magnet AC Synchronous electric	Permanent-magnet AC Synchronous electric	Permanent-magnet AC Synchronous electric	Permanent-magnet AC Synchronous electric	Induction Motor

*Note: Power and Torque combined for dual motor versions. Individual motor ratings are N/A

Tesla : https://www.thecarconnection.com/overview/tesla_model-3_2019
BMW i3 : https://www.bmwusa.com/vehicles/bmwi/i3/sedan/pricing-features.html
Bolt : https://media.chevrolet.com/media/us/en/chevrolet/vehicles/bolt-ev/2017.tab1.html
I-Pace : https://www.jaguar.com/jaguar-range/i-pace/specifications/index.html

30 July 2019 2

BMW i3- Rotor Configuration

MUNRO & ASSOCIATES, INC.

Stack assembly	: Formed depressions and pressed
Magnet slots	: 24
Number of Laminations	: 468 (approx.)
Lamination sections	: 6
Lamination section count	: 78
Lamination thickness	: 0.30 mm
Airgap from Stator	: 1.0mm

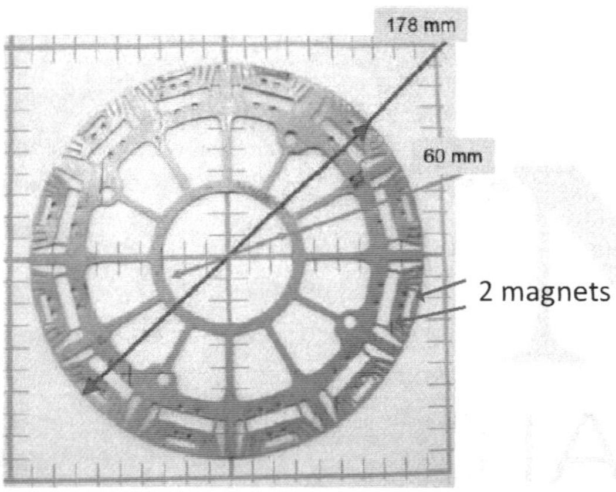

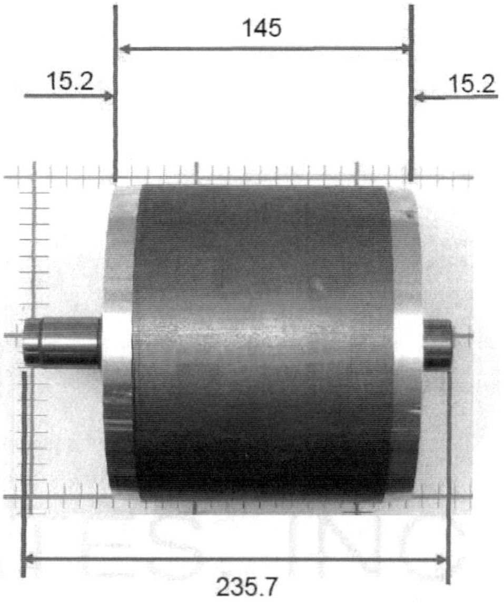

30 July 2019 15

BMW i3- Rotor Magnet Configuration

MUNRO & ASSOCIATES, INC.

Magnet material	: NdFeB, Sintered
Grade	: Unknown
Formation	: Two-pattern, parallel magnets
Total Magnets in Rotor	: (L) 72, (S) 72
Weight	: (L) 21.8 g, (S) 6.1 g
Density	: (L) 6.92 g/cc, (S) 7.45 g/cc
Total Magnet Weight	: 2.01 kg

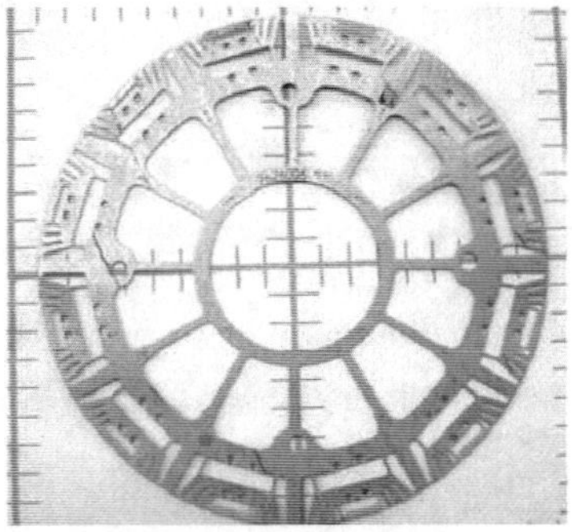

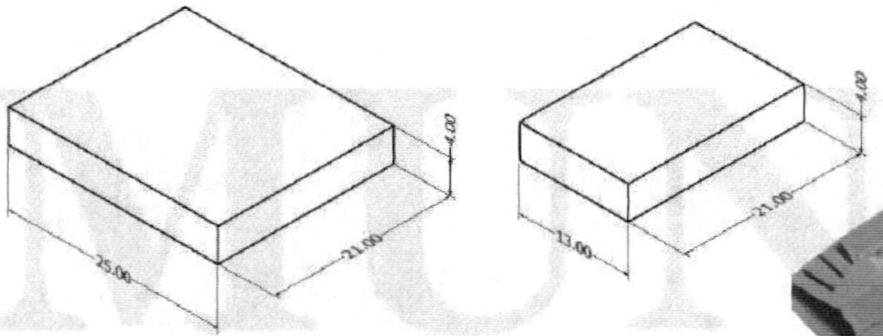

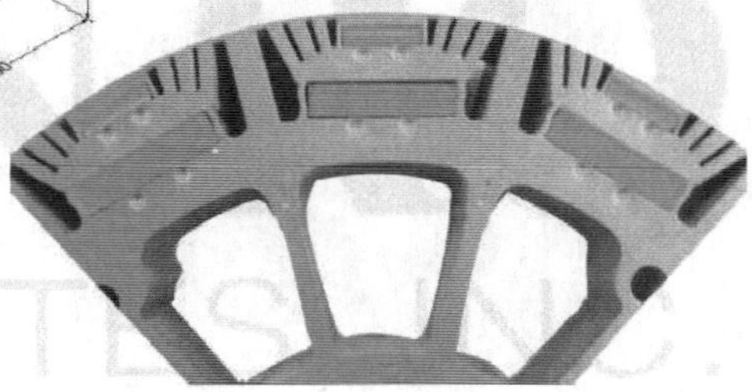

All dimensions in mm

I-Pace- Rotor Magnet Configuration

MUNRO & ASSOCIATES, INC.

Magnet material	: NdFeB, Sintered
Grade	: Unknown
Formation	: Single V
Weight	: 11.0g
Density	: 7.99g/cm^3
Total Magnets in Rotor	: 168
Total Magnet Weight	: 1.85kg

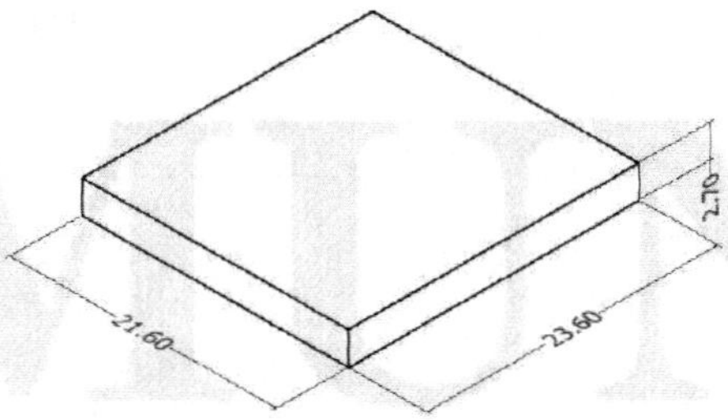

All dimensions in mm

Tesla 3 Rear- Rotor Configuration

MUNRO & ASSOCIATES, INC.

Stack assembly	: Glued and pressed
Magnet slots	: 12
Number of Laminations	: 540 (approx.)
Lamination sections	: 4
Laminations section count	: 135
Lamination thickness	: 0.25 mm
Airgap from Stator	: 0.80 mm

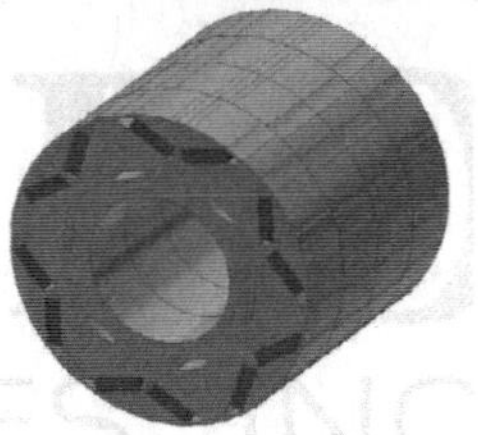

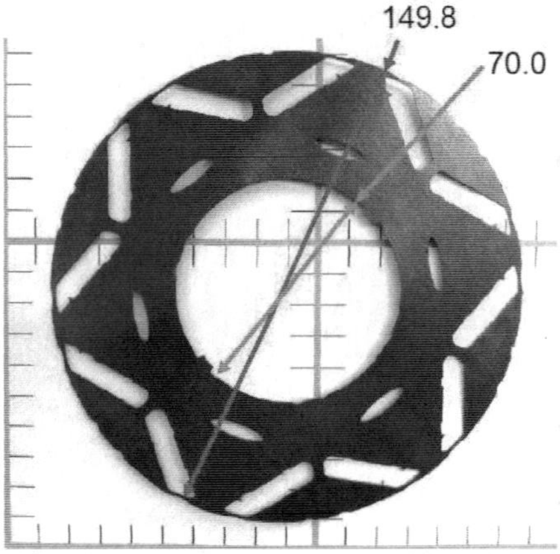

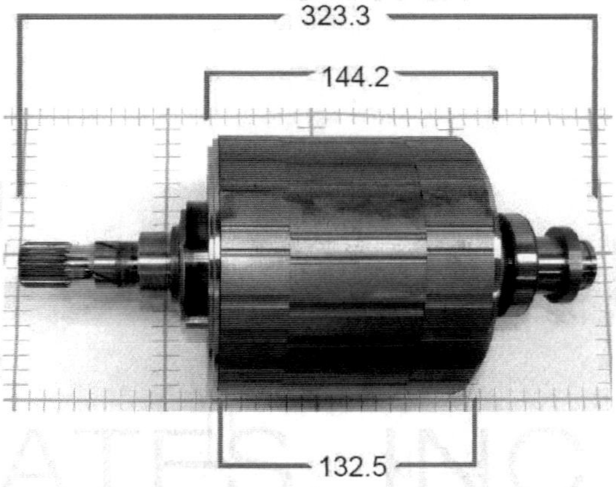

Based on magnet lengths

30 July 2019 Copyright © Munro & Associates, Inc. 2019 www.LeanDesign.com 6

Tesla 3 Rear- Rotor Assembly

MUNRO & ASSOCIATES, INC.

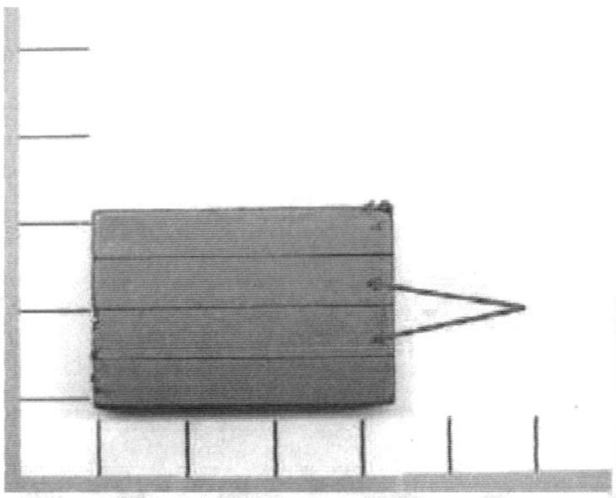

Component Summary

Vehicle	Tesla Model 3
System	Rotor
Part	T3R Magnet Inner

Quantity	96
Weight (kg)	0.0095
Total Weight (kg)	0.9120

Piece Cost **	$0.95
Total Cost *	$91.20

Total Cost for all 96 components

* Excluding tooling, ER&D, and logistics
** Includes material cost and purchased parts cost

30 July 2019 Copyright © Munro & Associates, Inc. 2019 www.LeanDesign.com 13

Tesla 3 Rear- Rotor Assembly

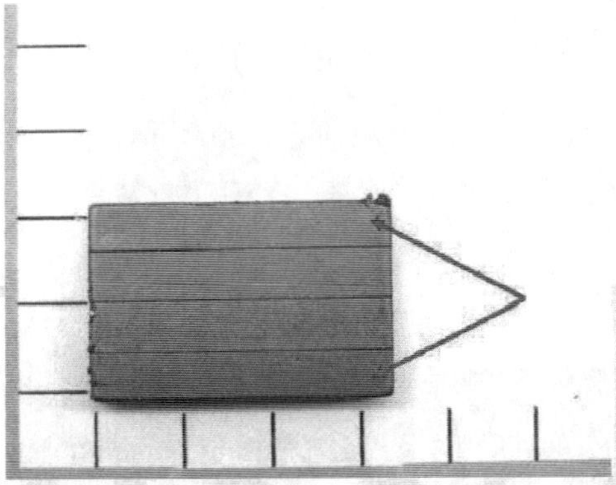

Component Summary

Vehicle	Tesla Model 3
System	Rotor
Part	T3R Magnet Outer

Quantity	96
Weight (kg)	0.0091
Total Weight (kg)	0.8736
Piece Cost **	$0.91
Total Cost *	$87.36

Total Cost for all 96 components

* Excluding tooling, ER&D, and logistics
** Includes material cost and purchased parts cost

30 July 2019 14

Prius- Rotor Magnet Configuration

Magnet material	: NdFeB, Sintered
Grade	: Unknown
Formation	: Single V
Weight	: 11.0g
Density	: 6.76g/cm^3
Total Magnets in Rotor	: 40
Total Magnet Weight	: 0.44kg

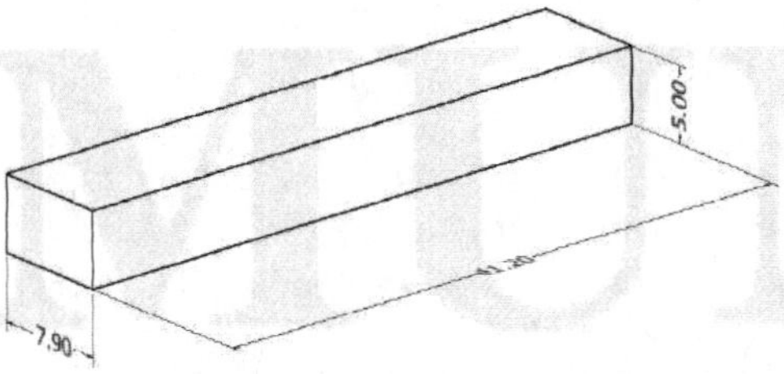

All dimensions in mm

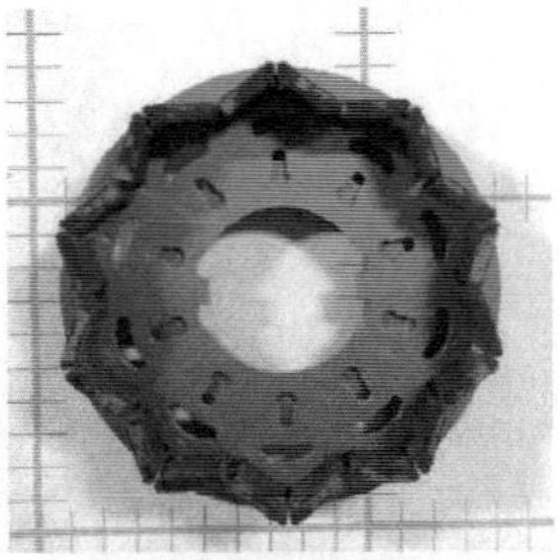

30 July 2019 54

Equipmake APM 200

MagnetoDynamics LLC
Consultancy in Magnetics

Motor Mass	40Kg
Reduction Gearbox Mass	9 Kg
Inverter Mass	8 Kg
Motor and Gearbox Diameter	318mm
Motor and Gearbox Length	247 mm
Maximum Power	220kW
Maximum Speed (motor)	10,000 rpm
Maximum Torque (motor)	450Nm
Gear Ratio	6:1
Maximum Torque (driveshaft)	2,475Nm

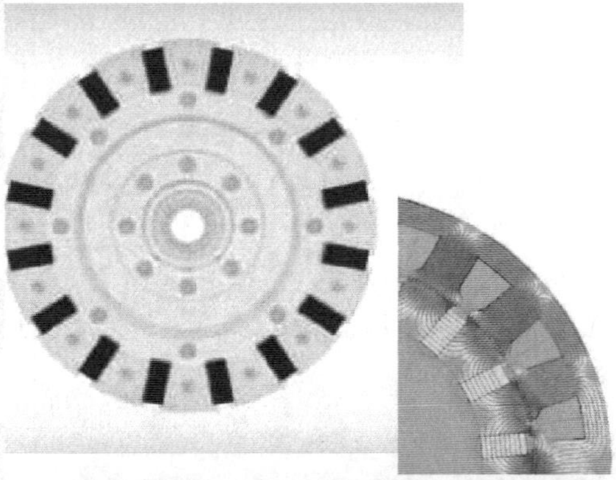

MagnetoDynamics LLC
Consultancy in Magnetics

EV motors – kW/kg of magnet material

	Power (kW)	Magnets (kg)	kW/kg
Jaguar iPace	394	3.44	115
Toyota Prius	60 (?)	0.46	130
Chevy Bolt	200	1.6	125
BMW i3	170	2.0	85
Tesla Model 3	258	1.8	143
Equipmake	220	1.6 (?)	137

MagnetoDynamics LLC
Consultancy in Magnetics

Back to 2009 Dayton.

MAGNET APPLICATIONS
TOTAL MAGNETIC SOLUTIONS

Hybrids – impact in 2020

- GM state they expect 80% of production by 2020 to be hybrids.

- Toyota expect 100% by 2020!

- Fuel cells will replace ICE.

- At 60 million vehicles per year, each consuming 1kg of NdFeB magnets, total ADDITIONAL requirement per year is 60,000 tonnes.

The Hybrid I am waiting for!

MAGNET APPLICATIONS
TOTAL MAGNETIC SOLUTIONS

Lexus LFA – 4.8 liter V10.

2020 Supra – 3 liter Straight 6.

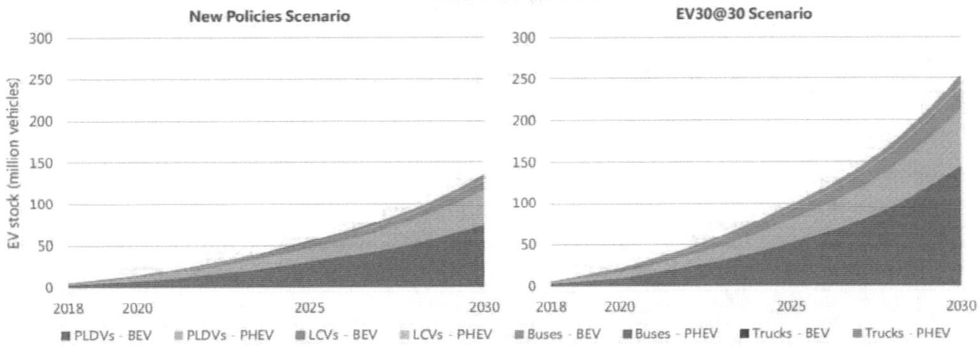

IEA – International Energy Agency

IEA (2019), "Global EV Outlook 2019", IEA, Paris,

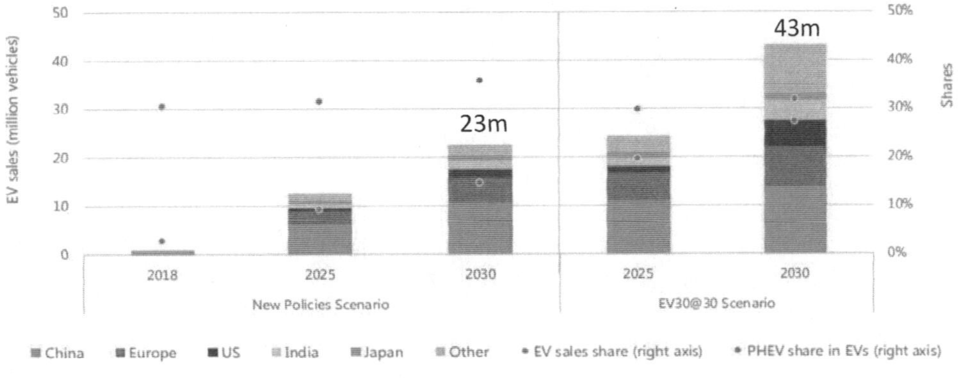

MagnetoDynamics LLC
Consultancy in Magnetics

Magnet and Nd requirements 2030.

IEA estimates 23 to 43 million vehicle production in 2030 – Assume 33 million.

About 85% EV / Hybrid PLDV + LCV using 1.2 kg magnet material. (At 150 kW/kg average motor output = 180 kW)

Remaining 15% (Bus, truck) average 3 kg.

Total magnet demand in 2030 = 48 million kg = 48,000 tonnes.

New TH Magnetics EV magnet plant – 5,000 tonnes capacity. (2020)

Total Nd demand (at 30%) = 15,000 tonnes.

天和磁材®
TIANHE MAGNETICS

DFP(HRE free process) Grade Chart

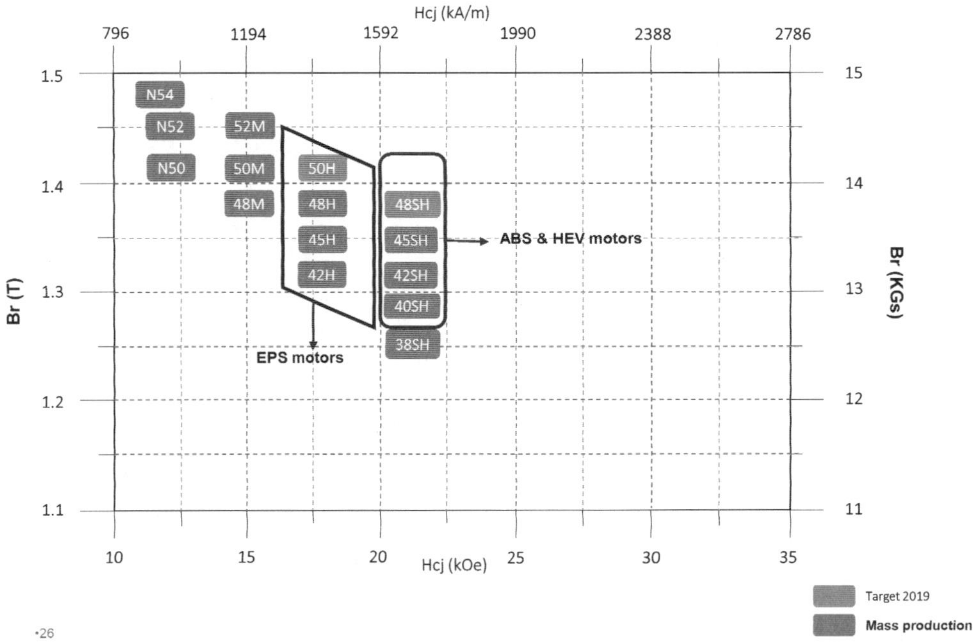

•26

DDP(HRE diffusion process) Grade Chart for EV Magnets

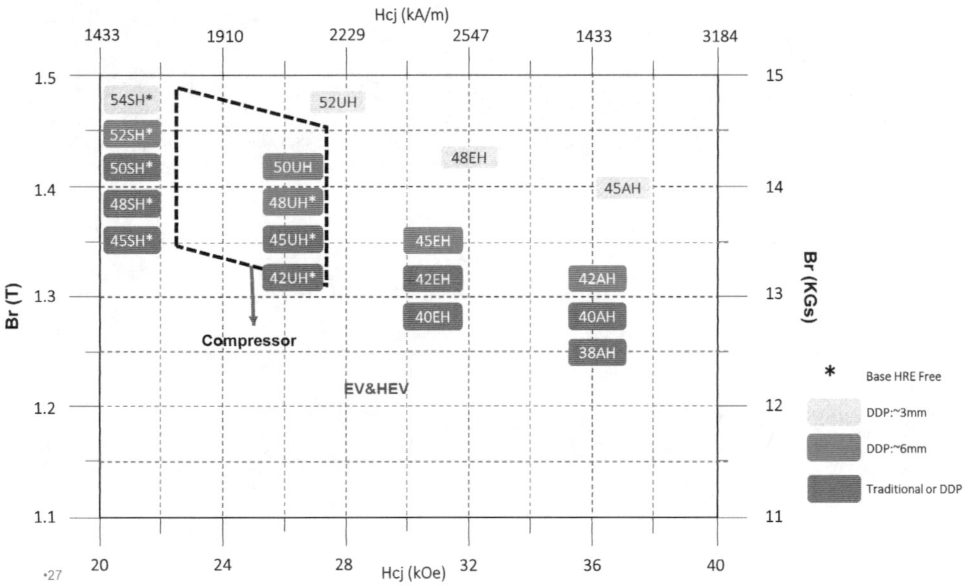

3.1 Tianhe (Baotou) Production Base Layout

Occupied area: 130,000 m² Floor area: 80,000 m²

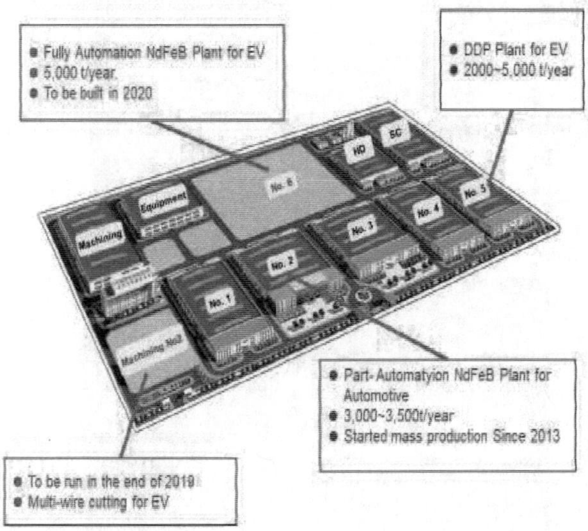

Plant	Description	2019 Capacity (tons)	2023 Capacity (tons))
SC Plant	SmCo Melting	300	500
	NdFeB Strips	8,000	15,000
HD Plant	HD Powder	8,000	15,000
Plant No.1	NdFeB Cylinder	1,500	3,000
Plant No.2	NdFeB Block for Automotive	3,000	3,500
Plant No.3	NdFeB Block	3,000	3,500
Plant No.4	SmCo Block	300	500
Plant No.5	NdFeB DDP for EV	2,000	5,000
Plant No.6	NdFeB Block for EV	--	5,000
NdFeB Tons in Total		**7,500**	**15,000**
DDP NdFeB in Total		**2,000**	**5,000**
SmCo in Total		**300**	**500**

•4

3.3 Integrated Rare Earth & Magnet Supply Chain

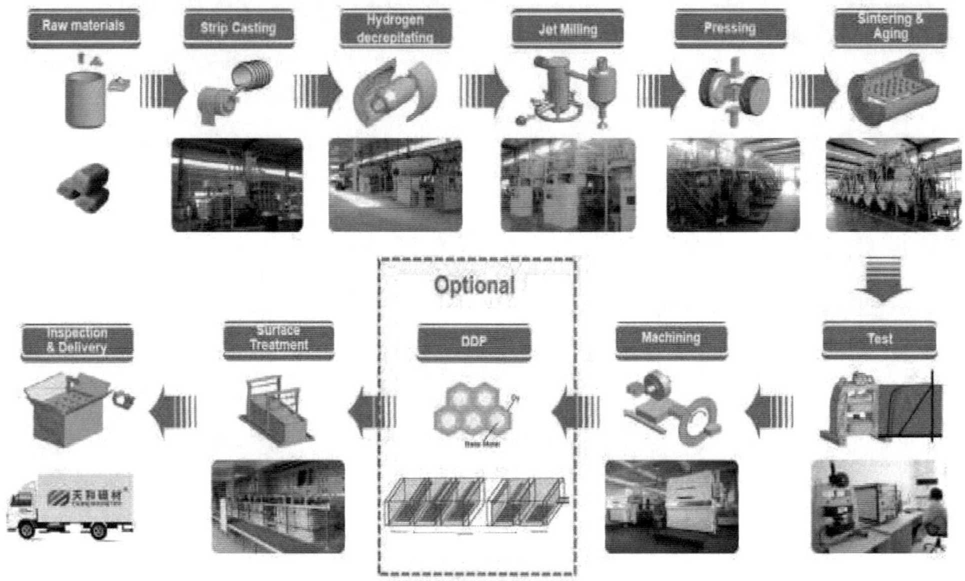

Automated Production Equipment

天和磁材®
TIANHE MAGNETICS

Multi-Wire Cutting

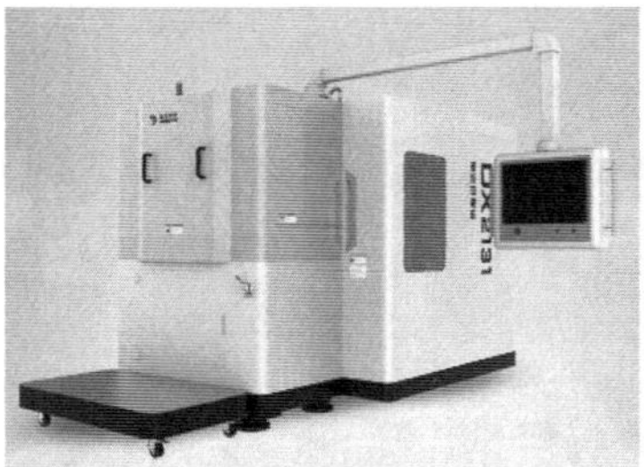

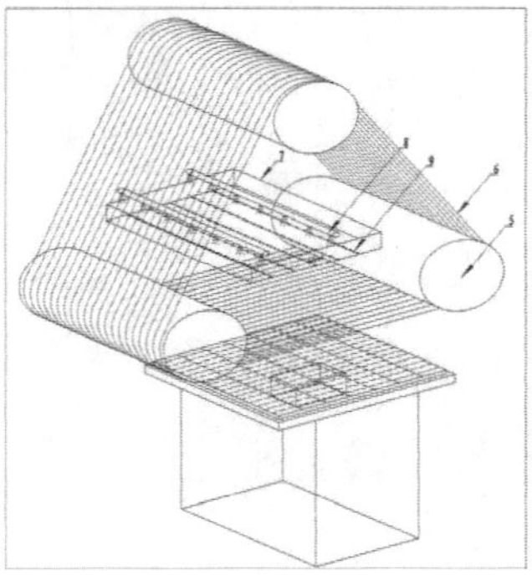

天和磁材®
TIANHE MAGNETICS

Automated Plating Lines

Characteristics of Surface Treatment

Coalting / Performance	Phosphating	Bluing	Zn	Ni	Double Ni	NiCuNi	Electrophoresic Epoxy	CuNi	Spraying Epoxy	ZnNi
Colour	Gray	Blue	Blue White	Silver	Silver	Silver	Black	Silver	Black	Blue White ~Silver
Thickness (μm)	0-2	0~2	5~10	10~15	10~20	12~25	15~30	12~20	15~25	5~10
Shear Stress			●	◎	◎	◎	●	◎	○	◎
Hardness	○	○	◎	●	●	●	○	●	○	◎
PCT			○	◎	◎	◎	◎	◎	●	◎
Salt Spray Test			○	○	◎	◎	●	◎	●	●
Cost	Electrophoresis epoxy > Sprayed epoxy > NiCuNi / CuNi / Ni > ZnNi > Zn > Phosphating / Bluing									

○ Good ◎ Better ● Best

MagnetoDynamics LLC
Consultancy in Magnetics

Summary

- IPM motor designs are becoming standard
- NdFeB magnet usage will be approx. 1.2kg per PLD vehicle
- EV/HEV motor magnet usage 48,000t by 2030.
- Highest quality manufacturing required and in progress.

Iron Oxide
PVS Steel Services, Inc.

PVS STEEL SERVICES, INC.

1

Steel Production

Steel mills produce "Hot Band".

- Rust is natural occurrence during processing
- Pickling
- Ferrous chloride, aka Waste Pickle Liquor (WPL)

PVS STEEL SERVICES, INC.

2

Acid Regeneration Plants (ARP)

- Years ago steel mills deep-welled their WPL
- Process created to manage WPL streams
- ARP's built on steel mill property to service pickle lines
- Main goal of each ARP is to regenerate HCl.
- By-product of ARP is Iron Oxide.

PVS STEEL SERVICES, INC.

3

Typical Iron Oxide Grades

	G1000(M)	G700(M)	G500(M)	G300(M)	GSA	G100	GHP
Cl wt. %	≤0.30	≤0.20	≤0.15	≤0.15	≤0.35	≤0.15	≤0.125
SiO2 wt. %	≤0.12	≤0.08	≤0.06	≤0.04	≤0.12	≤0.012	≤0.008
CaO wt. %	≤0.12	≤0.08	≤0.06	≤0.04	≤0.12	≤0.025	≤0.020
Na2O wt. %	≤0.05	≤0.04	≤0.03	≤0.02	≤0.05	≤0.015	≤0.010
Al2O3 wt. %	≤0.16	≤0.14	≤0.12	≤0.10	≤0.16	≤0.02	≤0.015
MnO wt. %	report	report	report	report	report	report	report
P2O5 wt. %	report	report	report	report	report	report	report
TiO2 wt. %	report	report	report	report	report	report	report
Cr2O3 wt. %	report	report	report	report	report	report	report
K2O wt. %	report	report	report	report	report	report	report
CuO wt. %	report	report	report	report	report	report	report
*Fe2O3 wt. %	≥98.5	≥98.6	≥98.8	≥99.0	≥98.5	≥99.3	≥99.4
Fe3O4 wt. %	report	report	report	report	report	report	report
Particle Size Microns	0.50 - 1.0	0.50 - 1.0	0.50 - 1.0	0.50 - 1.0	0.40 - 0.60	0.60 - 1.0	0.40 - 0.60
Surface Area m^2/g	≥2.5	≥2.75	≥3.0	≥3.0	4.5 – 6.0	≥2.5	≥2.5
Loss of Moisture wt. %	≤0.5	≤0.5	≤0.5	≤0.5	≤0.5	≤0.5	≤0.5
Bulk Density gm/cm^3	.40 - .60 .60 - .90(M)**	.40 - .60 .60 - .90(M)**	.40 - .60 .60 - .90(M)**	.40 - .60 .60 - .90(M)**	.40 - .60	.40 - .50	.40 - .50

*Reported as minimum value calculated by subtraction method of (100% Fe2O3 less LOI less Impurities by ICP = %Fe_2O_3)

**Milled; increases Bulk Density via vibratory rod mill

PVS STEEL SERVICES, INC.

4

Iron Oxide Applications

A. Hard Ferrite Applications (target lower chlorides, preferably without reducing surface area, and produce higher % Fe_2O_3, via incoming material segregation)

- Ceramic Magnets
- Bonded Magnets
- Injection Molded Magnets

Soft Ferrite Applications (higher purity, lower SiO_2 under 60 - 80 ppm and chlorides under 0.12%

- Power Ferrite (transformers)
- Noise Suppression (electronic)

C. Water Treatment Chemicals:

- Ferric Chloride Production
- Ferric Sulfate Production (target much lower chlorides preferably under 0.10%)

D. Pigment Applications Low End:

Brick, concrete, tile and mulch

Special Applications:

Batteries, electrical anodes, glass production

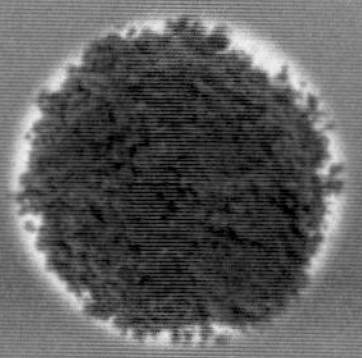

PVS STEEL SERVICES, INC. 5

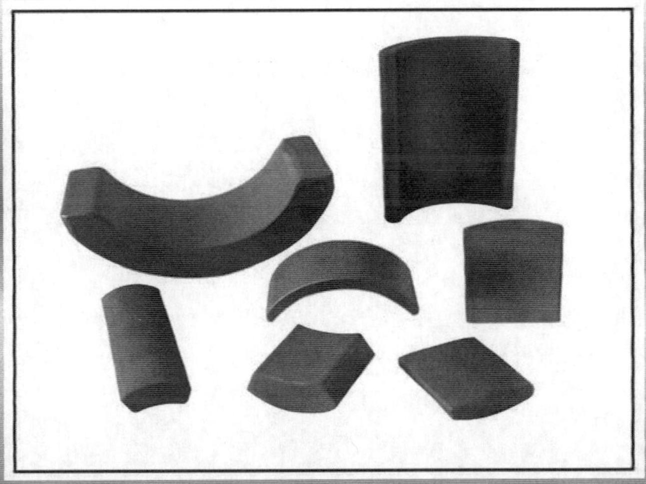

FERRITE MAGNETS

PVS STEEL SERVICES, INC.

OVERVIEW OF FERRITE MAGNETS

Grade	Br (KG)	Hcb (KOe)	Hci (KOe)	BHmax	Tmax
C1	2.3	1.86	3.5	1.05	250C / 482F
C5	3.8	2.4	2.5	3.4	250C / 482F
C7	3.4	3.23	4	2.75	250C / 482F
C8	3.85	2.95	3.05	3.5	250C / 482F
C8B	4.2	2.913	2.96	4.12	250C / 482F
C9	3.8	3.516	4.01	3.32	250C / 482F
C10	4	3.617	3.51	3.82	250C / 482F
C11	4.3	2.512	2.56	4.32	250C / 482F
C12	4	3.65	4	4.0	250C / 482F

Br (Remanence) The magnetic flux density remaining in a magnet after the magnetizing field **H** has been removed.

Coercivity HcB

The magnetic field strength required to bring the magnetic flux density back to 0.

Intrinsic Coercivity (Hci)

The demagnetizing field **H** necessary to cause a magnet which was previously saturated to have zero magnetization.

BHmax (Maximum Energy Product) On a **B-H** graph this is the point at which the product **B•H** reaches a maximum.

PVS STEEL SERVICES, INC.

CHANGING LANDSCAPE FOR MAGNETS

- Yesterday – motor magnets were a dime a dozen, and the attributes from the magnets was the same.
- Today – with increasing demands placed on motors (lighter weights, smaller packaging, improved performance, less heat, etc.), the demands on manufacturers are becoming far greater.
- Today, part 2 – higher magnet grades will be required for what used to be a generic motor for appliances. With all the bells and whistles being put into appliances and automobiles, motors are expected to generate more power in a smaller space.

PVS STEEL SERVICES, INC.

Joseph Holung, Ph.D., P.E.

11/8/2019

Analysis of the magnetic field and torque in radially magnetized permanent magnet Couplings: Exact 2D formulation

ABSTRACT

A two-dimensional formulation for the magnetic field and torque in radially magnetized, permanent magnet couplings is given. Expressions for the field quantities are developed from the magnetic scalar potential in the air gap between the shaft and cylinder. The cogging torque in such multi-pole couplings is derived and compared with experimental results.

INTRODUCTION

Magnetic couplings are interesting because they can transmit torque without mechanical contact. A radial magnetic coupling consists of a shaft, fitted with a circular array of permanent magnet arc segments, which is separated by an air gap from a similar array of permanent magnet arc segments attached to the bore of a cylinder. The magnetization of each arc segment is assumed to be in a purely radial direction, either positive or negative, with the number and arrangement determining the number of poles in the coupling.

In the case of axial magnetic couplings, closed-form expressions for the force and torque have been derived from the magnetic vector potential obtained by solving Laplace's and Poisson's equation for a two-dimensional (2D) analytical model [1]. The approach is well-suited to parametric studies often carried out in early engineering investigations to size geometry and lead to simpler expressions than other approaches such as a Coulombian formulation [2,3,4].

In this paper, the magnetic field and torque in radially magnetized couplings is derived from a two-dimensional analytical model. Exact closed-form expressions are obtained by solving Poisson's equation for the magnetic scalar potential in the permanent magnet regions and Laplace's equation in the air gap region.

PROBLEM DESRIPTION AND ASSUMPTIONS

A cross-section of an ideal, radially magnetized coupling is shown in Fig. 1. A circular array of permanent magnet arc segments extends radially to radius R_2, from a shaft of radius R_1. An air gap separates a corresponding array of permanent magnet arc segments attached to the bore of a cylinder with bore radius

R_4. The air gap radial clearance is R_3-R_2. The pole arc to pole pitch ratio is denoted by α. The alternating

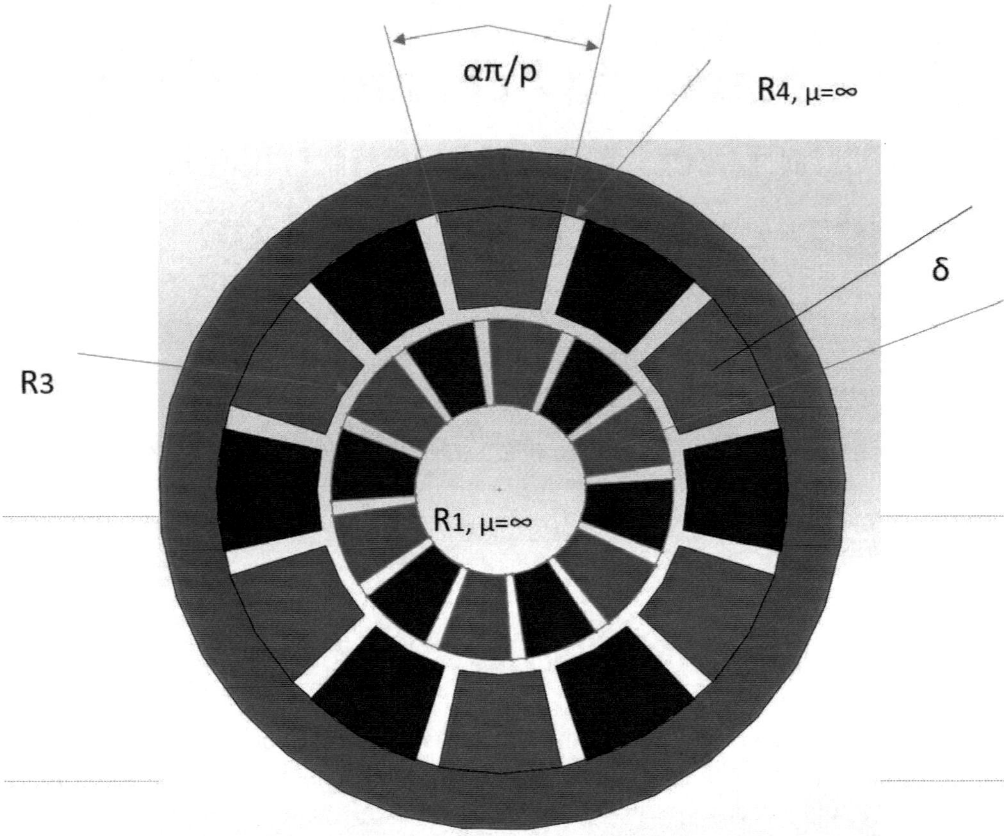

Fig 1. Cross-section of a radially magnetized coupling. The pole arc to pole pitch ratio is α, the number of poles is p (p=6). The shaft and housing have infinite permeability ($\mu=\infty$, at r= R_1 and R_4). δ is an angular offset (torque angle) used as a parameter in the torque expression.

colors denote the alternating positive and negative radial direction of the magnetization in each of the adjacent arc segments. With integer p denoting the number of pole pairs, Fig. 1 shows a p=6 pole-pair, radial, magnetic coupling. The cylinder is assumed to be sufficiently long and losses due to end effects and fringing negligible.

In order to simplify the two-dimensional analysis, the following additional assumptions are made:

1. The iron shaft and cylinder have infinite magnetic permeability, i.e., $\mu=\infty$
2. The radially magnetized permanent magnets have relative recoil permeability $\mu_r=1$.[1]

The analysis domain will be separated into three regions. Region 1 is the region occupied by permanent magnets attached to the shaft, $R_2 \leq r \leq R_1$, region 2 is the air gap region, $R_3 \leq r \leq R_2$, and region 3 is occupied by the outer constellation of permanent magnets, $R_4 \leq r \leq R_3$. The magnets of region 3 are

[1] This assumption is reasonable for the neodymium-iron-boron (NdFeB) magnets which have $\mu_r = 1.05$.

shown rotated by angle δ (torque angle) relative to the magnets in region 1. It is clear from the geometry that the magnetic field distribution is periodic with period T= 2π/p.

The constitutive law relating the magnetic flux density vector, **B,** to the magnetic field intensity vector, **H,** and the magnetization vector, **M,** in the permanent magnet regions is

$$\boldsymbol{B} = \mu(\boldsymbol{H} + \boldsymbol{M}) \tag{1}$$

where $\mu = 4\pi \times 10^{-7}$ henrys/meter, is the permeability of space. As explained in [6], this material model,

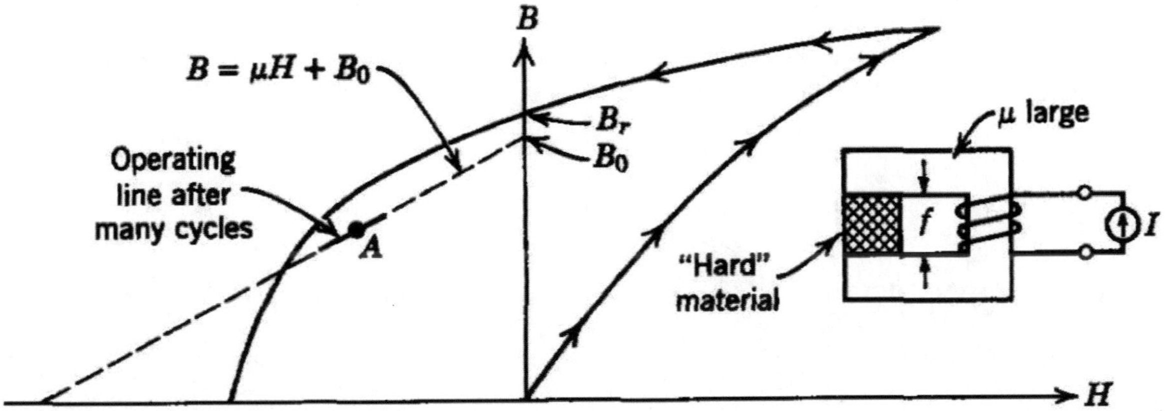

Fig. 2. (Reproduced from [6]). Hard magnetic material magnetized and then demagnetized by the current I.

shown in Fig. 2., represents "hard" magnetic materials with linear demagnetizing curve. The curve results when these materials are subjected to a field intensity **H** by means of an extremely large current as indicated by the inset. They explain that when the current (i.e., **H**) is removed, there is a residual flux density B_r. Then, if the sample is removed from the circuit and subjected to other magnetic fields, the **B-H** curve settles down to operate at some point, such as "A" shown in the figure. The straight line indicated by the dotted line is the representative model of the behavior.

ANALYSIS

The magnetic field problem will be formulated in terms of the scalar magnetic potential. The field intensity is defined as the negative gradient of a magnetic scalar potential, ψ

$$\boldsymbol{H} = -\nabla\psi \tag{2}$$

Gauss's law of magnetism states that the magnetic field has divergence equal to zero,

$$\nabla \cdot \mathbf{B} = \mathbf{0} \tag{3}$$

Substituting (2) into (1) and then imposing condition (3) results in the governing equations in each region. Thus, in the permanent magnet regions, 1 and 3, the governing equation is Poisson's equation, which, expressed in the two cylindrical coordinates (r, θ), is

$$\nabla \cdot \nabla\psi(r,\theta) = \frac{\partial^2\psi}{\partial r^2} + \frac{1}{r}\frac{\partial\psi}{\partial r} + \frac{\partial^2\psi}{\partial\theta^2} = \nabla \cdot \boldsymbol{M} \tag{4}$$

In the air gap region, region 2, **M**=0, and there is no current source, so the governing equation is Laplace's equation,

$$\frac{\partial^2\psi}{\partial r^2} + \frac{1}{r}\frac{\partial\psi}{\partial r} + \frac{\partial^2\psi}{\partial\theta^2} = 0 \tag{5}$$

The magnetization vector to be considered has only a radial component, (**M** = Mr e_r), where $\mathbf{e_r}$ is a unit vector in the radial direction, and is distributed ideally as shown in Fig. 3, for region 3. The square wave

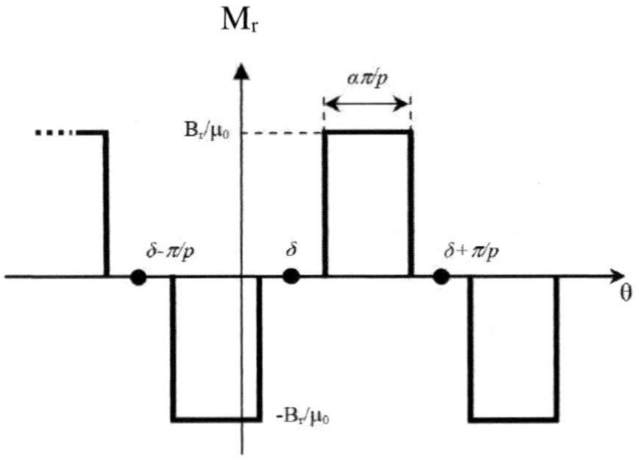

Fig.3. Radial component of magnetization vector in region 3.

can be represented as a Fourier series and substituted into the right side of Eq. (4); the result is

$$\frac{\partial^2\psi}{\partial r^2} + \frac{1}{r}\frac{\partial\psi}{\partial r} + \frac{\partial^2\psi}{\partial\theta^2} = \frac{1}{r}\, M_r \tag{6}$$

$$M_r = \sum_{k=1,3,5,\ldots}^{\infty} M_k * \sin kp\,(\theta - \delta) \tag{7}$$

where

$$M_k = \frac{4\,B_r}{k\,\pi\,\mu} * \cos \mathrm{k}\frac{\pi}{2}\,(1-\alpha) \tag{8}$$

M_r consists of an infinite sum of sine waves of odd harmonics. The governing equation in region 1 is similar and is obtained by setting δ equal to zero. To complete the analytical model, certain boundary conditions must be satisfied. The tangential component of **H** must be zero at the soft iron boundaries (since μ= ∞), and the tangential component of **H** and the normal component of **B** must be continuous at the interfaces.

Using superscripts and subscripts to identify the regions and components, these boundary conditions are summarized in Table 1.

Table 1. Boundary Conditions at Interface

Domain1	Domain2	Relation	Interface	Equation
Iron	Magnet	$H_\theta^3=-\frac{1}{r}\frac{\partial\psi 3}{\partial\theta}=0$	r=R_4	9
Magnet	Air gap	$H_\theta^3=H_\theta^2$ $(-\frac{1}{r}\frac{\partial\psi 3}{\partial\theta}=-\frac{1}{r}\frac{\partial\psi 2}{\partial\theta})$	r=R_3	10
Magnet	Air gap	$B_r^3=B_r^2$	r=R_3	11
Air gap	Magnet	$H_\theta^2=H_\theta^1$ $(-\frac{1}{r}\frac{\partial\psi 2}{\partial\theta}=-\frac{1}{r}\frac{\partial\psi 1}{\partial\theta})$	r=R_2	12
Air gap	Magnet	$B_r^2=B_r^1$	r=R_2	13
Magnet	Iron	$H_\theta^1=-\frac{1}{r}\frac{\partial\psi 1}{\partial\theta}=0$	r=R_1	14

General solution of the field equations.

The general solution for the potential will be obtained by superposition. The analytic model will be split into two parts which, when solved and summed together, provide the solution. The geometry of the first excludes the magnets of region 1, and the second excludes the magnets of region 3. The two cases are shown in Fig. 4. In each case, a preliminary solution is first obtained by considering a single term in the driving function. The complete solution will be obtained by summation of additional terms as indicated by Eq. (7) and Eq. (8).

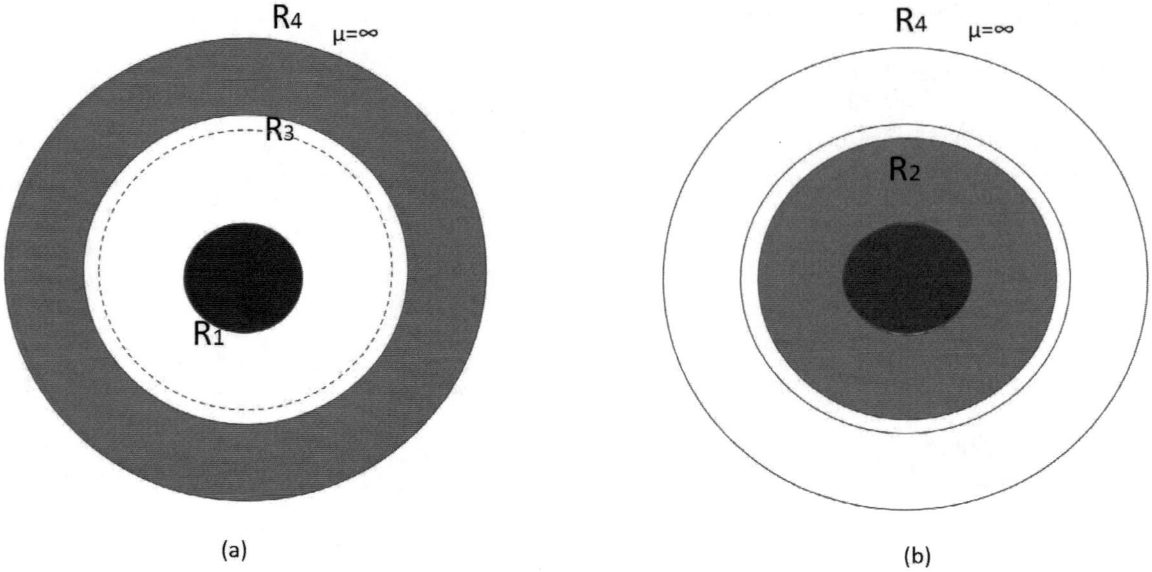

Fig. 4. The analytic model split into two parts: (a) the model geometry without the inner magnets of region 1, and (b), the model geometry without the outer magnets of region 3. The iron shaft has radius r= R_1, and the outer boundary is at r= R_4 for both.

Solution for case (a) and kp≠1

Referring to Fig. 4(a), and considering a single term in the driving function, the governing equation in the permanent magnet outer ring is Poisson's equation,

$$\frac{\partial^2 \psi}{\partial r^2} + \frac{1}{r}\frac{\partial \psi}{\partial r} + \frac{\partial^2 \psi}{\partial \theta^2} = \frac{1}{r} M_k \, sin \, kp(\theta - \delta) \tag{15}$$

The solution is

$$\psi^3(r,\theta) = \left[a \left(\frac{r}{R_4}\right)^{kp} + b\left(\frac{R_3}{r}\right)^{kp} + \frac{M_k * r}{1-(kp)^2}\right] \sin kp(\theta - \delta) \tag{16}$$

where a superscript on the scalar potential is used to denote the region, a and b are two arbitrary constants in the complementary solution, and the last term is the particular solution. This particular solution is valid for kp ≠1. The solution for kp=1 will be given later as a special case.

In the air region, ($R_3 \le r \le R_1$), the governing equation is Laplace's equation, Eq. (5), whose general solution is well-known. The solution must also be chosen to satisfy the boundary conditions, which for case (a) is given by Eqs. (9-11), and Eq. (14), in Table 1, adjusting the superscripts for the interface boundaries. Accordingly, the solution is of the form

$$\psi^{(a)}(r,\theta) = \left[A\left(\frac{r}{R_1}\right)^{kp} + B\left(\frac{R_3}{r}\right)^{kp}\right][C\sin(kp*\theta) + D\cos(kp*\theta)] \tag{17}$$

where a superscript (a) is used in this case to represent the scalar potential in the air region for case (a), and A, B, C, and D, are arbitrary constants. All the constants in Eq. (16) and Eq. (17) can be determined by applying the boundary conditions. The details are provided in the Appendix. The result for the scalar potential in the permanent magnet region is

$$\psi^{3}(r,\theta) = J(r) * \sin kp(\theta - \delta) \tag{18}$$

where

$$J(r) = b\left[\left(\frac{R_3}{r}\right)^{kp} - \left(\frac{R_3}{R_4}\right)^{kp}\left(\frac{r}{R_4}\right)^{kp}\right] - R_4\left(\frac{r}{R_4}\right)^{kp} * \frac{M_k}{1-(kp)^2} + \frac{M_k * r}{1-(kp)^2} \tag{19}$$

and

$$b = \frac{M_k * R_3}{2\,[1-(kp)^2\,][\left(\frac{R_3}{R_1}\right)^{2kp} - \left(\frac{R_3}{R_4}\right)^{2kp}]} * \left[2\left(\frac{R_3}{R_4}\right)^{kp-1} - \left(1 + \left(\frac{R_3}{R_1}\right)^{2kp}\right) - \left(1 - \left(\frac{R_3}{R_1}\right)^{2kp}\right)(kp)\right] \tag{20}$$

The result for the scalar potential in the air gap is

$$\psi^{(a)}(r,\theta) = \frac{J(r=R_3)}{\left(1 - \left(\frac{R_3}{R_1}\right)^{2kp}\right)}\left[\left(\frac{R_3}{r}\right)^{kp} - \left(\frac{R_3}{R_1}\right)^{kp}\left(\frac{r}{R_1}\right)^{kp}\right] sin\; kp(\theta - \delta) \tag{21}$$

The two components of the magnetic flux density vector in the air region can be computed from Eq. (21). The radial component is

$$\begin{aligned} B_r^{(a)}(r,\theta) &= -\mu\,\frac{\partial\psi^{(a)}}{\partial r} \\ &= \mu\,\frac{J(r=R_3)*(kp)}{\left(1 - \left(\frac{R_3}{R_1}\right)^{2kp}\right) * R_3}\left[\left(\frac{R_3}{r}\right)^{kp+1} + \left(\frac{R_3}{R_1}\right)^{kp+1}\left(\frac{r}{R_1}\right)^{kp-1}\right]\sin kp(\theta - \delta) \end{aligned} \tag{22}$$

and the tangential component is

$$B_\theta^{(a)}(r,\theta) = -\mu \frac{\partial \psi^{(a)}}{r\,\partial\theta}$$

$$= -\mu \frac{J(r=R_3)*(kp)}{\left(1-\left(\frac{R_3}{R_1}\right)^{2kp}\right)*r}\left[\left(\frac{R_3}{r}\right)^{kp} - \left(\frac{R_3}{R_1}\right)^{kp}\left(\frac{r}{R_1}\right)^{kp}\right]\cos kp(\theta-\delta) \tag{23}$$

Solution for case (b) and kp≠1

For case (b), set δ=0 in Eq. (15) to obtain the governing equation in the permanent magnet inner ring of region 1,

$$\frac{\partial^2\psi}{\partial r^2} + \frac{1}{r}\frac{\partial\psi}{\partial r} + \frac{\partial^2\psi}{\partial\theta^2} = \frac{1}{r}\, M_k\, sin\,(kp\theta) \tag{24}$$

The solution is

$$\psi^1(r,\theta) = \left[a\left(\frac{r}{R_1}\right)^{kp} + b\left(\frac{R_2}{r}\right)^{kp} + \frac{M_k * r}{1-(kp)^2}\right]\sin(kp\theta) \tag{25}$$

where a and b are two arbitrary constants (different from case (a)). In the air region, ($R_2 \le r \le R_4$), the solution to Laplace's equation must be chosen to satisfy the boundary conditions, which for case (b) is given by Eqs. (12-14), and Eq. (9) in Table 1. The solution is

$$\psi^{(b)}(r,\theta) = \left[A\left(\frac{r}{R_4}\right)^{kp} + B\left(\frac{R_2}{r}\right)^{kp}\right][C\sin(kp*\theta) + D\cos(kp*\theta)] \tag{26}$$

where the superscript (b) is used to represent the scalar potential in the air region for case (b), and A, B, C, and D, are arbitrary constants. All the constants in Eq. (25) and Eq. (26) can be determined by applying the boundary conditions as before. Considerable work can be avoided by noting similarities in the boundary conditions and equations compared with case (a). For example, we can replace R_4 and R_3 in the magnet region for case (a) with R_1 and R_2, to obtain the corresponding solution for case (b). Similarly, by replacing R_3 and R_1 in the air region for case (a) with R_2 and R_4, respectively, we can obtain the corresponding solution for case (b). With this in mind, we can write the solution for the scalar potential in the permanent magnet region

$$\psi^1(r,\theta) = L(r) * \sin(kp\theta) \tag{27}$$

where

$$L(r) = b\left[\left(\frac{R_2}{r}\right)^{kp} - \left(\frac{R_2}{R_1}\right)^{kp}\left(\frac{r}{R_1}\right)^{kp}\right] - R_1\left(\frac{r}{R_1}\right)^{kp} * \frac{M_k}{1-(kp)^2} + \frac{M_k * r}{1-(kp)^2} \tag{28}$$

and

$$b = \frac{M_k * R_2}{2\,[1-(kp)^2\,][\left(\frac{R_2}{R_4}\right)^{2kp} - \left(\frac{R_2}{R_1}\right)^{2kp}]} * \left[2\left(\frac{R_2}{R_1}\right)^{kp-1} - \left(1 + \left(\frac{R_2}{R_4}\right)^{2kp}\right) - \left(1 - \left(\frac{R_2}{R_4}\right)^{2kp}\right)(kp)\right] \tag{29}$$

The scalar potential in the air gap is

$$\psi^{(b)}(r,\theta) = \frac{L(r = R_2)}{\left(1 - \left(\frac{R_2}{R_4}\right)^{2kp}\right)}\left[\left(\frac{R_2}{r}\right)^{kp} - \left(\frac{R_2}{R_4}\right)^{kp}\left(\frac{r}{R_4}\right)^{kp}\right] sin\,(kp\theta) \tag{30}$$

For the magnetic flux vector in air, we have for the radial component

$$\begin{aligned} B_r^{(b)}(r,\theta) &= -\mu\,\frac{\partial\psi^{(b)}}{\partial r} \\ &= \mu\,\frac{L(r = R_2) * (kp)}{\left(1 - \left(\frac{R_2}{R_4}\right)^{2kp}\right) * R_2}\left[\left(\frac{R_2}{r}\right)^{kp+1} + \left(\frac{R_2}{R_4}\right)^{kp+1}\left(\frac{r}{R_4}\right)^{kp-1}\right]\sin(kp\theta) \end{aligned} \tag{31}$$

and for the tangential component

$$\begin{aligned} B_\theta^{(b)}(r,\theta) &= -\mu\,\frac{\partial\psi^{(b)}}{r\,\partial\theta} \\ &= -\mu\,\frac{L(r = R_2) * (kp)}{\left(1 - \left(\frac{R_2}{R_4}\right)^{2kp}\right) * r}\left[\left(\frac{R_2}{r}\right)^{kp} - \left(\frac{R_2}{R_4}\right)^{kp}\left(\frac{r}{R_4}\right)^{kp}\right]\cos(kp\theta) \end{aligned} \tag{32}$$

Scalar potential and torque, kp≠1

The solution for all field quantities is obtained by superposition. For example, the magnetic scalar potential in the air gap region of the coupling is

$$\psi(r,\theta) = \sum_{k=1,3,5...}^{\infty} (\psi^{(a)} + (\psi^{(b)}) \tag{33}$$

where Eqs. (21) and (30) can be substituted in the above, and as many harmonic terms of the forcing function can be included as desired, in accordance with Eqs. (7) and (8).

Of special interest is the torque in the coupling; this can be computed from the Maxwell stress tensor, which, in electromagnetism with only a magnetic field, takes the form

$$\sigma_{ij} = \frac{1}{\mu} B_i B_j - \frac{1}{2\mu} B^2 \delta_{ij} \tag{34}$$

where B_i, B_j are components of the flux density vector, and δ_{ij} is the Kronecker delta. The magnetic torque is obtained by considering a circular integration path of any radius, R, within the air gap around the shaft and the tangential component of stress $\sigma_{r\theta}$ from Eq. (34). The differential torque, dT, acting on an element of area $Rd\theta dz$ is $dT= R *\sigma_{r\theta} * (Rd\theta dz)$. Thus, the total magnetic torque per unit length acting on the cylindrical coupling is

$$T/_L = \frac{R^2}{\mu} \int_{-\pi}^{\pi} B_r(R,\theta) * B_\theta(R,\theta) d\theta \tag{35}$$

where L is the axial length of the magnet segments. By adding all the contributions to the field in the same manner as was done for the scalar potential, we now express the torque per unit length as

$$T/_L = \frac{R^2}{\mu} \sum_k^{\infty} \int_{-\pi}^{\pi} [B_r^{(a)}(R,\theta) + B_r^{(b)}(R,\theta)] * [B_\theta^{(a)}(R,\theta) + B_\theta^{(b)}(R,\theta)] d\theta \tag{36}$$

By expansion,

$$T/_L = \frac{R^2}{\mu} \sum_k^{\infty} \int_{-\pi}^{\pi} [B_r^{(a)} B_\theta^{(a)} + B_r^{(a)} B_\theta^{(b)} + B_r^{(b)} B_\theta^{(a)} + B_r^{(b)} B_\theta^{(b)}] d\theta \tag{37}$$

An expression for the torque is obtained by first substituting for each term using Eqs. (22), (23), (31), and (32), and carrying out the integration. The result is the first and fourth integral is zero and only the two middle terms contribute to the torque; therefore, it is the interaction of the two fields that give rise to the torque. The final resulting expression for the torque in the coupling can be written compactly as

$$T/_L = \frac{\pi R^2}{\mu} \sum_k^{\infty} \left(B_{r0}^{(b)} * B_{\theta 0}^{(a)} - B_{r0}^{(a)} * B_{\theta 0}^{(b)} \right) \sin\delta \tag{38}$$

where the extra subscript 0 indicates the amplitude of each respective sinusoid term, which we evaluated before; namely,

$$B_{r0}^{(a)} = \mu \frac{J(r=R_3)*(kp)}{\left(1-\left(\frac{R_3}{R_1}\right)^{2kp}\right)*R_3}\left[\left(\frac{R_3}{R}\right)^{kp+1} + \left(\frac{R_3}{R_1}\right)^{kp+1}\left(\frac{R}{R_1}\right)^{kp-1}\right] \tag{39}$$

$$B_{\theta 0}^{(a)} = -\mu \frac{J(r=R_3)*(kp)}{\left(1-\left(\frac{R_3}{R_1}\right)^{2kp}\right)*R}\left[\left(\frac{R_3}{R}\right)^{kp} - \left(\frac{R_3}{R_1}\right)^{kp}\left(\frac{R}{R_1}\right)^{kp}\right] \tag{40}$$

$$B_{r0}^{(b)} = \mu \frac{L(r=R_2)*(kp)}{\left(1-\left(\frac{R_2}{R_4}\right)^{2kp}\right)*R_2}\left[\left(\frac{R_2}{R}\right)^{kp+1} + \left(\frac{R_2}{R_4}\right)^{kp+1}\left(\frac{R}{R_4}\right)^{kp-1}\right] \tag{41}$$

$$B_{\theta 0}^{(b)} = -\mu \frac{L(r=R_2)*(kp)}{\left(1-\left(\frac{R_2}{R_4}\right)^{2kp}\right)*R}\left[\left(\frac{R_2}{R}\right)^{kp} - \left(\frac{R_2}{R_4}\right)^{kp}\left(\frac{R}{R_4}\right)^{kp}\right] \tag{42}$$

Special case: kp=1, case (a)

The results obtained in the preceding sections must be modified when kp=1. Poisson's equation for case (a) now becomes

$$\frac{\partial^2\psi}{\partial r^2} + \frac{1}{r}\frac{\partial\psi}{\partial r} + \frac{\partial^2\psi}{\partial\theta^2} = \frac{1}{r} M_k \, sin(\theta - \delta) \tag{43}$$

The solution is

$$\psi^3(r,\theta) = \left[a\left(\frac{r}{R_4}\right) + b\left(\frac{R_3}{r}\right) + \frac{M_k * \ln r * r}{2}\right]\sin(\theta - \delta) \tag{44}$$

Thus, it is seen that the new solution is obtained from the previous by setting kp=1, and replacing the term $M_k/(1-(kp)^2)$ in the particular solution with $M_k/2*\ln r$.

Similarly, in the air region the solution to Laplace's equation is now written as

$$\psi^{(a)}(r,\theta) = \left[A\left(\frac{r}{R_1}\right) \;+ B\left(\frac{R_3}{r}\right)\right][C\sin\theta + D\cos\theta] \tag{45}$$

All the constants are determined by applying the boundary conditions as before. The result for the scalar potential in the permanent magnet region is

$$\psi^3(r,\theta) = J(r) * \sin(\theta - \delta) \tag{46}$$

where

$$J(r) = b\left[\left(\frac{R_3}{r}\right) - \left(\frac{R_3}{R_4}\right)\left(\frac{r}{R_4}\right)\right] - R_4\left(\frac{r}{R_4}\right) * \frac{M_k}{2} * \ln R_4 + \frac{M_k * r}{2}\ln r \tag{47}$$

and

$$b = \frac{M_k * R_3}{2\,[2][\left(\frac{R_3}{R_1}\right)^2 - \left(\frac{R_3}{R_4}\right)^2]} * \left[\left(1 - \left(\frac{R_3}{R_1}\right)^2 - 2 * \ln\left(\frac{R_3}{R_4}\right)\right)\right] \tag{48}$$

The result for the scalar potential in the air gap is

$$\psi^{(a)}(r,\theta) = \frac{J(r = R_3)}{\left(1 - \left(\frac{R_3}{R_1}\right)^2\right)}\left[\left(\frac{R_3}{r}\right) - \left(\frac{R_3}{R_1}\right)\left(\frac{r}{R_1}\right)\right] sin\,(\theta - \delta) \tag{49}$$

The two components of the magnetic flux density vector in the air region can be computed from Eq. (49). The radial component is

$$\begin{aligned} B_r^{(a)}(r,\theta) &= -\mu\,\frac{\partial\psi^{(a)}}{\partial r} \\ &= \mu\,\frac{J(r = R_3)}{\left(1 - \left(\frac{R_3}{R_1}\right)^2\right) * R_3}\left[\left(\frac{R_3}{r}\right)^2 + \left(\frac{R_3}{R_1}\right)^2\right]\sin(\theta - \delta) \end{aligned} \tag{50}$$

and the tangential component is

$$B_\theta^{(a)}(r,\theta) = -\mu \; \frac{\partial \psi^{(a)}}{r\,\partial \theta}$$

$$= -\mu \frac{J(r = R_3)}{\left(1 - \left(\frac{R_3}{R_1}\right)^2\right) * r} \left[\left(\frac{R_3}{r}\right) \; - \left(\frac{R_3}{R_1}\right) \; \left(\frac{r}{R_1}\right) \; \right] \cos(\theta - \delta) \qquad (51)$$

Special case: kp=1, case (b)

Poisson's equation for case (b) is

$$\frac{\partial^2 \psi}{\partial r^2} + \frac{1}{r}\frac{\partial \psi}{\partial r} + \frac{\partial^2 \psi}{\partial \theta^2} = \frac{1}{r} \, M_k \, sin\theta \qquad (52)$$

Obtained by letting δ=0. The solution is

$$\psi^1(r,\theta) = \left[a \left(\frac{r}{R_1}\right) \; + b \left(\frac{R_2}{r}\right) \; + \frac{M_k * \ln r * r}{2} \right] \sin\theta \qquad (53)$$

Similarly, in the air region the solution to Laplace's equation is now written as

$$\psi^{(b)}(r,\theta) = \left[A \left(\frac{r}{R_4}\right) \; + B \left(\frac{R_2}{r}\right) \; \right] [C \sin\theta + D \cos\theta] \qquad (54)$$

All the constants are determined by applying the boundary conditions as before. The result for the scalar potential in the permanent magnet region is

$$\psi^1(r,\theta) = L(r) * \sin\theta \qquad (55)$$

where

$$L(r) = b \left[\left(\frac{R_2}{r}\right) \; - \left(\frac{R_2}{R_1}\right) \; \left(\frac{r}{R_1}\right) \; \right] - R_1 \left(\frac{r}{R_1}\right) \; * \frac{M_k}{2} * \ln R_1 + \frac{M_k * r}{2} \ln r \qquad (56)$$

and

$$b = \frac{M_k * R_2}{2\,[2][\left(\frac{R_2}{R_4}\right)^2 - \left(\frac{R_2}{R_1}\right)^2]} * \left[\left(1 - \left(\frac{R_2}{R_4}\right)^2 - 2 * \ln(\frac{R_2}{R_1})\right) \right] \qquad (57)$$

The result for the scalar potential in the air gap is

$$\psi^{(b)}(r,\theta) = \frac{L(r=R_2)}{\left(1-\left(\frac{R_2}{R_4}\right)^2\right)}\left[\left(\frac{R_2}{r}\right) - \left(\frac{R_2}{R_4}\right)\left(\frac{r}{R_4}\right)\right] sin\,\theta \qquad (58)$$

The two components of the magnetic flux density vector in the air region can be computed from Eq. (58). The radial component is

$$B_r^{(b)}(r,\theta) = -\mu\frac{\partial\psi^{(a)}}{\partial r} = \mu\frac{L(r=R_2)}{\left(1-\left(\frac{R_2}{R_4}\right)^2\right)*R_2}\left[\left(\frac{R_2}{r}\right)^2 + \left(\frac{R_2}{R_4}\right)^2\right]\sin\theta \qquad (59)$$

and the tangential component is

$$B_\theta^{(a)}(r,\theta) = -\mu\frac{\partial\psi^{(a)}}{r\,\partial\theta} = -\mu\frac{L(r=R_2)}{\left(1-\left(\frac{R_2}{R_4}\right)^2\right)*r}\left[\left(\frac{R_2}{r}\right) - \left(\frac{R_2}{R_4}\right)\left(\frac{r}{R_4}\right)\right]\cos\theta \qquad (60)$$

RESULTS

To illustrate the utility of the derived closed-form expressions, computations were done on a radially magnetized, multi-pole coupling, with parameters given in Table 2.

The torque calculations were carried out by taking a contour in the air gap with radius equal to the mean radius, (i.e., $R= (R_2+R_3)/2$). Table 3 shows the amplitude of the cogging torque per unit length, computed from the torque expressions, for different number of pole-pairs as well as the contribution of the first four terms of k included in the summation. The sum converges rapidly and even a single term (k=1) approximation would yield a sufficiently accurate estimate for most preliminary sizing study. Within the range examined for this coupling, the maximum cogging torque that could be achieved is 29.37 N-m per meter of axial length of the magnet segments. This corresponds to a 3 pole-pair design, as shown in Fig. 5.

Torque measurements were taken on several couplings prepared by BJA Magnetics, [7]. The magnet segments were constructed from N52 (NdFeB) magnets and all samples correspond to the 6 pole-pair geometry of Table 2. The steel shaft and housing were made from SUS403. The magnet arc segments were magnetized diametrically (i.e., in a uniform direction) rather than in a truly radial direction. As others have noted [2], this is due to difficulty in producing a radial magnetization field. As the number of arc segments increases, the field will better approximate a true radial field.

The torque measurements are shown in Fig. 6. Measurements were made in both clockwise and counter-clockwise directions and cover one full revolution of the shaft. The average amplitude was approximately 70 Kgf-mm. From Table 3, the predicted amplitude of the cogging torque for an ideal, radially magnetized, 6 pole-pair coupling with this geometry would be 95.9 Kgf-mm. It is interesting to note that the prediction could be adjusted and brought into better correlation with the experimental measurements by replacing the value of B_r with a reduced value B_0, (Refer to Fig. 2 and the discussion of it).

Table 2. Parameters of radial coupling studied

Item	Description	Value
R_1	Inner radius of shaft magnets	1.5×10^{-3} m
R_2	Outer radius of shaft magnets	3.0×10^{-3} m
R_3	Inner radius of cylinder magnets	3.25×10^{-3} m
R_4	Outer radius of cylinder magnets	5×10^{-3} m
L	Axial length of magnets	37×10^{-3} m
B_r	Residual flux density, N52 magnet	1.44 Tesla
α	Pole arc to pole pitch ratio	0.9
p	Number of pole-pairs	variable

Table 3. Computed torque amplitude per unit length, N-m/m, on coupling of Table 2.

	Number of pole-pairs, p					
Index, k	1	2	3	4	5	6
1	15.95	24.60	27.33	27.27	26.08	24.48
3	1.76	2.21	1.76	1.39	1.09	0.86
5	0.11	0.37	0.25	0.17	0.11	0.07
7	0.07	0.06	0.03	0.02	0.01	0.01
∑(T/L) =	17.89	27.24	29.37	28.85	27.29	25.42

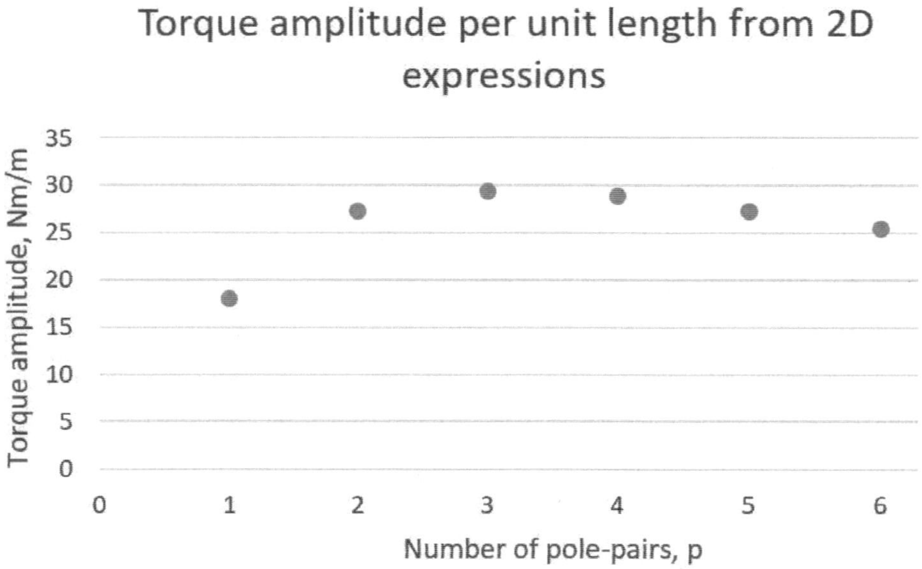

Fig. 5. Torque amplitude computed from closed-form expressions for the coupling of Table 2.

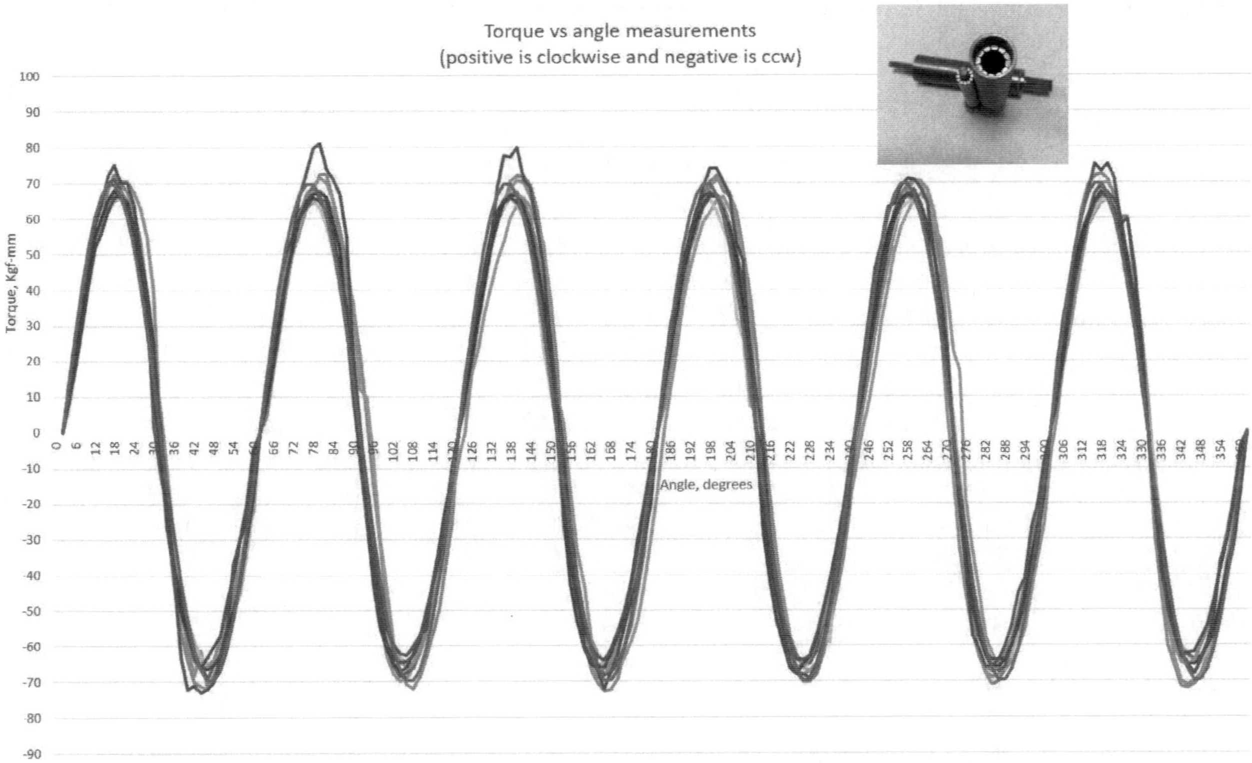

Fig. 6. Torque measurements on several samples of the 6 pole-pair, radially magnetized coupling of Table 2.

CONCLUSION

The scalar potential for multi-pole, radially magnetized couplings have been derived from the solution of Poisson's equation in the permanent magnet regions, and Laplace's equation in the air-gap region. All field quantities of interest can be obtained from the scalar potentials. In particular, the closed-form expression for the cogging torque was developed, which shows the sinusoidal behavior. The theoretical prediction for a 6 pole-pair coupling was carried out, compared with measurements taken on several samples, and the utility of the closed-form expression illustrated with a simple parametric study. Finally, it was explained how the model can be correlated to experimental findings in practice.

ACKNOWLEDGEMENT

The author gratefully acknowledges the funding support from Kenneth Seethaler, Manager, Strategic Technology and Innovation Center, Lenovo Corporation, Morrisville, NC, USA. Thanks also to Richard Helle and Daniel Bliss, BJA Magnetics, for many hours spent on this project, and for preparing all the samples for evaluation, and to Dr. Ryan Murray, Department of Mathematics, NC State University, for his helpful advice.

APPENDIX

All the constants can be determined from the boundary conditions and will be illustrated for case (a), kp $\neq$ 1. First, apply boundary condition, Eq. (9), ($\frac{\partial\psi 3(R4,\theta)}{\partial\theta} = 0$), together with Eq. (16), then

$$a = -b\left(\frac{R_3}{R_4}\right)^{kp} - \frac{M_k * R_4}{1-(kp)^2} \tag{A1}$$

Eqs. (18) and (19) follows from substituting Eq. (A1) into Eq. (16):

$$\psi^3(r,\theta) = J(r) * \sin kp(\theta - \delta) \tag{18}$$

$$J(r) = b\left[\left(\frac{R_3}{r}\right)^{kp} - \left(\frac{R_3}{R_4}\right)^{kp}\left(\frac{r}{R_4}\right)^{kp}\right] - R_4\left(\frac{r}{R_4}\right)^{kp} * \frac{M_k}{1-(kp)^2} + \frac{M_k * r}{1-(kp)^2} \tag{19}$$

Apply boundary condition, Eq. (14), ($\frac{\partial\psi a(R1,\theta)}{\partial\theta} = 0$), together with Eq. (17), then

$$A = -B\left(\frac{R_3}{R_1}\right)^{kp} \tag{A2}$$

Substitute Eq. (A2) into Eq. (17)

$$\psi^{(a)}(r,\theta) = \left[\left(\frac{R_3}{r}\right)^{kp} - \left(\frac{R_3}{R_1}\right)^{kp}\left(\frac{r}{R_1}\right)^{kp}\right][BC\sin(kp * \theta) + BD\cos(kp * \theta)] \tag{A3}$$

Apply boundary condition, Eq. (10), $(-\frac{1}{r}\frac{\partial\psi 3(R3)}{\partial\theta} = -\frac{1}{r}\frac{\partial\psi a(R3)}{\partial\theta})$

$$J(r = R_3)\cos kp(\theta - \delta) = \left[1 - \left(\frac{R_3}{R_1}\right)^{2kp}\right][BC\cos(kp * \theta) - BD\sin(kp * \theta)] \tag{A4}$$

Equating coefficients of the sine and cosine terms, we obtain the two relations

$$J(r = R_3)\cos kp\delta = \left[1 - \left(\frac{R_3}{R_1}\right)^{2kp}\right]BC \tag{A5}$$

$$J(r = R_3)\sin kp\delta = -\left[1 - \left(\frac{R_3}{R_1}\right)^{2kp}\right]BD \tag{A6}$$

We can eliminate δ by squaring both sides of Eqs. (A5) and (A6) and adding to get

$$[J(r = R_3)]^2 = \left[1 - \left(\frac{R_3}{R_1}\right)^{2kp}\right]^2[BC^2 + BD^2] \tag{A7}$$

Apply boundary condition, Eq. (11), $B_r^3 = B_r^a$ or $(-\frac{\partial\psi 3(R3)}{\partial r} + M_r = -\frac{\partial\psi a(R3)}{\partial r})$

$$\left(M_k - \frac{\partial J}{\partial r}\Big|r = R_3\right) \sin kp\,(\theta - \delta) = \frac{kp}{R_3}\left[1 + \left(\frac{R_3}{R_1}\right)^{2kp}\right] [BC \sin(kp * \theta) + BD \cos(kp * \theta)] \quad (A8)$$

Equating coefficients of the sine and cosine terms, we obtain the two relations

$$\left(M_k - \frac{\partial J}{\partial r}\Big|r = R_3\right) \cos kp\delta = \frac{kp}{R_3}\left[1 + \left(\frac{R_3}{R_1}\right)^{2kp}\right] BC \quad (A9)$$

$$-\left(M_k - \frac{\partial J}{\partial r}\Big|r = R_3\right) \sin kp\delta = \frac{kp}{R_3}\left[1 + \left(\frac{R_3}{R_1}\right)^{2kp}\right] BD \quad (A10)$$

Squaring both sides and adding,

$$\left(M_k - \frac{\partial J}{\partial r}\Big|r = R_3\right)^2 = \left({}^{kp}/_{R_3}\right)^2 \left[1 + \left(\frac{R_3}{R_1}\right)^{2kp}\right]^2 [BC^2 + BD^2] \quad (A11)$$

We can now eliminate $[BC^2 + BD^2]$ using Eqs. (A7) and (A11) to get

$$\frac{J(r = R_3)}{1 - \left(\frac{R_3}{R_1}\right)^{2kp}} = \frac{\left(\frac{R_3}{kp}\right)\left(M_k - \frac{\partial J}{\partial r}\Big|r = R_3\right)}{1 + \left(\frac{R_3}{R_1}\right)^{2kp}} \quad (A12)$$

By substituting Eq. (19) into Eq. (A12), the equation can be solved to determine the constant b. The result is Eq. (20).

$$b = \frac{M_k * R_3}{2\,[1-(kp)^2\,][\left(\frac{R_3}{R_1}\right)^{2kp} - \left(\frac{R_3}{R_4}\right)^{2kp}]} * \left[2\left(\frac{R_3}{R_4}\right)^{kp-1} - \left(1 + \left(\frac{R_3}{R_1}\right)^{2kp}\right) - \left(1 - \left(\frac{R_3}{R_1}\right)^{2kp}\right)(kp)\right] \quad (20)$$

With b determined, we can compute $J(r{=}R_3)$ from Eq. (19). Then, for every value of δ, we can compute BC and BD from Eqs. (A5) and (A6). Then we have ψ, B_r and B_θ. For example, substituting for BC and BD from Eqs. (A5) and A(6) into Eq. (A3), we arrive at Eq. (21):

$$\psi^{(a)}(r,\theta) = \frac{J(r = R_3)}{\left(1 - \left(\frac{R_3}{R_1}\right)^{2kp}\right)}\left[\left(\frac{R_3}{r}\right)^{kp} - \left(\frac{R_3}{R_1}\right)^{kp}\left(\frac{r}{R_1}\right)^{kp}\right] \sin kp(\theta - \delta) \quad (21)$$

REFERENCES

[1] T. Lubin, S. Mezani, and A. Rezzoug, "Simple Analytical Expressions for the Force and Torque of Axial Magnetic Couplings," IEEE Transactions on Energy Conversion, Institute of Electrical and Electronic Engineers, 2012, 11 p.

[2] R. Ravaud, G. Lemarquand, V. Lemarquand, and C. Depollier, "Torque in PM Couplings: Comparison of Uniform and Radial Magnetization," Journal of applied Physics 105, 2009.

[3] D. R. Mack, "Electricity and Magnetism," Advanced Course in Engineering, General Electric Company, 1972 (revised).

[4] D. R. Mack, "Mathematics for the advanced Course in Engineering," Advanced Course in Engineering, General electric Company, 1976.

[5] E. Kreyszig, "Advanced Engineering Mathematics," John Wiley & Sons, 4th Edition, N.Y., 1979.

[6] H. H. Woodson, and R. Melcher, "Electromechanical Dynamics," 3 vols. (Massachusetts Institute of Technology: MIT OpenCourseWare.) http://ocw.mit.edu (accessed 01/12/2018). License: Creative Commons Attribution - NonCommercial-Share Alike.

[7] BJA Magnetics, A wholly owned subsidiary of Bob Johnson Associates, Inc., www.bjamagnetics.com

Rare Earth Magnet Recycling – The Missing Link in a Circular Economy

Magentics 2020
Orlando, Florida
February 11, 2020

GEOMEGA
Rare Earths · Refining · Recycling

Forward Looking Statement

Our presentation contains "forward-looking statements" not based on historical facts. Forward-looking statements express, as of the date of this presentation, our estimates, forecasts, projections, expectations and opinions as to future events or results. The forward looking statements that are contained in this presentation are based on various assumptions and estimates by the Corporation and involve a number of risks and uncertainties. As a consequence, actual results may differ materially from results forecast or suggested in these forward-looking statements and readers should not place undue reliance on forward-looking statements. We caution you that such forward-looking statements involve known and unknown risks and uncertainties, as discussed in the Corporation's filings with Canadian Securities Administrators. Various factors may prevent or delay our plans, including but not limited to, contractor availability and performance, weather, access, mineral prices, success and failure of the exploration and development carried out at various stages of the program, and including as regards the commercialization of any of the technology, general business, economic, competitive, political and social conditions. The Corporation expressly disclaims any obligation to update any forward-looking statements, except as required by applicable securities laws.

Neodymium Oxide

Neodymium Metal

NdFeB Magnets

Electric Motors

A few definitions...

- **Why the world cares about Rare Earth Elements (REE)?**

  REE = Magnets

  Magnets = Motors

  Motors = Electrification ✓

- **Which REE we focus on?**

  Magnets = NdFeB

  NdFeB = Nd, Pr, Dy, Tb (magREO)

  Nd, Pr, Dy, Tb = 30% by demand volume of REE & 80% of REE market value ✓

Nd, Pr, Dy, Tb & magnets are the main drivers of the REE industry

REE Circular Economy

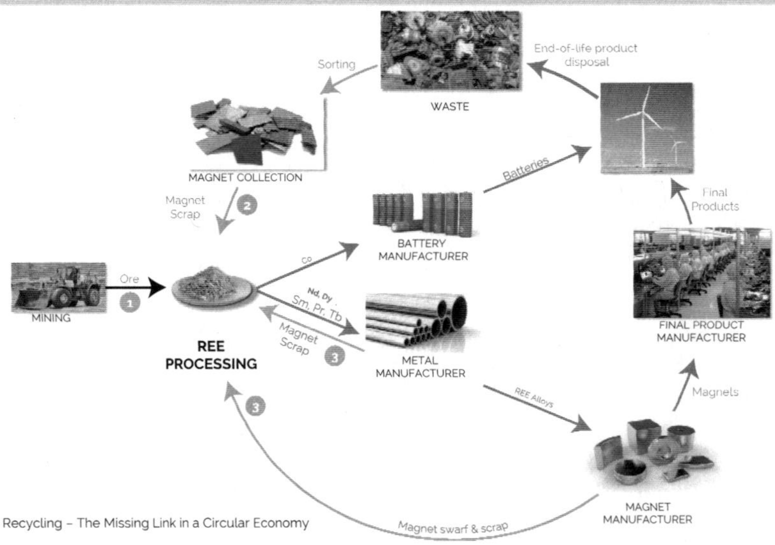

How much is recycled today?

- **The traditional view:**
  - <1% - Research publications by Meyer and Bras, 2011; Tanaka et al., 2013; Anderson et al., 2012
  - Typically only around 1% of the REE are recycled - Jowitt et al. 2018
  - Commercial recycling of rare earths is still very much in its infancy – Roskill 2018
- **The reality:**
  - China, which controls over 90% of REE Separation capacity, is attributing 31.25% of that to Recycled Waste – BAIINFO, June 2019
  - 25% & 20-30% magREO from swarf (Adamas Intel. & Roskill, 2019)
  - China is the leader in REE recycling
  - Estimated at over $1.2B of REO are recycled today

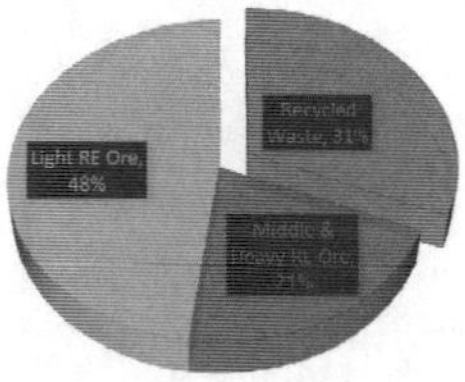

REE Recycling in China

- **Main drivers of REE recycling in China**
  - Infrastructure already in place
  - Recycled at existing Solvent Extraction (SX) facilities
  - Some exclusively used for recycling feed
  - Other facilities process both mining and recycling feeds
  - Minimal restrictions on impurities
  - No difference in purity and magnet performance relative to product derived from primary ore

REE Recycling in China

- **Sources of magnet recycling**
  - Collection of swarf and scrap from magnet manufacturing easily available (China largest producer of NdFeB magnets)
  - Swarf is considered as Dangerous Waste but easy to handle internally within China
  - > 50,000 tpy with majority in China

Swarf

Scrap

Source: Rocklink GMBH

REE Recycling in China

- **Sources of magnet recycling**
  - Several established programs for collecting end of life magnets from motors and wind turbines
  - Manufacturers get back material back from clients
  - Low cost labour for separating and handling complex assemblies
  - >15,000 tpy available worldwide with volumes increasing in some application and decreasing in others

Pre & Post Consumer assemblies

Source: Rocklink GMBH

REE Recycling in China

- **Cost & Environmental aspect of recycling in China**
  - HCl based process with iron rich "red mud" waste
  - Organic solvent-based pollutants in aqueous discharges
  - Disposal is low cost in traditional tailings
  - Acid for leaching readily available, often spent HCl, which significantly lowers the operating costs
  - High volume & continuous process lowers operating costs

REE Recycling – Rest of the World

- **Main drivers of REE recycling**
  - Security of supply
  - Environmental & socially responsible movement (circular economy)
  - Government funding of academia research
  - Department of Defence regulations (McCain Act)
  - Import ban by China on magnet scrap, metal ashes & concentrates as well as most WEEE categories

Not really driven by economics or the industry

REE Recycling – Rest of the World

- **Main obstacles of REE recycling**
  - Minimal SX availability for recycling (e.g. Vietnam)
  - Operating costs higher than in China due to consumables and stricter regulations
  - Difficult to operate as a batch process (high cost)
  - Much lower volumes of swarf available, limited to countries with magnet manufacturing capabilities (e.g. Japan)
  - Minimal collection & disassembly network
  - Labour costs prohibitive in the western world
  - Low labour costs in developing countries but then requires shipping
  - Stricter environmental regulations

REE Recycling – Rest of the World

- **What is needed to increase REE recycling**
  - Requires low cost & environmental process that operates in batches
  - Economics of recycling is "elastic"
  - Low CAPEX plant to justify economics based on the feed that is easily available outside of China
  - An operational plant will create an active market with recycling companies
  - Will establish a more extensive collection network
  - Infrastructure is there to make homogeneous and segregated collection process
  - Government regulations to promote, educate & support REE recycling
  - Most recyclers don't even know the value of the magnet in their recycling stream

It's not a low REO price problem,
It's a chicken and the egg problem

Progress in REE Recycling - Collection

- **MAGCYCLE**
  - First magnet take back program worldwide for NdFeB, AlNiCo, SmCo
  - Founded by Rocklink in 2018
  - Collection of magnet scrap by mail starting from 25 kgs annually
  - ~ 70 participants and 16 tons magnet scrap collected annually
  - Strategic partnership with North American rare earth recycler Geomega Resources

Magcycle
MAGNET
RÜCKNAHME
SYSTEM

Source: Rocklink GMBH

Progress in REE Recycling - Collection

- **MAGCYCLE**
  - First magnet take back program worldwide for NdFeB, AlNiCo, SmCo
  - Founded by Rocklink in 2018
  - Collection of magnet scrap by mail starting from 25 kgs annually
  - ~ 70 participants and 16 tons magnet scrap collected annually
  - Strategic partnership with North American rare earth recycler Geomega Resources
- **Hypromag –** Hydrogen decrepitation for extraction of small magnets
- **Greentec** – Escrap recycling, robotic disassembly of HDD
- **Apple** – Disassembly for reuse and recycle of magnets from smartphones
- Over 10 of other companies worldwide identified who are collecting from various sources as little as hundreds of kg to tens of tons per year
- New companies entering the field every year = more supply

Progress in REE Recycling - Processing

- **Geomega**
  - ISR process – proprietary technology
  - No liquid effluent and iron as a by-product
  - 95% recovery of the main reagents
  - 1st plant expected to start in Quebec, Canada in 2020 with 1.5 tpd feed capacity
- **Urban Mining** – magnet to magnet recycling
- **REE4EU, AMES Laboratory, CMI, Momentum Technologies** and other initiatives both government and academia supported in Europe and North America – various scales of development
- Significant interest in the industry since 2010 generated research that is now starting to produce results

Conclusion

- China is the clear leader in magnet recycling today
- A low OPEX and CAPEX solution can easily penetrate the market
- Recycled oxide will help produce more "non-China sourced" magnets
- Low pricing environment creates the perfect conditions for REE recycling:
  - Higher demand & more applications
  - Prices too low to justify new mine developments
- First commercial production outside of Asia will kickstart the common recycling sector
- New production of magnets outside of China will require recycling
- Government support is critical in increasing collection
- OEMs and major companies are looking for solutions that are clean and cost effective

Build it and they will come…

Developing a Rare Earths Hub in Quebec
GEOMEGA
Rare Earths · Refining · Recycling
Kiril Mugerman – President & CEO
kmugerman@geomega.ca
(450) 641-5119 ext 5653
www.geomega.ca
Developing a Rare Earths Hub in Quebec
Page 17 | Geomega (GMA.V)

IN-LINE MECHANICAL PRODUCTION TEST EQUIPMENT FOR CRACK DETECTION IN PERMANENT MAGNETS AND MAGNET BLANKS

SENIS magnetic & current measurement

GMW

S. Spasic (SENIS),
Yu Miao (MAS-Intelligent Technology),
Zhen Xu (GMW),
Ian Walker (GMW)

MAGNETICS 2020

1

CRACKS CAUSE COSTS!

SENIS magnetic & current measurement

GMW

- Magnets with cracks or defects on surface or inside inhomogeneities can break during magnetizing, processing, assembly or in operation.
- Crack induced failure inside the magnet system can be dangerous, e.g. high continuous torque motor
- It might be costly to replace the complete assembled magnet system, such as motor/rotor, sensor systems
- Detection of cracks during the production process can improves the yield and reduces the maintenance costs.

2

HOW DO CRACKS LOOK LIKE?

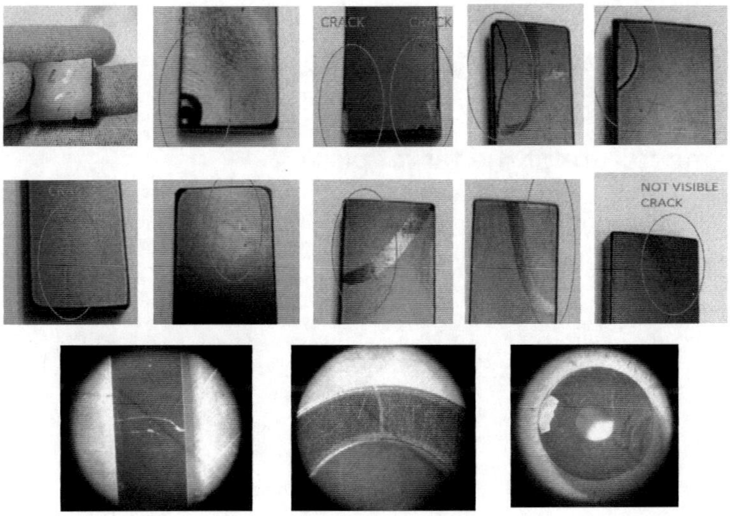

3

EDDY CURRENT - CRACK DETECTION

- Alternating current injected into a coil creates a magnetic field.
- When the coil is placed over a conductive part, opposed alternating currents are generated.
- Defects in the part disturb the path of the eddy currents.
- This disturbance can be measured by pickup coils, either through single coil or differential pick coils.

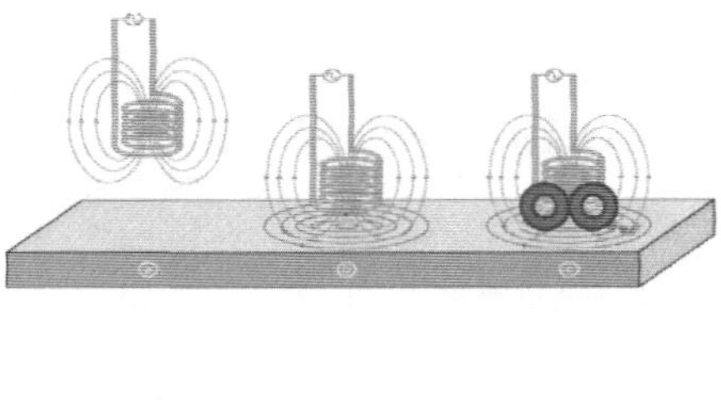

4

INFLUENCING FACTORS

- Conductivity of the target plate
- Permeability of the target plate
- Temperature of the target plate
- Coil geometry
- Operating frequency (excitation)

SENIS magnetic & current measurement

GMW

5

Probe Design and Simulation

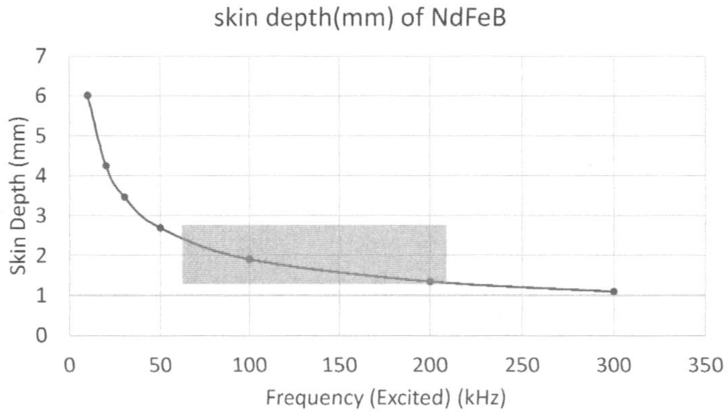

$$J = J_S\, e^{-(1+j)d/\delta}$$

$$\delta = \sqrt{\frac{2}{\omega\mu\sigma}}$$

d: Distance relative to sample surface

J_S: Surface density

Properties if NdFeB:

Conductivity: 6.67E+05 S/m

Relative permeability: 1.05

Sensor Configurations: 20kHz to 220kHz in the steps of 10kHz

SENIS magnetic & current measurement

GMW

6

Simulation Example

Sample Size: 100mm*40mm

Parameters

Name	Expression	Value	Description
a2	6.15[mm]	0.00615 m	Inner Radius of Coil
a1	12.4[mm]	0.0124 m	Outer Radius of Coil
b	6.15[mm]	0.00615 m	Length of Coil
N	3790	3790	Number of Turns
l	0.88[mm]	8.8E-4 m	Lift-Off
Sigma_Test	6.67e5[S/m]	6.67E5 S/m	Conductivity of Test Spec...
Thickness_Test	6[mm]	0.006 m	Thickness of Test Specim...
Height_Defect	3[mm]	0.003 m	Height of Defect
Depth_Defect	12.6[mm]	0.0126 m	Depth of Defect
Width_Defect	0.28[mm]	2.8E-4 m	Width of Defect
Freq	200000[Hz]	2E5 Hz	Frequency
Position	0[mm]	0 m	Initial Position of Coil

Top View

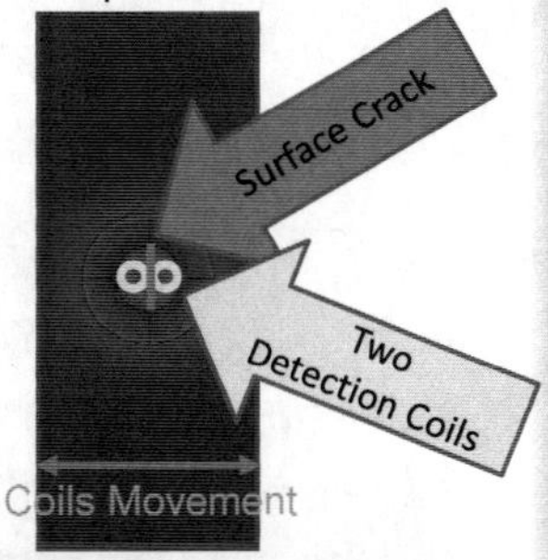

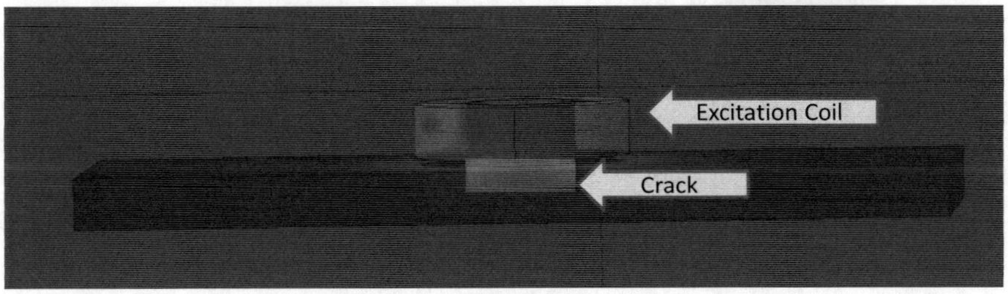

Side View

7

Current Density Distribution

Position: -4mm

Current Density (A/m2)

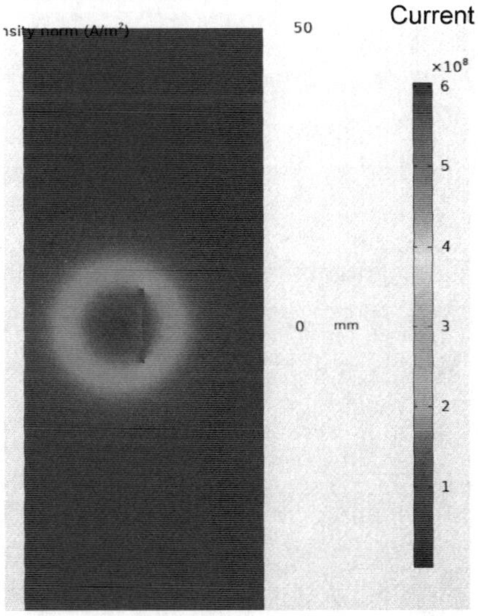

Crack

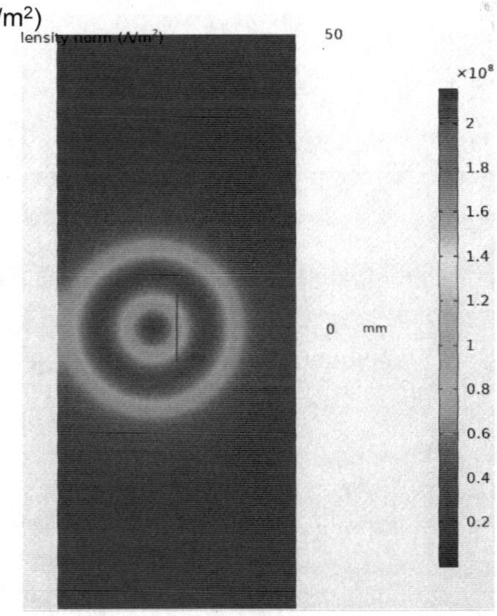

No Crack

8

Magnetic Flux Density on sample surface

Crack

Position: -4mm

No Crack

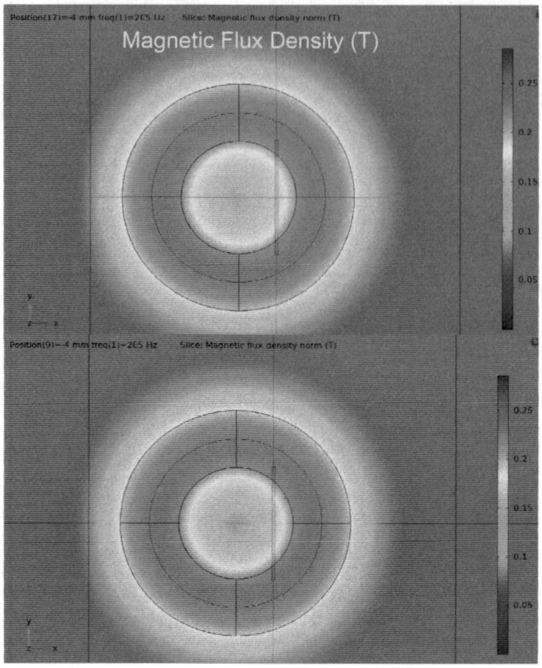

SENIS magnetic & current measurement

GMW

9

Current Density Distribution

Position: 4mm

Current Density (A/m^2)

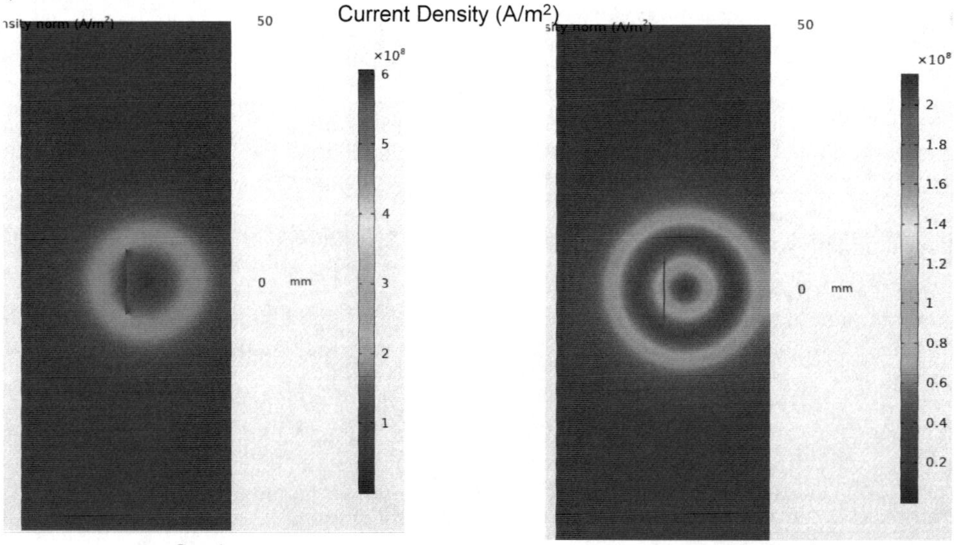

Crack

No Crack

SENIS magnetic & current measurement

GMW

10

Crack & No Crack

$$V = -\frac{d\varphi}{dt} = -\frac{d(N \cdot \vec{B} \cdot \vec{S})}{dt} = -N \cdot f \cdot \vec{B} \cdot \vec{S}$$

Crack Influences

Sample Edge Influences

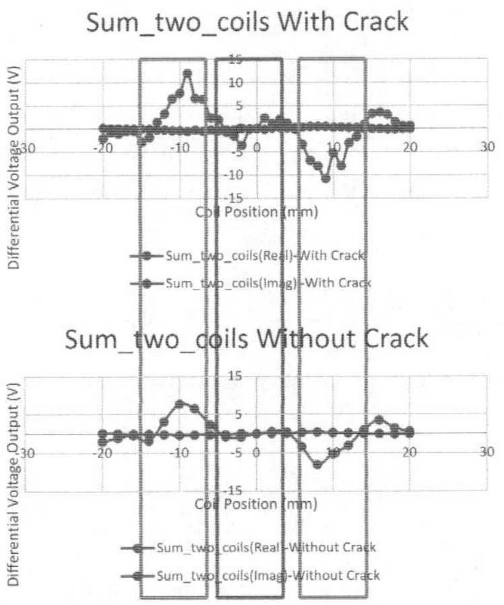

Sample Size
100mm*40mm

SENIS magnetic & current measurement

GMW

Current Density Distribution (XY)

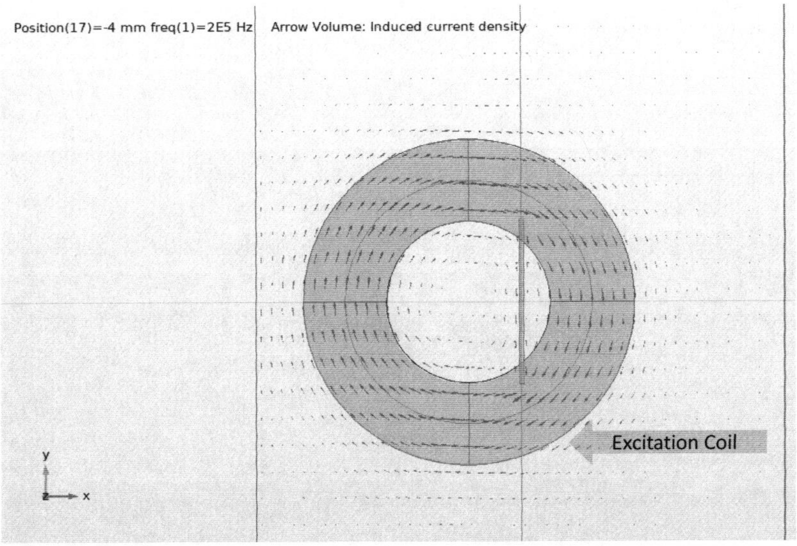

SENIS magnetic & current measurement

GMW

12

Current Density Distribution (YZ)

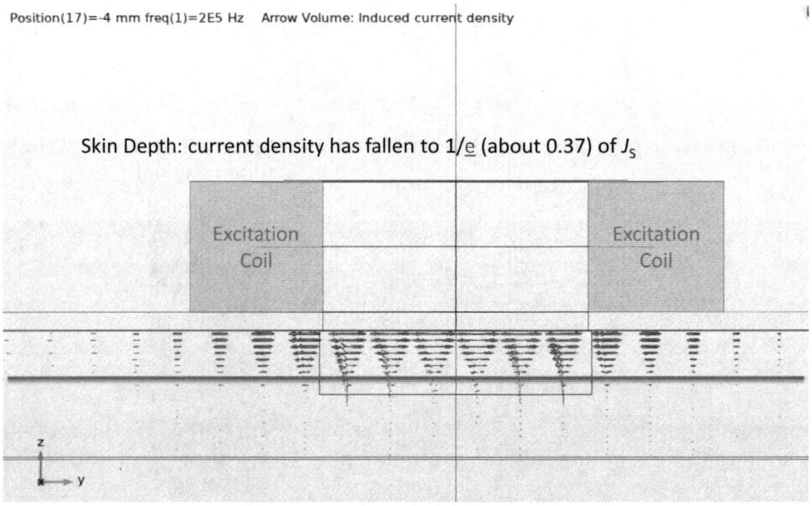

Skin Depth ~ 2mm (Total Sample Thickness 6mm)

SENIS magnetic & current measurement GMW

13

Current Density Distribution (XZ)

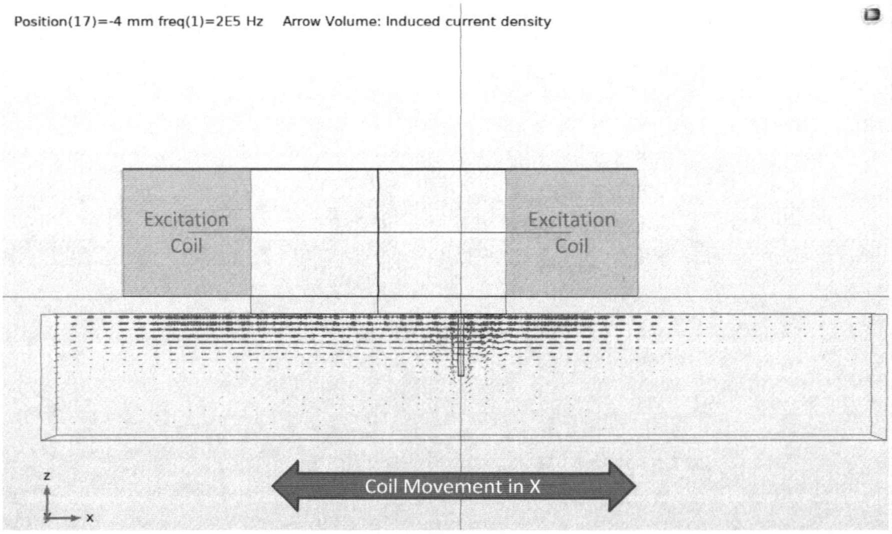

SENIS magnetic & current measurement GMW

14

MAPPER + EDDY-CURRENT PROBE

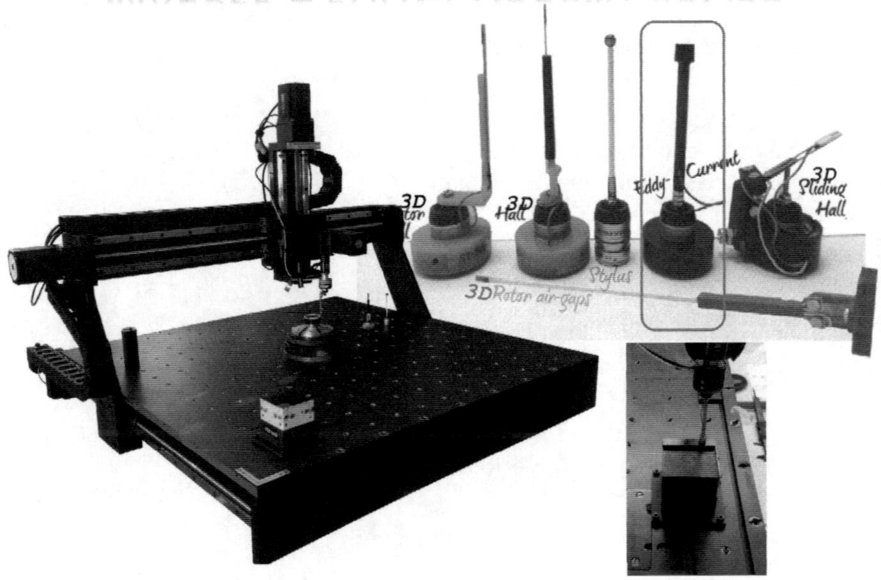

15

SENIS EDDY-CURRENT PROBES

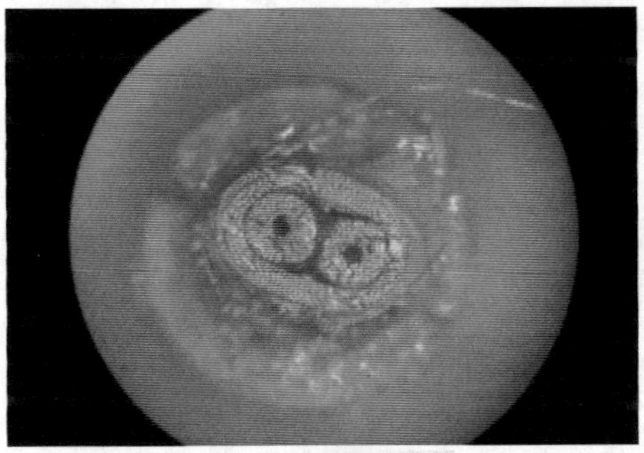

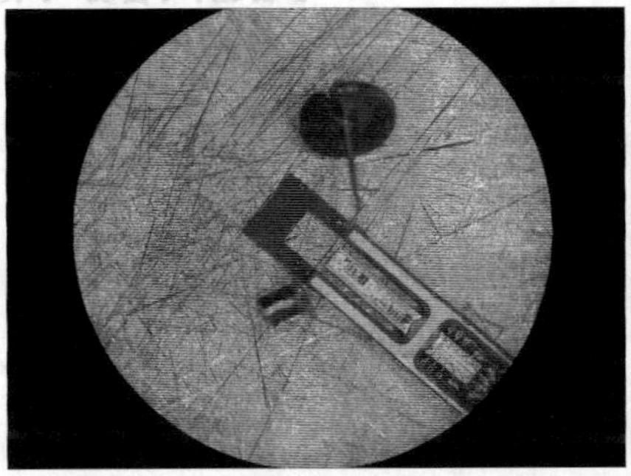

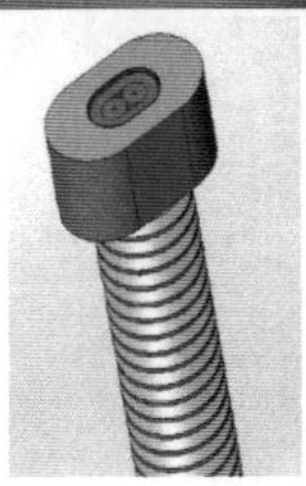

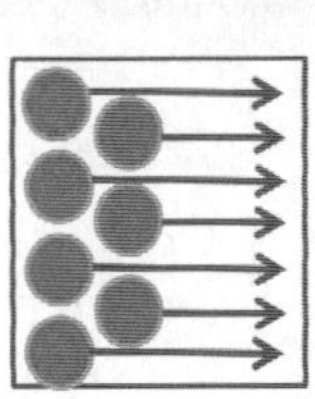

16

NEW PROJECT REQUIREMENTS

- Non-magnetised and epoxy coated magnet blanks of different sizes need to be separated from each other and put on the linear transport system
- Only the edge part of magnet need to be measured (6mm area on all four edges from both sides of the magnet blanks, i.e. length and width)
- The magnet thickness will be measured to adjust the distance (air-gap) between magnets and eddy current probe arrays
- An operator interface software for entering the magnet and test data, such as Article, Date, Op. Name, Lot number...
- GOOD / BAD decision will be made based on a SENIS proprietary algorithm for crack detection
- A calibration software using 5 golden parts to periodical compensate offset
- 100% in-line production test – test duration: <7sec per magnet

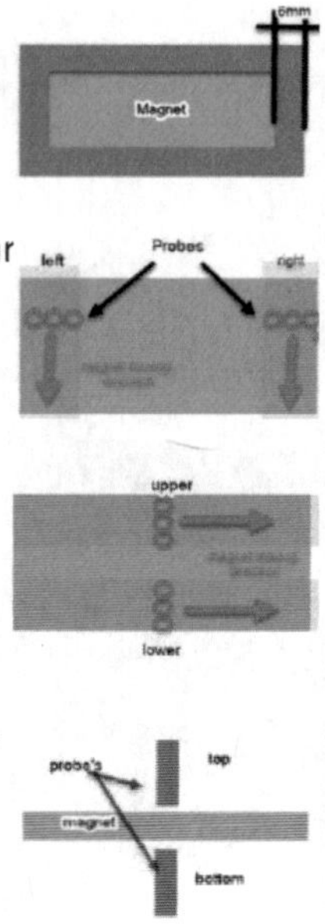

SENIS magnetic & current measurement

GMW

17

PARTS FLOW

optical position sensors detect the magnet on the transportation system with encoders

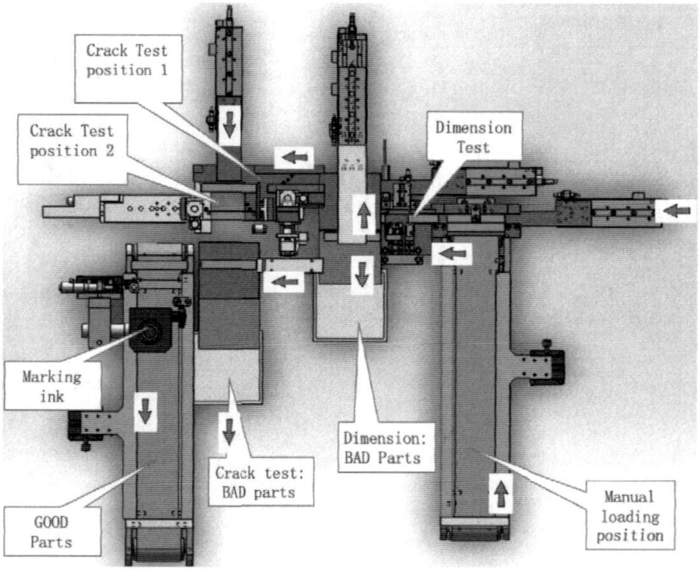

SENIS magnetic & current measurement

GMW

18

IMPLEMENTATION

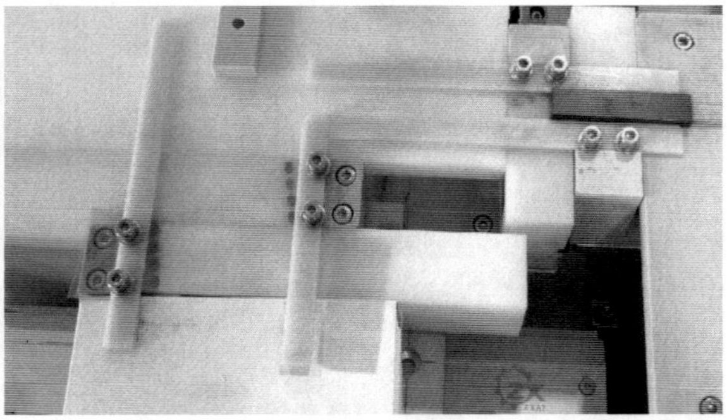

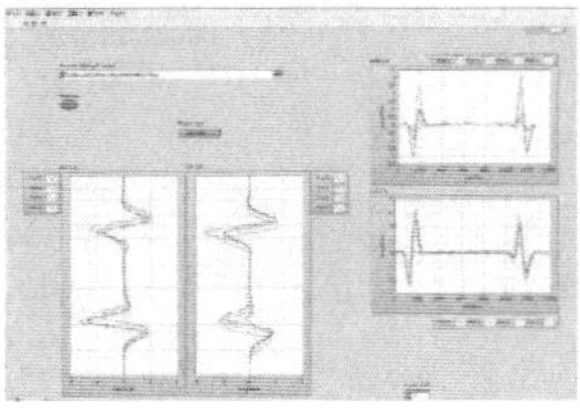

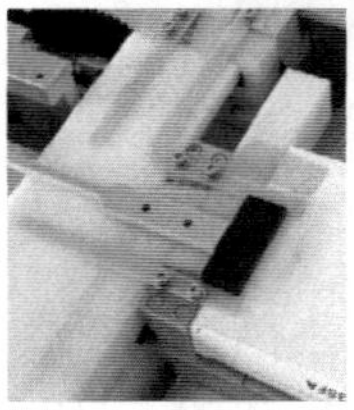

SENIS magnetic & current measurement

GMW

19

RESULT – CRACK DETECTION

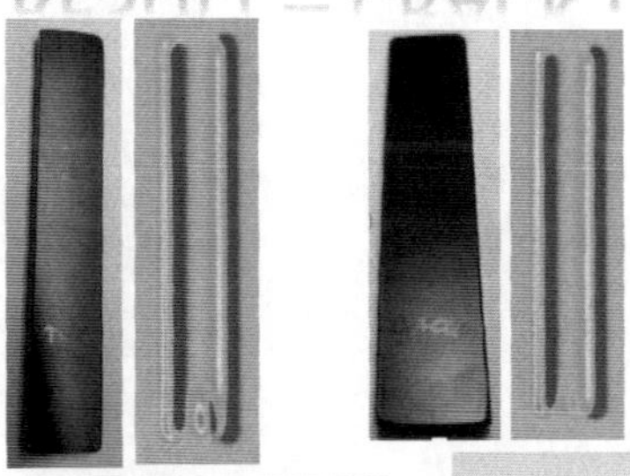

- The contrast reflects the voltage difference between two coils.
- Compared with cracks, magnet edges shows higher color contrast.

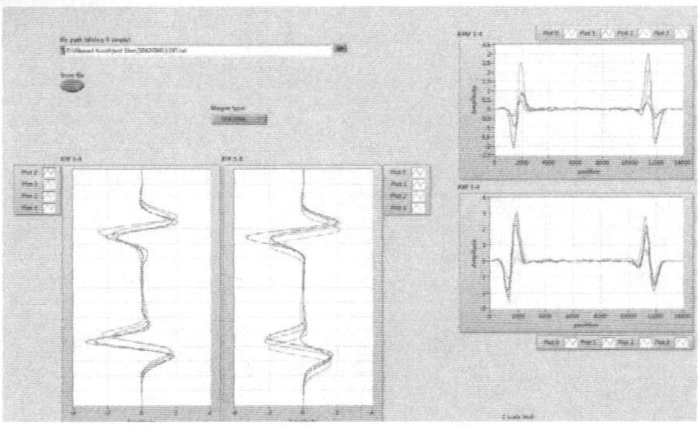

SENIS magnetic & current measurement

GMW

20

Website
Senis: http://www.senis.ch/
GMW Associates: https://gmw.com/

Email:
Sasa Spasic: spasic@senis.ch
Zhen Xu: zhen.xu@gmw.com

SENIS magnetic & current measurement

GMW

21

Application of Alternate Hard and Soft Magnetic Materials in Traction Motor Designs to Reduce Rare Earth Content

Michael Rubbo
Principal Consultant
Electric Machine Specialists

Electric Machine Specialists
CREATIVE POWER CONVERSION SOLUTIONS

Agenda

- Motivation and Methods
- Common Vehicle Specification / Base Motor Specification
- Benchmark Design (B1)
  - BPM-IR: High Energy Magnets w/ Si-Fe lams
  - Construction / Weights / S1 Heat Run Results / S1 Temp Performance
- Comparison of Alternate Hard and Soft Magnetic Materials
  - Lamination Permeability Impacts on Motor Performance – Saturation Factor
  - Lamination - Magnet Combinations for Alternate Designs
- Alternate Designs (A1, A2, A3)
  - Construction / Weights / S1 Heat Run Results / S1 Temp Performance
- Adding Thermal Performance to Output Performance Factors
- Performance Summary
  - Observations
  - Conclusions

Electric Machine Specialists
CREATIVE POWER CONVERSION SOLUTIONS

Motivation and Methods - 1

The "New Normal" -

- Machine designers face uncertainty using high-energy, rare earth permanent magnets in electric machines due to material shortages and price volatility.

What can we do?

- Can alternative designs w/ lower energy magnet and high permeability lams ***lower our*** risk exposure to rare earth materials and still perform at cost?
  - Might BPM designs (both inner and outer rotor) using Alnico or Ferrite magnets with high permeability "thin Si-Fe" or CRS lams be candidates?
  - Can we apply a practically informed "systems perspective" that includes design changes to electrical and cooling systems to achieve performance?

How to decide?

- We can compare some alternatives with a benchmark design (using RE magnets and Si-Fe lams) using a performance metric that includes thermal effects.

Electric Machine Specialists
CREATIVE POWER CONVERSION SOLUTIONS

Motivation and Methods - 2

- ***Why use a Direct Drive Wheel Motor for this design study?***
  - Electric wheel drives have many commercial and industrial applications (personal transport, material handling, etc.).
  - Wheel drive topologies allows for variable wheel "traction control", lower floor heights, independent steering and suspension capability, lower driveline NVH issues, etc.
  - *Wheel motors are torque dense, with limited installation volume that challenges material and cooling performance and amplifies difference between alternatives.*
- ***Methods***
  - A "Base Motor Specification" was developed from a general purpose, Low Speed Electric Vehicle (LSEV) application with a top speed of 25mph for a variety of grades and duties.
  - Multiple, manually optimized machine designs were developed from this Base Motor Specification and system level changes were then implemented as needed to achieve performance, including changes to drive current ratings and cooling system designs.

Electric Machine Specialists
CREATIVE POWER CONVERSION SOLUTIONS

Common Vehicle Specification

- Vehicle Details:
  - 500 kg Unladen Curb Weight
  - Capacity for varying payload, grade, and towing capacities
  - 23.4" tire outer diameter on 16" or 17" wheel
  - Frontal Area: 18 square feet
  - Drag Coefficient with Open Cab: 0.6
- *Nominal Vehicle Performance:
  - Maximum Speed: 25 mph,
  - Average Speed: 12.5 mph
  - 30% grade at 7.4 mph, $\mu_{rolling}$ = 0.15 (grass)
  - 10% grade at 25 mph, $\mu_{rolling}$ = 0.018 (cement)
  - 15% grade at 12.5 mph, $\mu_{rolling}$ = 0.018 (cement)

"Anaheim Police vehicle" by Richard Masoner / Cyclelicious is licensed under CC BY-SA 2.0
"Glasgow Airport" by James F Clay is licensed under CC BY-NC 2.0
** Vehicle performance based on method from "Build your own electric vehicle", 1994, First Edition, author: Bob Brandt, McGraw-Hill, Inc. ISBN 0-8306-4243-3*

Electric Machine Specialists
CREATIVE POWER CONVERSION SOLUTIONS

Base Motor Specification - 1

- Preliminary Power System Details:
  - 48 Volt Battery
  - 600A rms maximum inverter switch rating
  - Sin Triangle PWM with 3rd harmonic injection
  - 3.4:1 constant power speed range
    - 154 rpm (base speed) to 524 rpm (maximum speed)
    - Ideal candidate for "PM assisted reluctance motor"
    - SPM motors also work with higher OCV at max rpm
- Key Operating Points
  - S2-1 minute: 10.5kW
    - 650Nm at 154rpm
  - S2-60 minute: 10.7kW
    - 390Nm at 262 rpm
    - 195Nm at 524 rpm
  - S1 continuous rating: 4.6kW
    - 169Nm at 262 rpm

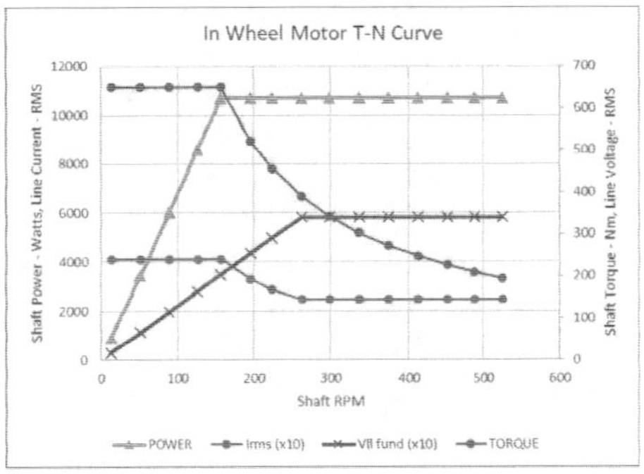

Electric Machine Specialists
CREATIVE POWER CONVERSION SOLUTIONS

Base Motor Specification - 2

- Potential Wheel Sizes:
  - 23.36" (+/- 0.1") Common Tire for LSEV platforms
  - Wheel bead diameter will be slightly larger than the maximum motor OD (inner rotor designs)
    - Assuming 1" difference (0.5" per side) between motor outer diameter and wheel bead diameter
    - This provides room for cooling channels on motor OD
  - Maximum overall motor length is nominally the section width but a longer motor may project towards center of vehicle

- Final Motor Layout Assumptions:
  - ***Motor Outer Diameter (w/o fins): 15" (381mm)***
  - ***Est. Motor Overall Length: 200mm +/- 40mm***

Protean PD18

Tire Sizes*	205/45R16	205/40R17
Wheel Bead OD (in)	16"	17"
Tire Sidewall (in)	3.63 x 2	3.23 x 2
Tire OD (in)	23.26"	23.46"
Section Width (in)	8.07"	8.07"

- *Size information : https://www.discounttire.com/learn/tire-size-calculator*
- *Picture (taken by the author) of a Protean PD-18 Wheel Motor*

Electric Machine Specialists
CREATIVE POWER CONVERSION SOLUTIONS

Benchmark Motor Construction

- Motor Topology
  - Three phase, Two Bearing IPM
    - Inner Rotor / Outer Stator
    - TEAO: 8mm fins on MOD w/ 5.6m/s airflow (at 12.5 mph)
    - Common ~3% Si-Fe Lamination Steel
    - 381 MOD x 179 OAL (flange to ODE head)
  - Stator / Rotor
    - 72 slot / Dual Layer, Random-Wound, Dist. Winding with 14 pole rotor
    - Two row "V" magnet array w/ N38UH Magnets
  - Total / Active Material: 81.7 kg / 50.3 kg
    - Cu: 8.00 kg
    - Lamination: 39.9 kg
    - Magnet: 2.40 kg

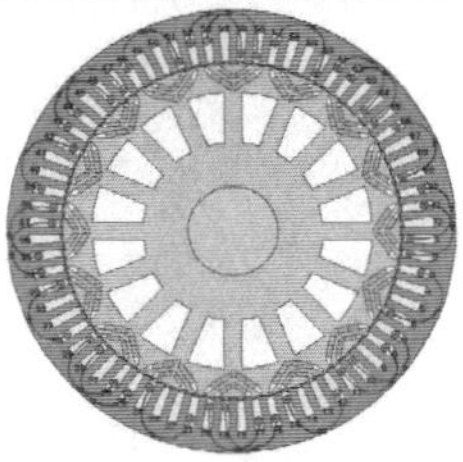

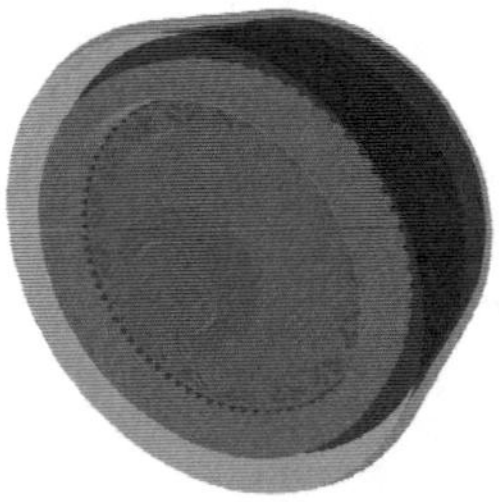

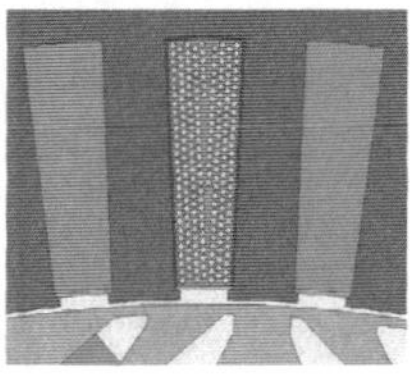

Electric Machine Specialists
CREATIVE POWER CONVERSION SOLUTIONS

Benchmark Motor S1 Thermal Perf @ (169Nm / 262 rpm)

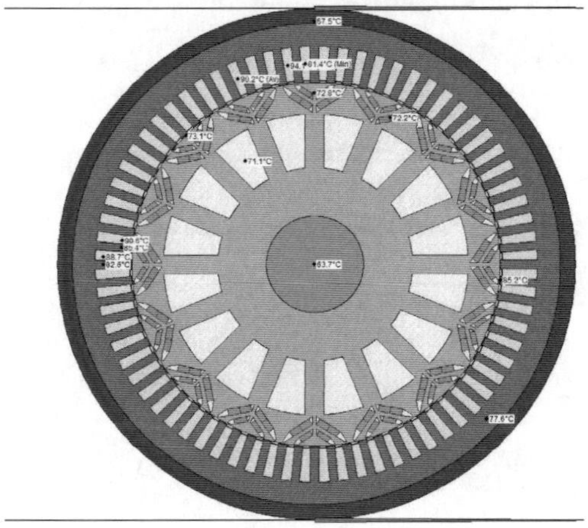

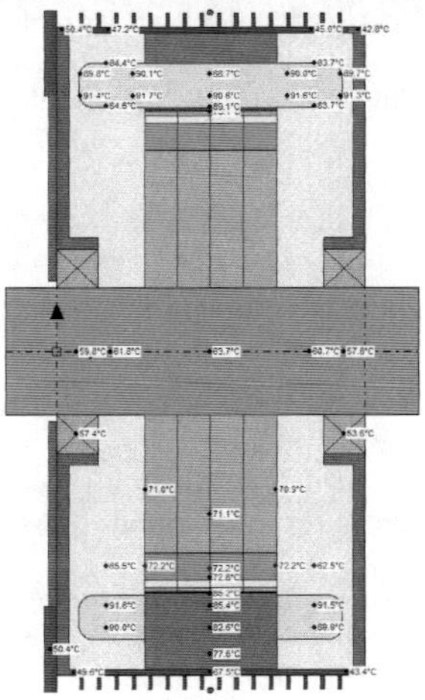

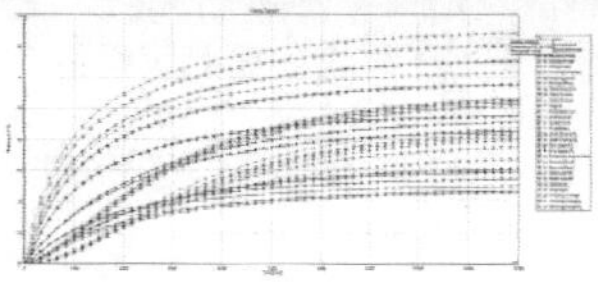

- Line Current = 111Arms
- OCV = 75.33 VLLpk at 600 rpm
- RLL = 0.0324 ohms at hot temp.
- Ke = 1.099 Vs/rad (fundamental)
- Kt = 1.074 Nm/Apk line current
- Mean Temperatures @20C Ambient:
  - Winding: 90.2C
  - Magnet: 72.2C
- Losses at temp:
  - Total: 769W
  - Cu: 599W
  - Core: 170W

Electric Machine Specialists
CREATIVE POWER CONVERSION SOLUTIONS

Benchmark Motor T-N Performance at S1 Temperatures

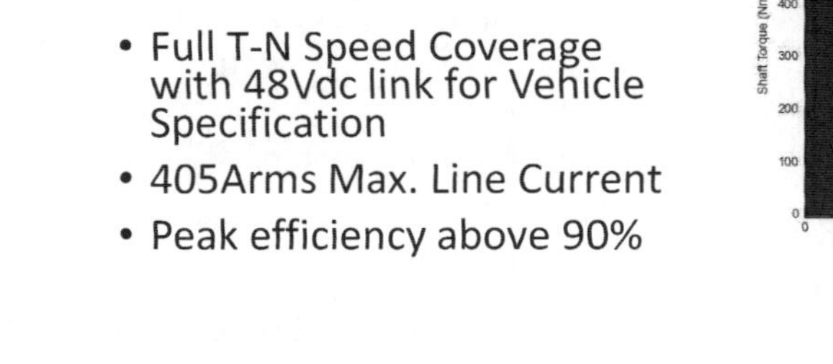

- Full T-N Speed Coverage with 48Vdc link for Vehicle Specification
- 405Arms Max. Line Current
- Peak efficiency above 90%

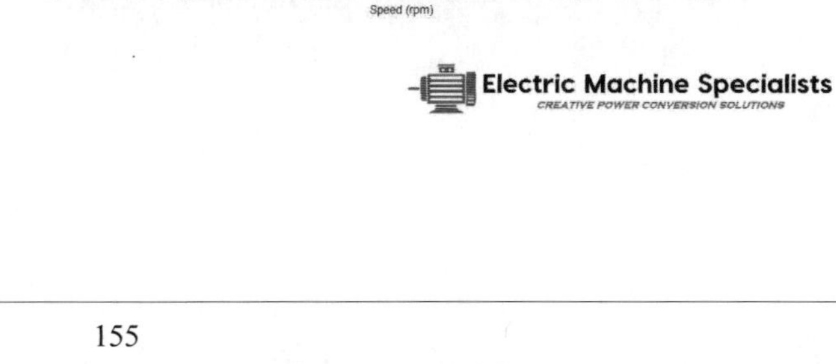

Electric Machine Specialists
CREATIVE POWER CONVERSION SOLUTIONS

Permeability and Performance – Saturation Factor - 1

- A metric and method for evaluating alternate materials ***in situ*** - the "Saturation Factor" – K_{sat}:
  - $\frac{E_{pk}}{w_e N'_{ph}} = B_{g_{pk}} \left(\frac{2}{\pi}\right) A_p$; Relating Terminal Flux Linkages at the motor winding terminals to Flux per pole with sinusoidal airgap flux density distribution across a rotor pole
  - $H_{g_{pk}} = \frac{B_{g_{pk}}}{\mu\_o}$; Relating Peak Gap Flux Density to peak Magnetic Intensity
  - $F_{p_{pk}} = H_{g_{pk}} g''$; Relating Peak Amp Turns per Pole to Magnetic Intensity and effective magnetic air gap
  - $g'' = gK_{cf}K_{sat}$; Relating effective airgap to mechanical airgap, Carter's Coefficient, and Saturation Factor

A high saturation factor (K_{sat}) makes the magnetic airgap of "longer" which for a fixed air gap peak flux density (and magnetic intensity) requires higher peak amp turns per pole (or more magnet).

In practice, this makes the slope of the Volts vs. current curve of an induction machine at a no-load, constant speed become nonlinear and draw more and more current as voltage is increased.

Electric Machine Specialists
CREATIVE POWER CONVERSION SOLUTIONS

Permeability and Performance – Saturation Factor - 2

- How to calculate Saturation Factor – K_{sat}
  - $K_{sat} = 1 + \left(\frac{K_{Bt}K_{lt}}{\mu_{tr}}\right)_s + \left(\frac{K_{By}K_{ly}}{\mu_{yr}}\right)_s + \left(\frac{K_{Bt}K_{lt}}{\mu_{tr}}\right)_r + \left(\frac{K_{By}K_{ly}}{\mu_{yr}}\right)_r$
  - K_{Bt}, K_{By}; Ratio relating ratio Peak Flux Density in teeth and yoke to that in the airgap.
  - K_{lt}, K_{ly}; Relating ratio of average mechanical path length of the teeth and yoke magnetic to the airgap (after accounting for airgap fringing effects)
  - μ_{tr}, μ_{yr}; Relative permeability of the average teeth and yoke sections of the motor iron at respective peak flux densities in each section and

    Relative permeability is the ratio of B/H data (steel curves) to that of air.
  - s, r; Subscripts for stator and rotor respectively

Electric Machine Specialists
CREATIVE POWER CONVERSION SOLUTIONS

Permeability and Performance – Saturation Factor - 3

- Methodology for Saturation Factor Studies:
  - Saturation factor was analytically calculated for four reference motor lamination geometries with the same outer diameter, slot number, and mechanical airgap length..
  - Each design has a unique pole number (4,8,12,&16), rotor diameter, and a core length equal to one pole pitch.
  - Slot depths and tooth widths (using parallel tooth construction) were chosen to allow each machine to have identical flux densities in the stator and rotor teeth and back iron.
  - Core Loss was not considered in this study as frequencies are fairly low (<100Hz)
  - Each design was analyzed over a range of air gap flux densities (which establishes torque per amp capability) with B/H data for each of the following materials:
    - *A ~3% Si-Fe standard lamination materials in a common material thicknesses (29 Ga)*
    - *Co-Fe Alloy (49% Co, remainder Fe plus other elements) at 0.15mm, with Jsat > 2.4T*
    - *"Thin" Si-Fe electrical steels (≤ 0.007") with higher permeability than standard Si-Fe materials*
    - *Cold Rolled Steel lamination material in common material thickness (24Ga)*

Electric Machine Specialists
CREATIVE POWER CONVERSION SOLUTIONS

Permeability and Performance – Saturation Factor - 4

- Study #1 Results : $B_{g_{pk}}$ = 1.0T, K_{Bt} = 1.8, K_{By} = 1.6; held constant, vary poles

K_{sat}	poles			
Steel Type	*4*	*8*	*12*	*16*
~3% Si-Fe	1.80	1.46	1.28	1.24
Co-Fe Alloy	1.02	1.01	1.01	1.01
"Thin" Si-Fe	1.30	1.17	1.11	1.09
CRS	1.44	1.25	1.15	1.14

- Generally speaking, with pole counts higher than 8, K_{sat} varied little as a function of pole count for the reference machines in Study #1, and steel selection is independent of pole count.
- At 8 poles or less, the differences in K_{sat} can be interpreted as a statement on relative PM material content needed to sustain the airgap flux density.
  - For example in a 4 pole design: Co-Fe requires ~ 60% the magnet mass of ~3% Si-Fe.

Electric Machine Specialists
CREATIVE POWER CONVERSION SOLUTIONS

Permeability and Performance – Saturation Factor - 5

Study #2 Results : $B_{g_{pk}}$ = 0.9T and p=16 held constant, vary K_{Bt} which = K_{By}

- At constant gap flux density of 0.9T in the 16 pole design varying Bt, By through changes in tooth and back iron dimensions.
- Comparisons of ~3% Si-Fe and Thin Si-Fe Moving from 1.8T to 2.0T:
  - ~3% Si-Fe:
    - Gain of 25% slot area, which is 20% reduction of 1.8T wdg. temperature rise
    - Magnet size increase 2x
  - Thin Si-Fe:
    - Same gain of 25% slot area
    - But, same size as 1.8T magnet from the ~3% Si-Fe design

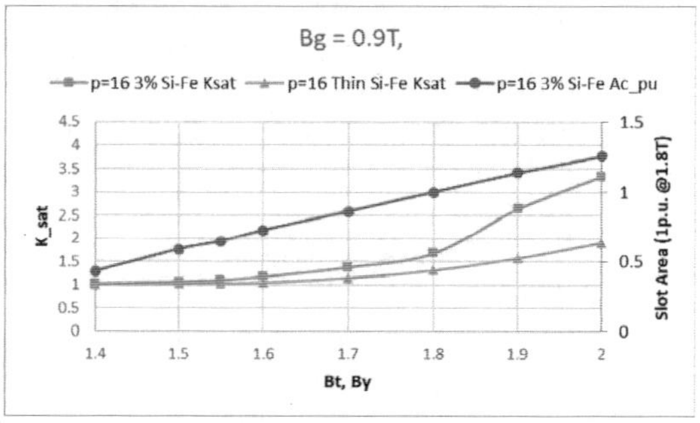

Electric Machine Specialists
CREATIVE POWER CONVERSION SOLUTIONS

Permeability and Performance – Saturation Factor - 6

- Study #3 Results : $B_{g_{pk}}$ = (0.9T – 1.15T), K_{Bt} = 1.8, K_{By} =1.6, p=12

K_{sat}	$B_{g_{pk}}$					
Steel Type	*1.15T*	*1.1T*	*1.05T*	*1.0T*	*0.95T*	*0.9T*
~3% Si-Fe	2.57	1.87	1.58	1.28	1.14	1.07
Co-Fe Alloy	1.01	1.01	1.01	1.01	1.01	1.01
"Thin" Si-Fe	1.56	1.37	1.22	1.11	1.05	1.03
CRS	2.04	1.65	1.35	1.15	1.08	1.04

- Relative changes in gap flux density are changes in Torque at equal currents, so changes from 1.0 to 1.05T is an increase in torque of 5%.
- At $B_{g_{pk}}$ >1.05T and low Hz: Co-Fe, Thin Si-Fe, then CRS are good options.
- At $B_{g_{pk}}$ <1.05T and low Hz: Thin Si-Fe, CRS, and ~3% Si-Fe are good options.
- At higher frequencies (equal gap flux) would tend toward Co-Fe or Thin Si-Fe.

Electric Machine Specialists
CREATIVE POWER CONVERSION SOLUTIONS

Permeability and Performance – Saturation Factor - 7

Study #3 Results : Vary $B_{g_{pk}}$ (and Bt, By) with K_{Bt} = 1.8 K_{By} = 1.6 and p=12

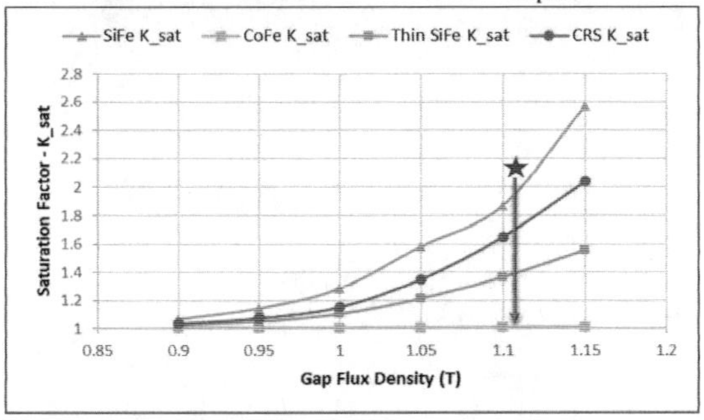

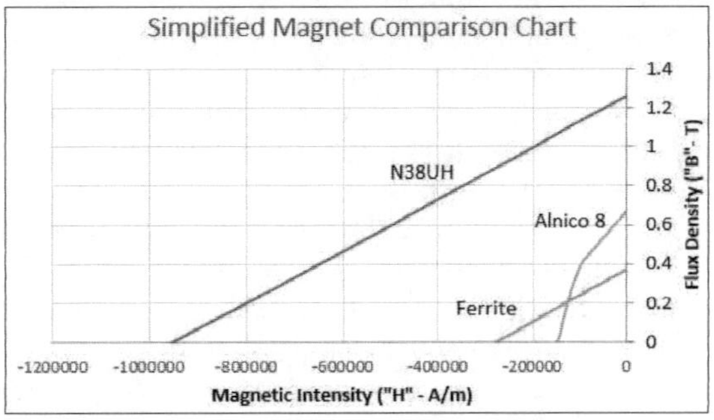

At gap flux densities of ≥1.1T, by changing from ~3% Si-Fe to Thin Si-Fe we can reduce magnet size 30% (Ksat 2 -> 1.4), or magnet size can be retained and extra flux can be used to offset some of the flux loss moving from N38UH to a non RE magnet material.

Electric Machine Specialists
CREATIVE POWER CONVERSION SOLUTIONS

Lamination-Magnet Combinations for Alternate Designs

- Material Study Observations and Challenges:
  - In torque dense machines ($B_{g_{pk}}$> 1.05T), one of the Thin Si-Fe steels may provide enough permeability to offset some of the loss of remanence moving from RE magnets (>1.05T Br) to high coercivity Alinco magnets (>0.65T Br).
  - Increasing slot area with a higher permeability material will help with additional current required to make up for loss of torque per amp with non-RE materials
  - The non-linear "normal BH curve" of Alnico requires us to limit field weakening currents (to remain along linear recoil permeability) if the gap flux density goal is maintained. In the following work 0.3T is the knee point for Alnico and most combinations are SPM machines with little reluctance torque.
  - The low remanence of Ferrite (>0.37T) with better demagnetization capability than Alnico are ideal for highly salient machines PM assisted synchronous reluctance machines, or when used in Halbach arrays in SPM applications.

Electric Machine Specialists
CREATIVE POWER CONVERSION SOLUTIONS

Alternate Design #1 - Motor Construction

- Motor Topology
  - Three phase, Two Bearing IPM
    - Inner Rotor / Outer Stator
    - 8mm fins on MOD with 5.58 m/s airflow at 12.5 mph
    - "Thin" Si-Fe Lamination Steel
    - 3" solid steel shaft
    - 381 MOD x 223 OAL (flange to ODE head)
  - Stator / Rotor
    - 72 slot / Dual Layer, Rectangular Wire, Dist. Winding
    - Three row V / 12 pole / 8HC Sintered Alnico Magnets
  - Total / Active Material: 99.2 kg / 63.07 kg
    - Cu: 11.05 kg
    - Lamination: 47.79 kg
    - Magnet: 4.18 kg

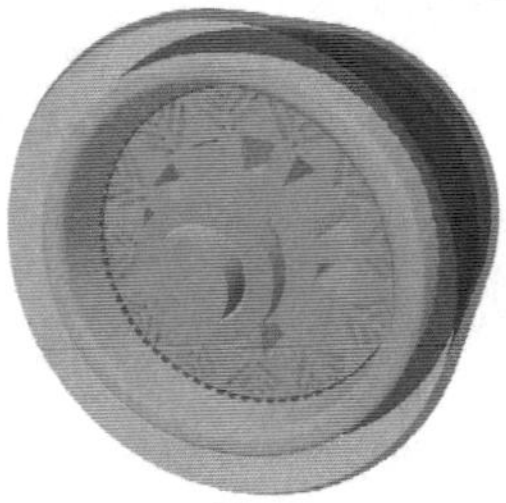

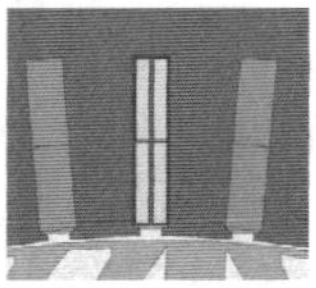

Electric Machine Specialists
CREATIVE POWER CONVERSION SOLUTIONS

Alt. Design #1 - S1 Thermal Perf @ (169Nm / 262 rpm)

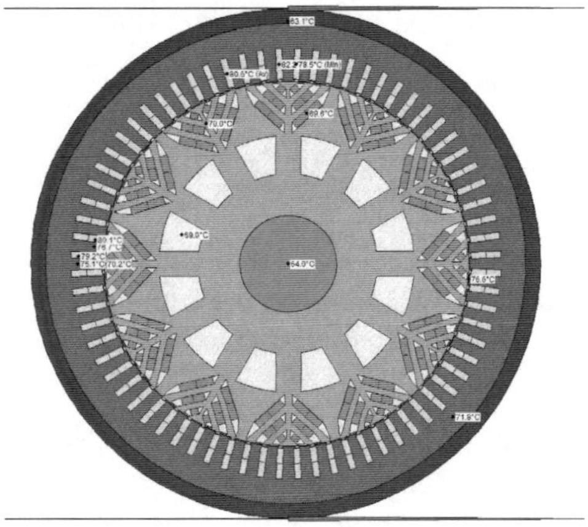

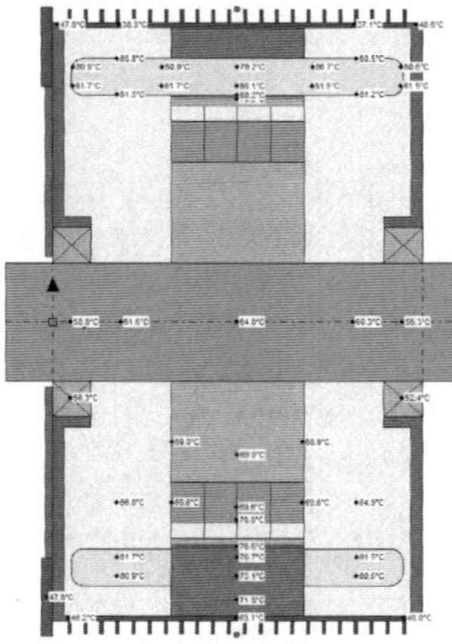

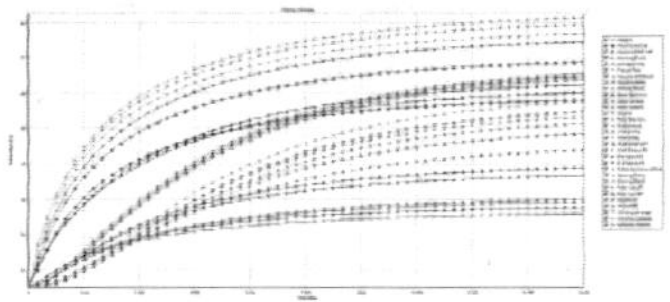

- Line Current: 171.8Arms
- OCV = 23.44 VLLpk at 600 rpm
- RLL = 0.01424 ohms at hot temp.
- Ke = 0.3439 Vs/rad (fundamental)
- Kt = 0.6952 Nm/ Apk line current
- Mean Temperatures:
  - Winding: 80.6C
  - Magnet: 69.6C
- Losses at temp:
  - Total: 790W
  - Cu: 630W
  - Core: 160W

Electric Machine Specialists
CREATIVE POWER CONVERSION SOLUTIONS

Alt. Design #1 - T-N Performance at S1 Temperatures

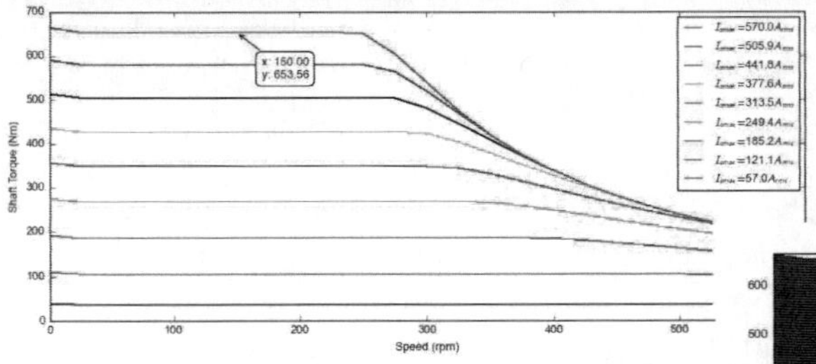

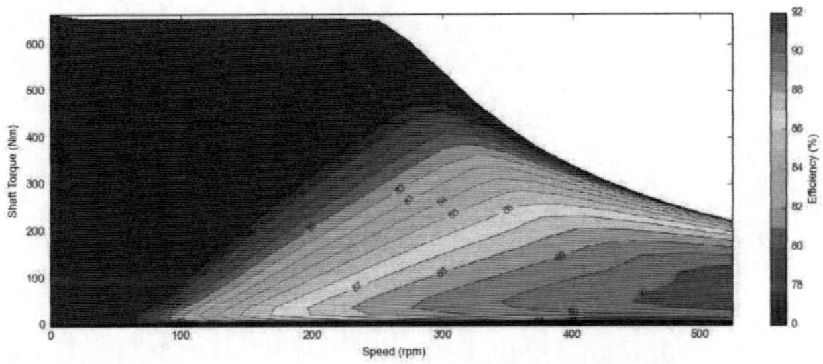

- Full T-N Speed Coverage with 48Vdc link for Vehicle Specification
- 570Arms Max. Line Current
- Peak efficiency above 91%
- Id_rms max <300A to prevent demagnetization of buried magnets

Electric Machine Specialists
CREATIVE POWER CONVERSION SOLUTIONS

Alternate Design #2 - Motor Construction

- Motor Topology
  - Three phase, Two Bearing SPM
    - Outer Rotor / Inner Stator
    - Rotor assembled to and rotates with wheel with no significant heat transfer at rotor OD
    - Thin Si-Fe Lamination with Mild Steel Hub and 3" solid shaft
    - 381 MOD x 199 OAL
  - Stator / Rotor
    - 72 slot / Dual Layer, Rectangular Wire, Distributed Winding
    - Slot Cooling
      - (*0.5 - 1 liter/min Hydraulic Fluid*)
      - Without slot cooling temperatures exceed 170C
    - 24 pole / 8HC Sintered Alnico Magnets
  - Total / Active Material: 77.4 kg / 52.15 kg
    - Cu: 8.50 kg
    - Lamination and Rotor Hub: 39.52 kg
    - Magnet: 4.131 kg

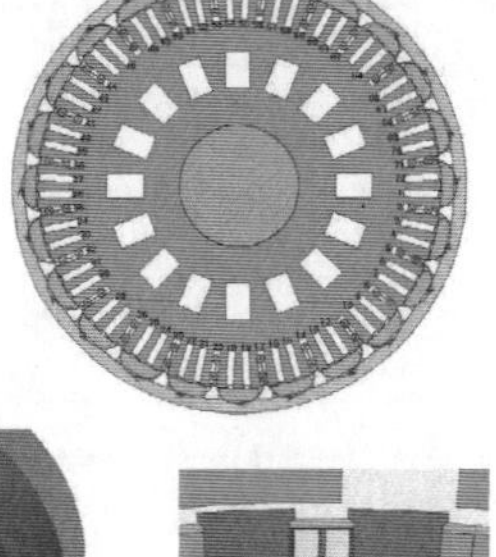

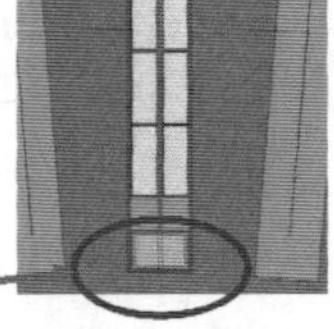

Electric Machine Specialists
CREATIVE POWER CONVERSION SOLUTIONS

Alt. Design #2 - S1 Thermal Perf @ (169Nm / 262 rpm)

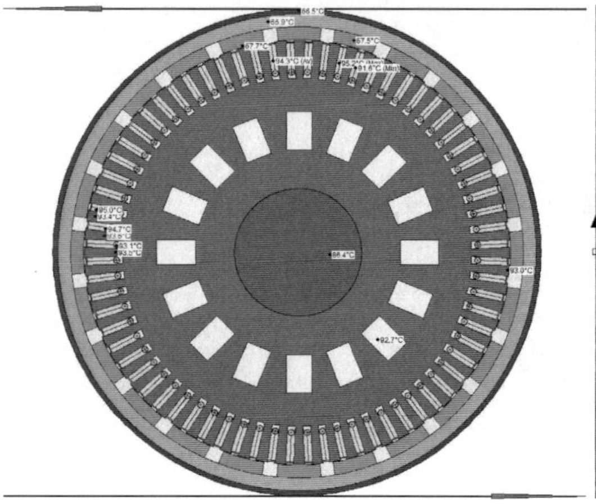

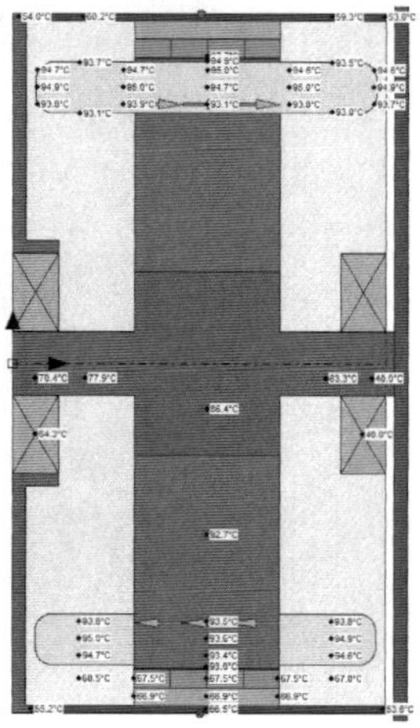

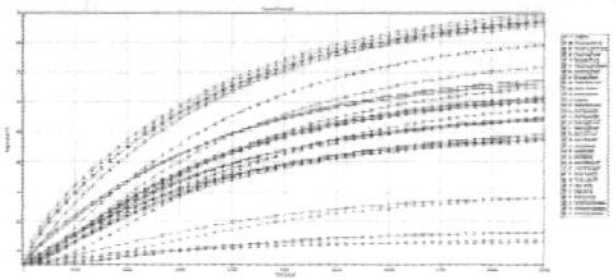

- Line Current: 118A
- OCV = 68.61 VLLpk at 600 rpm
- RLL = 0.02014 ohms at hot temp.
- Ke = 1.199 Vs/rad (fundamental)
- Kt = 1.048 Nm/A
- Mean Temperatures:
  - Winding: 90.6C
  - Magnet: 68.2C
- Losses at temp:
  - Total: 501W
  - Cu: 426W
  - Core: 75W

Electric Machine Specialists
CREATIVE POWER CONVERSION SOLUTIONS

Alt. Design #2 - T-N Performance at S1 Temperatures

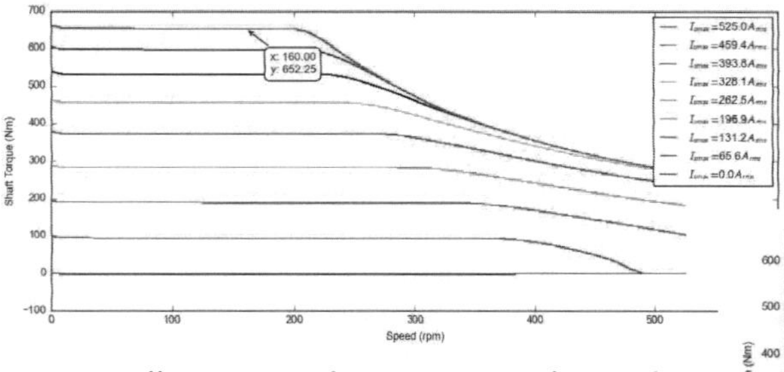

- Full T-N Speed Coverage with 48Vdc link for Vehicle Specification
- 525Arms Max. Line Current
- Peak efficiency above 94%

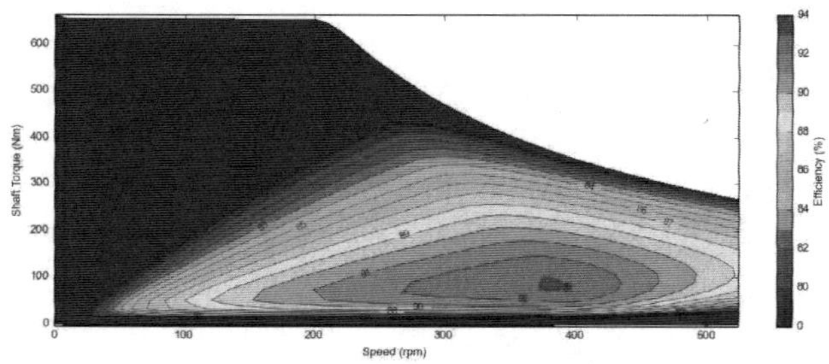

Electric Machine Specialists
CREATIVE POWER CONVERSION SOLUTIONS

Alternate Design #3 - Motor Construction

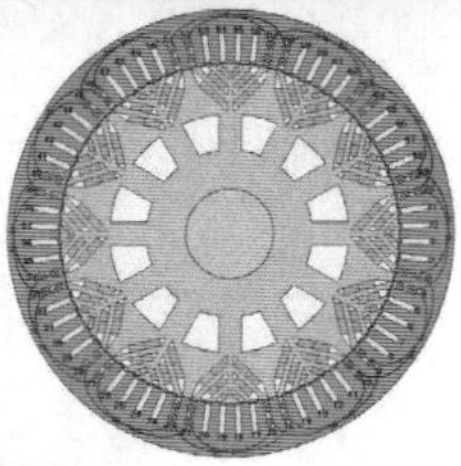

- Motor Topology – Dual Motor Approach
  - Three phase, Two Bearing IPM
    - Inner Rotor / Outer Stator
    - 8mm fins on MOD with 5.58 m/s airflow at 12.5 mph
    - CRS Lamination Steel
    - 3" solid steel shaft
    - 381 MOD x 230 OAL (flange to ODE head)
  - Stator / Rotor
    - 72 slot / Dual Layer, Random Wound, Dist. Winding
    - Three row V / 12 pole / HF084 Ferrite Magnet
  - Total / Active Material: 94.1kg / 57.8 kg (per motor)
    - Cu: 8.235 kg
    - Lamination: 46.66 kg
    - Magnet: 2.893 kg

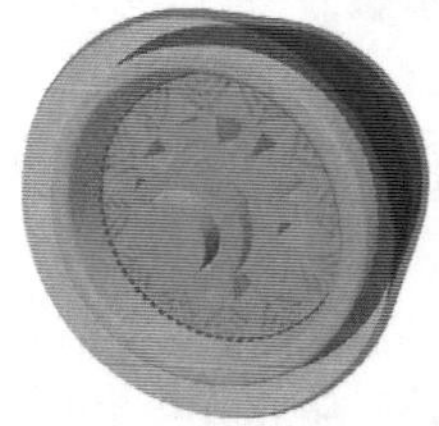

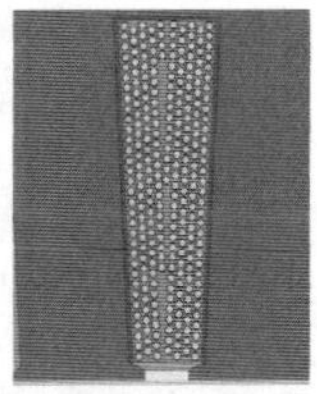

Electric Machine Specialists
CREATIVE POWER CONVERSION SOLUTIONS

Alt. Design #3 - S1 Thermal Perf @ (80.5Nm / 262 rpm)

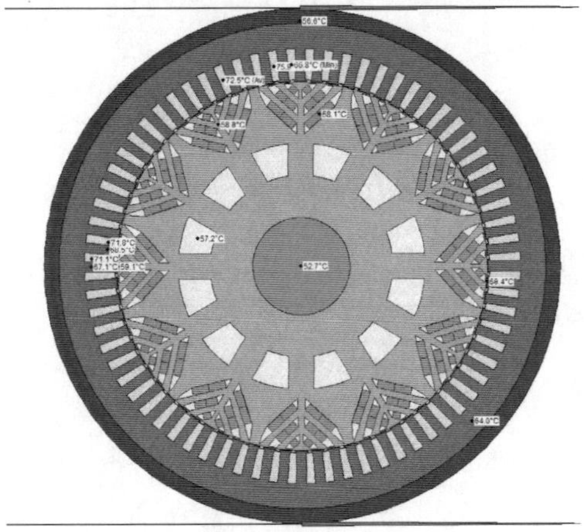

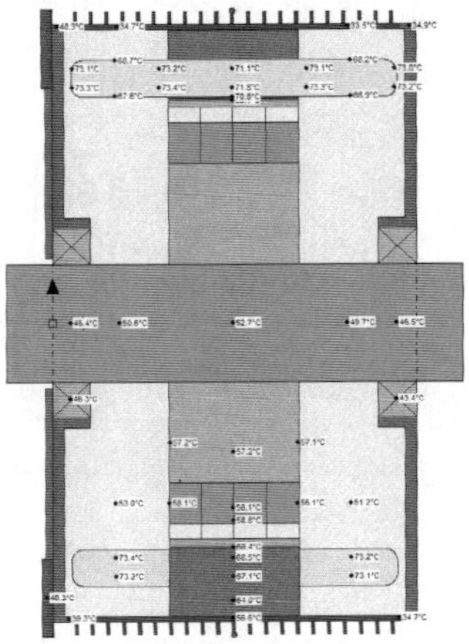

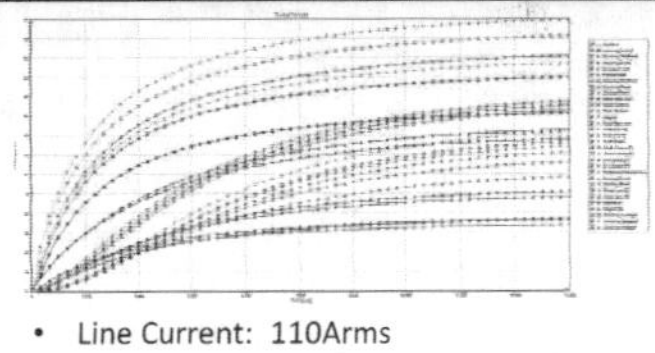

- Line Current: 110Arms
- OCV = 6.058 VLLpk at 600 rpm
- RLL = 0.02495 ohms at hot temp.
- Ke = 0.0941 Vs/rad (fundamental)
- Kt = 0.5656 Nm/Apk
- Mean Temperatures:
  - Winding: 72.4C
  - Magnet: 59.8C
- Losses at temp:
  - Total: 627W
  - Cu: 452W
  - Core: 175W

Electric Machine Specialists
CREATIVE POWER CONVERSION SOLUTIONS

Alt. Design #3 - T-N Performance at S1 Temperatures

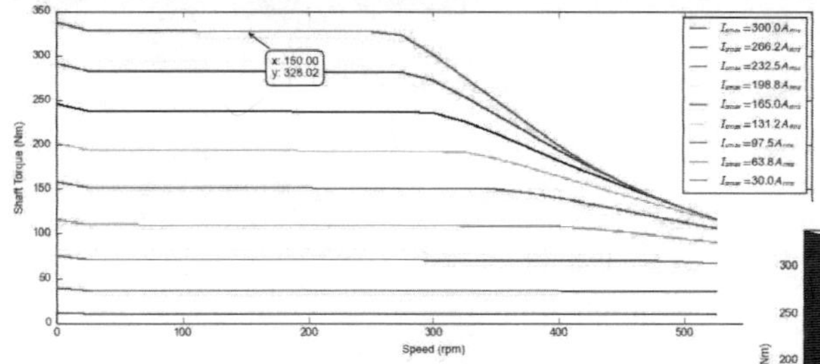

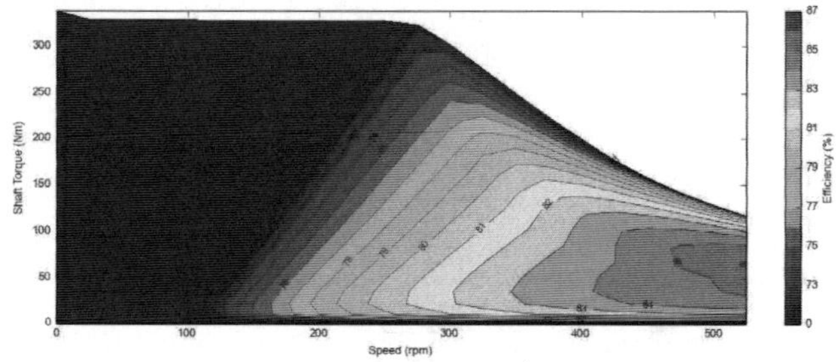

- Full T-N Speed Coverage with 48Vdc link for Vehicle Specification using two motors
- 300Arms Max. Line Current per motor, for a total of 600A rms max when two motors are used on the vehicle.

Electric Machine Specialists
CREATIVE POWER CONVERSION SOLUTIONS

Adding Thermal Performance to Output Factors - 1

- Let's take a closer look at the winding temperature rise of a machine using the simple model of a BLDC motor:
  - $\frac{P_{out}}{P_{in}} = \frac{1}{\{1+(\frac{T_O R_{ll}}{{K_t}^2 w_r})\}}$; Efficiency of trapezoidal drive BLDC machine in SI units.
  - $\frac{P_{loss}}{P_{out}} = \left(\frac{T_O R_{ll}}{{K_t}^2 w_r}\right)$; Relating P_{loss} to Output Power
  - $\frac{T_{out}}{P_{loss}} = \left(\frac{{K_t}^2}{T_O R_{ll}}\right)$; Relating Output Torque to P_{loss}
  - $\frac{T_{out}}{P_{loss}} = \left(\frac{K_t}{I_{dc} R_{ll}}\right)$; Relating Output Torque to P_{loss} as a function of load current
  - $R_{th} = \frac{1}{h_b A_s}$; Thermal Resistance (°C/Watt) of Winding
  - $°C_{rise} = P_{loss} R_{th}$; Steady State Temperature Rise of Winding (°C)
  - $\frac{T_{out}}{°C_{rise}} = \left(\frac{K_t}{I_{dc} R_{ll} R_{th}}\right)$; Torque/°C as a function of load current

Electric Machine Specialists
CREATIVE POWER CONVERSION SOLUTIONS

Adding Thermal Performance to Output Factors - 2

- Lets draw an analogy between $\frac{T_{out}}{°C_{rise}}$ and the Motor Constant (K_m):
  - $\frac{T_{out}}{°C_{rise}} = \left(\frac{K_t}{I_{dc} R_{ll} R_{th}}\right)$; Torque/°C as a function of load current
  - $K_m = \left(\frac{T_{out}}{(I_{dc}{}^2 R_{ll})^{0.5}}\right)$; Definition of the Motor Constant (K_m)
  - $K_m = \left(\frac{K_t}{R_{ll}{}^{0.5}}\right)$; Simplified Version of Motor Constant (K_m) independent of current
  - $K_{m_{th}} = \left(\frac{K_t}{R_{ll}{}^{0.5} R_{th}}\right)$; Motor Constant ($K_m$) modified for motor thermal performance.

K_m is a figure of merit for comparing motor designs, independent of speed or load that does not incorporate cooling system effectiveness.

$K_{m_{th}}$ a figure of merit that resembles K_m , and its relationship of Torque and temperature rise, but is independent of load, loss and speed.

Electric Machine Specialists
CREATIVE POWER CONVERSION SOLUTIONS

Performance Summary - Observations

Design	B1	A1	A2	A3	
Topology	IPM - IR	IPM - IR	SPM - OR	2 x IPM - IR	
Matl Combination	RE + SiFe + Random Wound	Alnico + Thin SiFe + Rect Wire	Alnico + Thin SiFe + Rect Wire	Ferrite + CRS + Random Wound	
Cooling System	TEAO	TEAO	*TELC*	TEAO	
Tmax - Nm	654	653	653	328	← 1
I max - Arms	405	570	525	300	
Bg_pk_fundamental - Tesla	1.039	1.249	0.74	1.07	
Ke_Vpk_LL_fundamental - Vs/rad	1.11	0.47	1.20	0.10	
Kt Pk - Nm/A_line_pk	1.14	0.81	0.88	0.77	
Copper Loss -Pcu @ T_max - Watts	7972	6940	8327	3368	
RLL °C_S1 - ohms	0.0324	0.0142	0.0201	0.0250	← 2
R_thermal_wdg (C Rise_S1/Watt)	0.091	0.077	0.141	0.084	
MV - Motor Volume - cubic meters	0.0204	0.0254	0.0227	0.0262	
RV - Rotor Volume - cubic meters	0.0048	0.0053	0.0018	0.0052	
Kg AM - active material (AM)	50.3	63.0	52.2	57.8	
T_max / MV - kNm/m^3	***32.0***	25.7	28.8	*12.5*	← 3
T_max / kg AM - Nm/kg	***13.0***	10.4	***12.5***	5.7	
T_max/RV - kNm/m^3	135.5	122.7	***368.5***	63.1	
Km_max - (T_max/(Pcu @ Tmax)^0.5)	***7.3***	***7.8***	***7.2***	5.7	← 4
Km_max / R_thermal_wdg	80.2	***102.2***	*50.7*	67.6	
Relative AM Cost ROM - Author's Opinion	1.00	1.25	1.10	***0.80***	
if change Thin Si-Fe to other Common Si-Fe or CRS		***+/-.35***	***+/-.30***	***(inc. 2 motor)***	
T_max / kg AM / Relative Cost ROM	***13.0***	8.3	***11.4***	7.1	← 5

1. Non RE designs need higher line current which adds cost to the inverter. Changes in drive current rating can add up to 50% to drive cost.
2. The BPM-OR machine (TELC) still has a higher thermal impedance from winding to ambient, despite a brake fluid conductor cooling loop.
   **Increasing surface area or fluid flow will help but may increase cooling system cost.*
3. B1, the RE-IPM machine has the highest torque/motor volume, but A2, the BPM-OR machine has similar torque/kg.
4. The Km values for three motors with similar capability for the application. Including thermal effects with (Km_th) changes the comparison. *(See * above)*
5. Other lower cost materials may have enough permeability to make non RE designs more competitive.

Electric Machine Specialists
CREATIVE POWER CONVERSION SOLUTIONS

Performance Summary - Conclusions

- The application of different lamination materials as a function of peak gap flux density and material permeability can be used reduce magnet volume, or offset loss of gap flux using Non RE magnet materials.
- Modifying traction motor designs to eliminate RE materials involve trade-offs beyond the motor design and impact the inverter drive, manufacturing methods and cooling systems.
- Non RE designs with similar torque density (volume or mass) may have a system cost as high as those with RE machines, though perhaps with less economic or sourcing risk .
- Creating motor designs with Alnico magnets that are competitive with RE materials is possible, but avoiding irreversible losses in the magnet by limiting field weakening currents is essential. SPM designs with Alnico (or ferrite Halbach arrays) are other approaches.
- TRV or T/kg measures alone do not overtly include the effectiveness of cooling system design, and a modified Motor Constant ($K_{m_{th}}$) is proposed that includes cooling systems effects is proposed that highlights the impacts of those systems.

Electric Machine Specialists
CREATIVE POWER CONVERSION SOLUTIONS

Contact Information

Electric Machine Specialists
CREATIVE POWER CONVERSION SOLUTIONS

Michael Rubbo
Principal Consultant
Electric Machine Specialists
Solon, OH, USA
440-991-6369
michael.rubbo@electric-machine-specialists.com

Some Thoughts on the Future of Soft Magnetic Materials

DR. MILLARD S. MASTELLER
MASTELLER SPECIAL MATERIALS CONSULTING, LLC

MAGNETICS 2020
FEBRUARY 11-12, 2019, ORLANDO, FL

Outline

- What is a soft magnetic material?
- Key families of materials
- Overview of fabrication processes
- Potential of additive manufacturing
- Electrical steels
- 4 Predictions

Soft Magnetic Material

Per the IEC – "A magnetic material having a low coercivity". The delineation of soft, semi-hard and hard magnetic materials is imprecise but most soft magnetic materials have a coercivity of less than 1 kA/m (12.5 Oe).

Desirable attributes are:

- Low coercivity
- High magnetic permeability
- High magnetic saturation
- High electrical resistivity

Compositional Effects

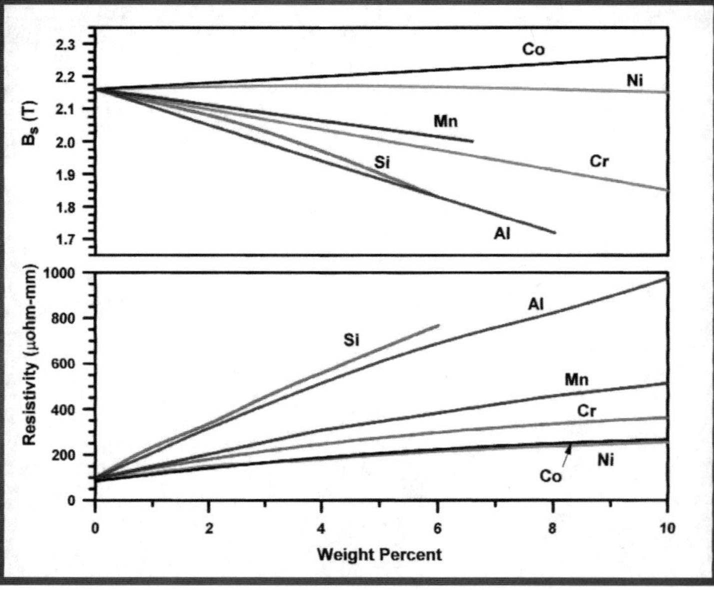

Key Families

- Pure iron and low carbon, low alloy steel
- Iron – silicon alloys with up to 6.5% Si
- Soft ferrites – Mn_a or $Ni_aZn_{(1-a)}Fe_2O_4$
- Iron – chromium alloys (ferritic stainless steel) with 8 – 29% Cr
- Iron – nickel alloys with 30 to 80% Ni
- Iron – cobalt alloys with 15 to 49% Co

"Magic" Compositions

- 6.5% Si – Fe
- 9% Si – 6% Al – Fe (Sendust)
- 50% Ni – Fe
- 75-80% Ni – Cu, Mo, Cr – Fe
- 36% Co – Fe
- 49% Co – 2% V – Fe

Developments Since 1951

Materials

- CRML steel
- Amorphous & nanocrystalline materials
- Soft magnetic composites (SMC)

Processes

- Oxygen steelmaking
- Continuous casting
- Vacuum melting and degassing
- Computer process control
- Rapid solidification
- Metal injection molding
- Additive manufacturing

Parts Production Processes

- **Conventional stamping, laser cutting, EDM, photoetching, fine flow blanking, adiabatic stamping of laminations**
- **Pressed and sintered powder (inc. soft ferrites, SMC, and dust cores)**
- **Wound cores (esp. amorphous and nanocrystalline)**
- **Machining (solenoid and relay cores)**
- **Sheet metal operations like deep drawing, spinning, bending**
- **Metal injection molding**
- **Casting – including AM**
- **Misc. technologies like sputtering, plating, CVD**

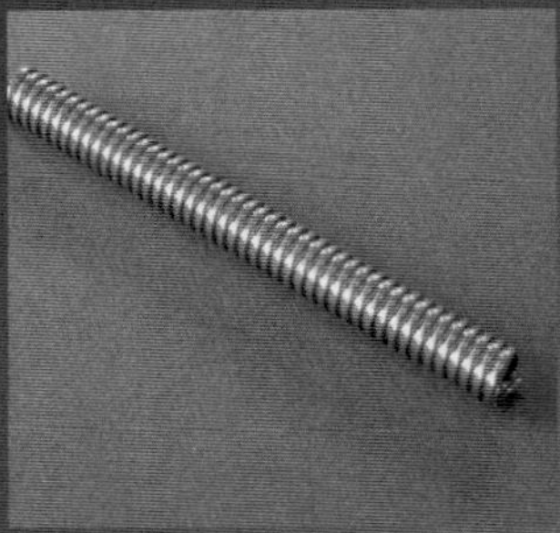

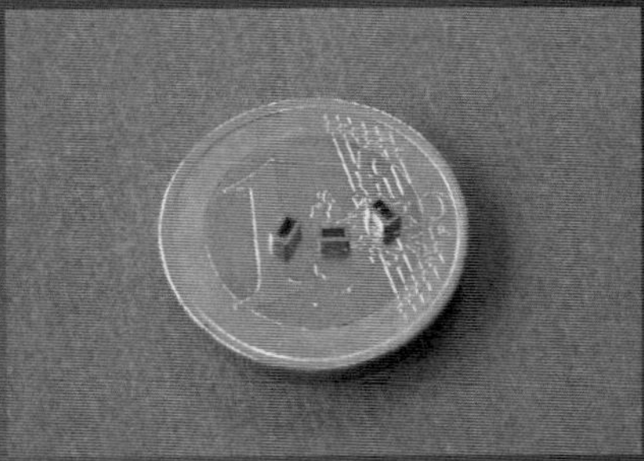

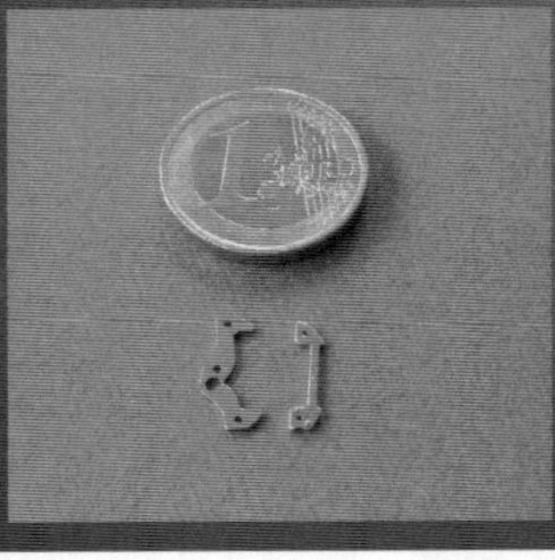

Additive Manufacturing

Some Pros of Additive Manufacturing

- Minimum scrap generation
- Rapid prototyping
- Economical production of small runs
- Ability to make very large parts
- Simplified raw material inventory
- Ability to make parts incorporating different materials
- Does not require skilled tool and diemakers and machinists

Some Cons of Additive Manufacturing

- Cast structure
  - Porosity
  - Residual stresses
  - Inhomogeneous structure (anisotropy)
- Heat treatment may be required
- Limited magnetic data for design
- Low rate of production
- Production parts made by another process may not behave as predicted by the AM prototype

Three AM Questions

- What are the magnetic properties?
- Is the process control sufficient to ensure product consistency?
- Are material specifications even possible?

B(H) Data for 50 Ni - Fe

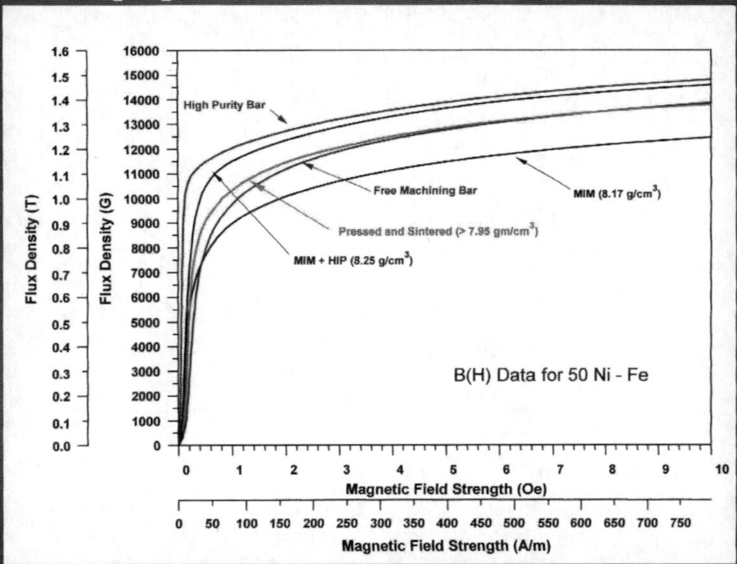

Specifications for 50 Ni-Fe

Specification	Condition	Relative Maximum Permeability	Coercive Field Strength H_{cB} (A/m)
ASTM A753 Bar > 12.7 mm dia.	Wrought	50000 min	6.0 max
IEC 60404-8-6 - Bar	Wrought	No requirement	6 to 12 max
MPIF 35-MIM Grade 1	MIM	47500 min	11.9 max
MPIF 35-MIM Grade 2	MIM	27000 min	19.9 max
ASTM A 904	Pressed and Sintered 7.5 gm/cm^3	No requirement 9900 typical	32 max
IEC 60404-8-9 Grade S-FeNi-20	Pressed and Sintered – Density 7.6 gm/cm^3 min	No requirement 20000 typical	20 max
IEC 60604-8-9 Grade S-FeNi-15	Pressed and Sintered – Density 7.9 gm/cm^3 min	No requirement 30000 typical	15 max

Electrical Steels

EV Motor Materials

Property	50 Ni-Fe	CRML 36D145	FPNO 36F145	49Co-2V-Fe	SMC
B_s(T)	1.6	2.1	2.0	2.4	2.1
Resistivity (μohm-mm)	480	340	500	420	90000?
dc μ_{max}	> 200000	> 14000	8000	8000	720
400 Hz Core Loss (W/kg) 1.0 T	10	22	19	21	31
400 Hz Core Loss (W/kg) 1.5 T	26	57	44	43	65
Yield Strength (MPa)	150	310	360	410	20

For nominal 0.36 mm strip except for SMC

ASTM Electrical Steels

ASTM Standard	Material Type	Minimum Thickness mm (in.)	Maximum Thickness mm (in.)
A677	Fully processed nonoriented silicon iron	0.36 (0.014)	0.64 (0.025)
A683	Semiprocessed nonoriented silicon iron	0.47 (0.0185)	0.64 (0.025)
A726	Cold rolled motor lamination steel	0.36 (0.014)	0.79 (0.031)
A876	Fully processed grain-oriented silicon iron	0.18 (0.007)	0.35 (0.0138)
A1086	Thin fully processed nonoriented silicon iron (graded at 400 and 1000 Hz)	0.10 (0.004)	0.30 (0.012)

Possible Developments

- Even thinner steel (< 0.2 mm) for reduced losses and increased ac permeability
- Reduced rotational losses through creation of more favorable crystallographic textures thus reducing anisotropy
- The sheet thickness effect on grain size may require temper mill processing of nonoriented silicon iron for further loss reduction

Rolling Mills

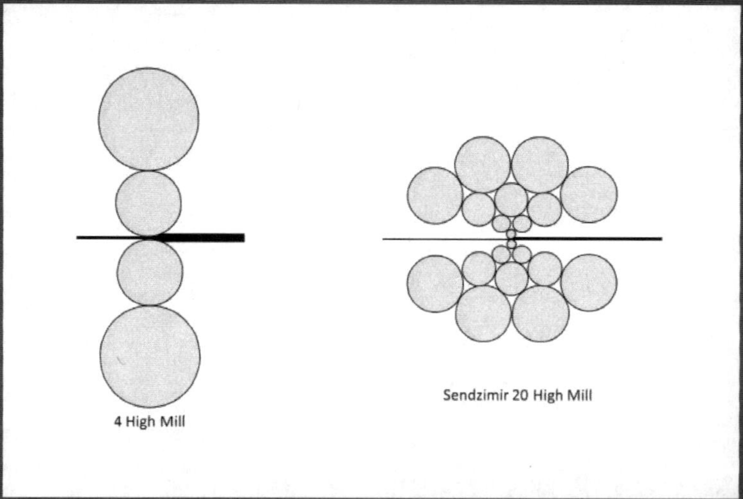

Sheet Thickness Effect

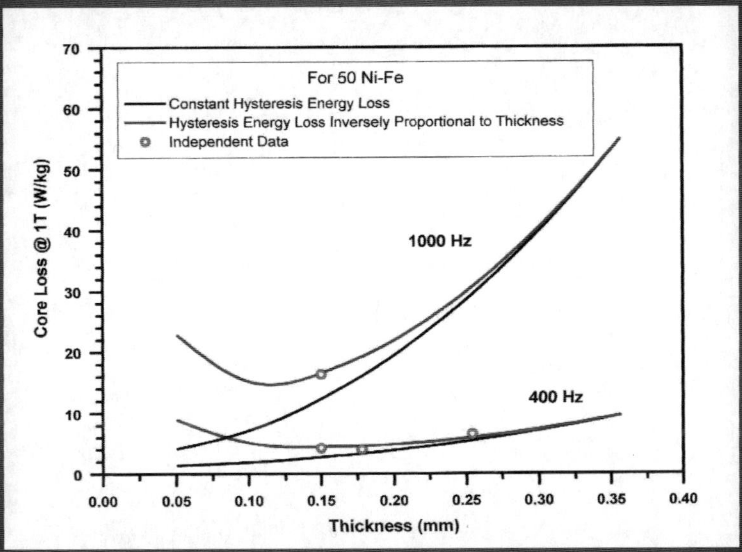

Prediction #1

It is unlikely that fundamentally new soft magnetic materials will be developed since the underlying physics & materials science are well understood and the economic incentives are few. Unlike permanent magnets there is not an issue with raw materials availability since Fe, Si, Al, Mn, Zn, B and O are readily available worldwide at low cost.

Prediction #2

Issues with control of magnetic properties will limit the use of additive manufacturing for soft magnetic component production.

Prediction #3

There may be some additional incremental improvements in electrical steels but with the current availability of 0.2 to 0.3 mm thick steels, we are probably nearing what is practically achievable.

Prediction #4

Due to future improvements in battery technology, EV motor cost, reliability and durability will become more important considerations than electrical efficiency (range) for automakers.

AUTHOR INDEX

TWST Events
622 3rd Ave, 34th FL
New York, NY 10017
USA

ISBN 978-1-7138-0805-3

CURRAN ASSOCIATES INC.
proceedings.com